IMAGES
of America

DAVENPORT

JEWEL OF THE MISSISSIPPI

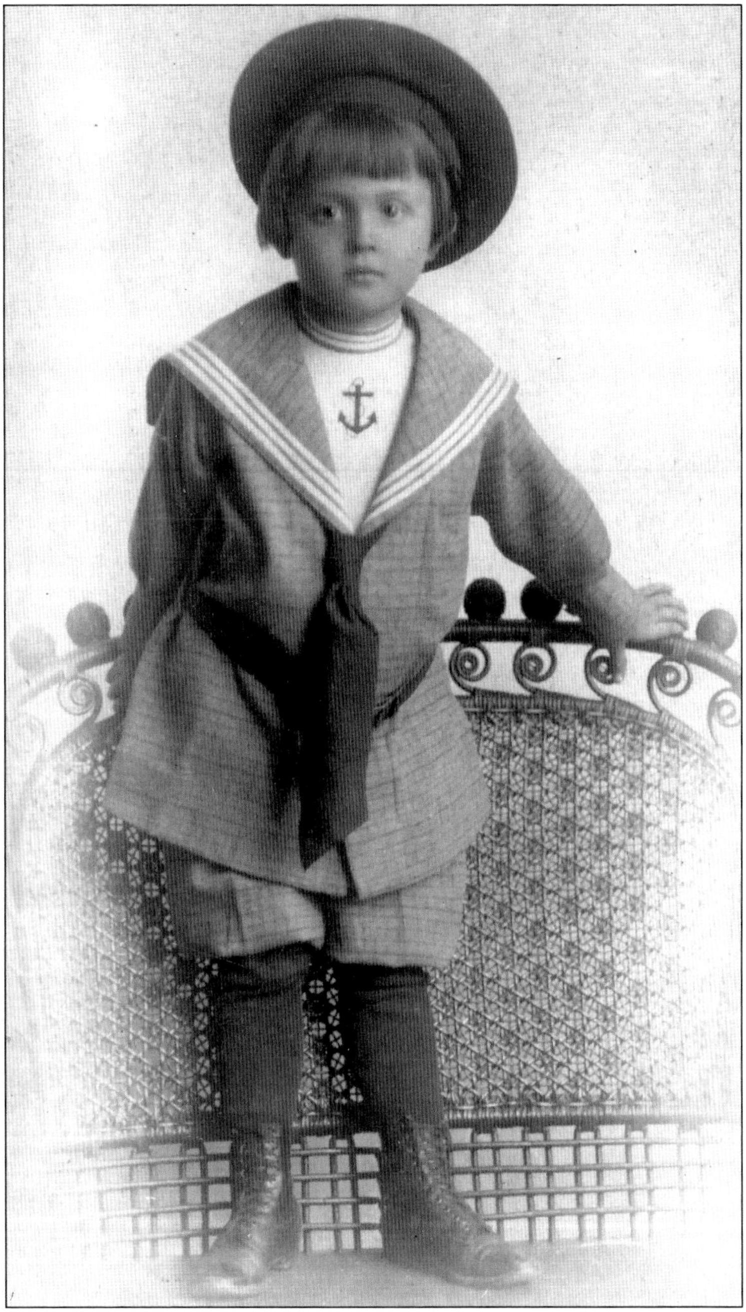

At age five, Leon Bix Beiderbecke already showed signs of a unique musical talent. While both his parents smiled their approval at their young pianist, "Little Bixie" entertained guests with the familiar favorites "Pop Goes the Weasel" and "Yankee Doodle Came to Town." However, once he picked up the cornet in high school, the instrument fit his hands and mouth as if it were made for him. "No one ever played that horn like Bix," declared fellow master musician Louie "Satchmo" Armstrong. Who would have ever thought this urchin, attired in his new "Anchors Aweigh!" outfit in 1908, would help make the '20s roar with the sound of ear pleasin', soul stirrin' jazz?

IMAGES
of America

DAVENPORT

JEWEL OF THE MISSISSIPPI

David Collins, Rich Johnson,
Mary Louise Speer, and John Willard

ARCADIA
PUBLISHING

ISBN 978-0-7385-0728-6

Published by Arcadia Publishing
Charleston, South Carolina

Printed in the United States of America

Library of Congress Catalog Card Number: 00104290

For all general information contact Arcadia Publishing at:
Telephone 843-853-2070
Fax 843-853-0044
E-mail sales@arcadiapublishing.com
For customer service and orders:
Toll-Free 1-888-313-2665

Visit us on the Internet at www.arcadiapublishing.com

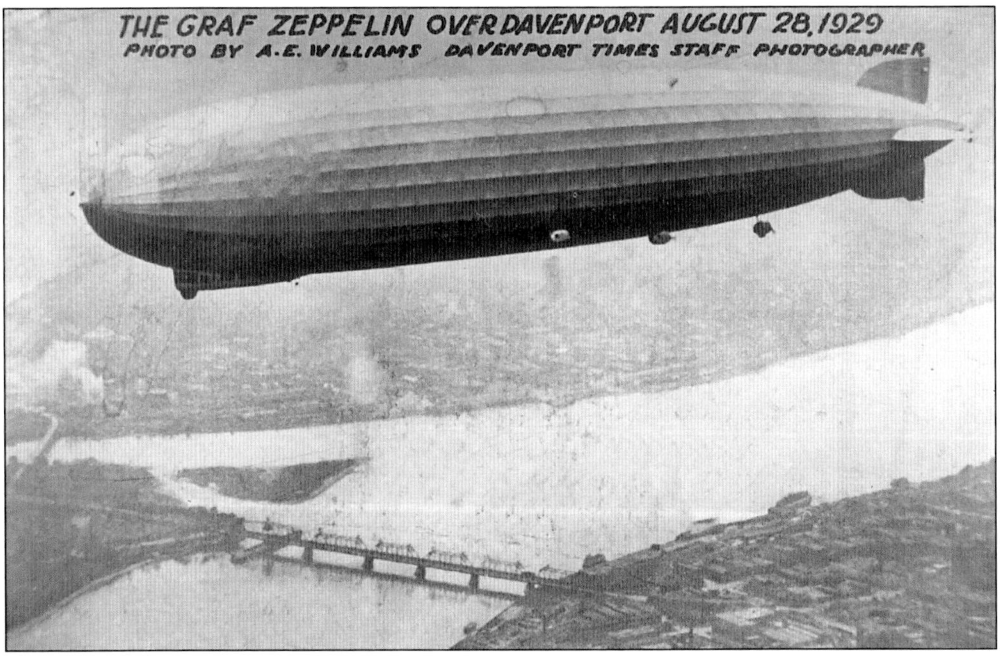

"Look up in the sky! It's a bird! It's a plane! It's the Graf Zeppelin!" On August 28, 1929, thousands of eager spectators in the Mississippi Valley area gazed skyward to watch the giant dirigible coast leisurely at the height of 1,000 feet. Davenport Mayor John Berwald received credit for bringing the craft to this area on its way to Chicago, where it then continued to Lakehurst, New Jersey. "I just thought it looked like a funny-shaped balloon," remembers Arthur Brack, who watched the spectacle seated on his father's shoulders.

Contents

ACKNOWLEDGMENTS

The Sauk/Fox were here first, living on the lands where the snake-like Mississippi River bends east to west in the middle of America's heartland. Then the settlers arrived, discovering the rich soil for farming and the strategic location for transportation use. Time has brought changes and, thankfully, those changes have been preserved in photo and prose.

Naturally, it is impossible in only 128 pages to capture every person, place, and event that has been part of this river town's history. However, it is the hope of those who assembled this volume that it will provide an enjoyable glimpse into the past and at the present. If this goal is achieved, the following should share recognition for their contributions:

Sharlott Blevins; Roy Booker and Craig Chandler, *Quad-City Times*; Betty Christian, Dale Focus and Sara Quartile, North High School; Faye Clow, Bettendorf Public Library; Lorna Dawson, Amy Groskopf, Mary Ann Moore, and Pat Richardson, Davenport Public Library Special Collections Department; Lettie Ernst, Carolyn Anderson, and Tom Stranger, Family Museum; Walter Fichter; Lois Free, Hostetler Studio of Photography; Sara Gadzik, Associate Director of Communications, St. Ambrose University; Martha Haire, Davenport Mayor's Office; Jane Hart, Davenport West High School; University Relations Office, Marycrest International University; The Maas Family Photo Collection; Julie Jensen McDonald; Florence Jones; Morgan-Reynolds Publishing House; Rochelle Murray, Children's Department Director, Davenport Public Library; Alverna Rekemeyer; Dr. William Roba; Kay Runge, Director, Davenport Public Library; Theresa Speer; Dick Stahl, Davenport Central High School; Marlys Svendsen; Marjorie Sullivan Tobin and Fred and Georgia Wallace, Picturesque Quad-Cities; Henry Vargas; and Henry Weber.

INTRODUCTION

Davenport traces its beginnings to an 1832 treaty signed by Chief Keokuk. The treaty transferred a 50-mile strip of land along the Mississippi River from the Yellow River in the north to the Des Moines River in the south. The area was dubbed the "Black Hawk Purchase."

The town stumbled as it took its baby steps. By 1836, land surveys in the new territory had been completed. Mindful that the region was ripe for development, seven frontiersmen gathered at the home of Colonel George Davenport to map out a town. However, when the first lots appeared on the market that same year, sales stalled. Land speculators feared they were not getting clear titles. An economic panic the next year did not help matters.

Fortunately, the city worked past its shaky start. After the potential buyers balked at buying lots, Antoine LeClaire, who had acquired vast land holdings as a government interpreter, secured clear titles. The city was on its way. At LeClaire's suggestion, they named the new town Davenport after Colonel Davenport. Davenport was widely known as the quartermaster for the U.S. Army garrison at nearby Fort Armstrong.

Three years after its 1836 incorporation, the population stood at six hundred. The city council passed its first ordinances. A ferryboat company, a flour mill, cottages, and an imposing brick hotel filled the landscape. Scarlet-blanketed Sauk warriors on horseback and rumbling wagons rode past the building where the first lawyer had hung out his shingle. The first merchant sold dry goods, groceries, and hardware from a log house. At Brimstone Alley, located by the corner of Ripley and Third, preachers admonished settlers about their need for repentance and salvation. The momentum never stopped.

The population grew steadily in the 1840s and 1850s, as settlers descended daily on the "Queen City of the West." A boon to commerce was the selection of the city as the site for the first railroad bridge across the Mississippi, built in 1856. As the "iron horse" began its first river crossings, mighty steamboats loaded with passengers and goods plied the waters.

During the 19th century, the city also helped open the West and provided opportunities for immigrants who founded department stores, construction companies, and breweries. Immigrants found a haven in the rapidly growing city, where smoke rising from the chimneys of its booming manufacturing plants attested to its industrial might. The Germans, fleeing political unrest and military conscription in their homeland, comprised the largest ethnic group. Coming mainly from the northern German provinces of Schleswig and Holstein, the new arrivals were industrious, prosperous, and well educated. Irish, and a small number of Swedes and Hungarians, also moved into the city. Freed black slaves represented another ethnic force. By 1895, three hundred African Americans were living in Davenport. The new arrivals established businesses, banks, churches, and cultural institutions.

As westward expansion prompted a demand for building materials, Davenport became a lumber center, giving rise to a new class of millionaires with names like "Lindsay," "Renwick,"

"Mueller," "French," and "Reimers." Also contributing to Davenport's prosperity in the 1860s were returning veterans from the Civil War, who took advantage of cheap land in the region. The city's population had swelled to more than 20,000 by 1870.

At the end of the 19th century, Davenport was the most important city in eastern Iowa. As the population swelled to 30,000 at the turn of the century, residents built substantial homes in places like McClellan Heights, a Civil War training camp-turned luxury housing subdivision.

In the early part of the 20th century, Davenport prospered as a banking and financial center, touting itself as "the richest and busiest city in Iowa." Downtown Davenport reshaped its riverfront. Mayor G.W. Scott ordered a mid-winter sweep out of prostitutes from 2nd Street bordellos. Orphans knew a well-ordered life at the Soldiers Orphan Home, and Reverend Ned Lee cared for the city's indigent. Under the leadership of department store magnate W.D. Petersen, the city's blighted riverbank was transformed into LeClaire Park during 1911–1912. As the icing on the cake, Petersen furnished the park with a music pavilion, LeClaire Park Bandshell, where outdoor concerts are enjoyed to this day.

In the years just before and after World War I, Davenport enhanced its image as a bustling midwestern city with impressive building projects, such as the headquarters for the Commercial Club (Chamber of Commerce). The First National Building and other office towers took their place on the skyline after the war.

The bubble burst during the Great Depression of the 1930s. Thousands of Davenporters lost their jobs. Many had to trade comfortable middle-class lives for shantytowns. However, even during the depths of the Great Depression, Davenport built civic projects, commercial buildings, and schools. The city made progress with such projects as the 1931 Mississippi Hotel and Orpheum Theater. New schools went up, thanks to federal programs intended to put people to work. Major bridge projects were completed, such as the Iowa-Illinois Memorial (Interstate 74 Bridge) in 1935 and the Centennial Bridge in 1940.

Davenporters mobilized for World War II and celebrated victory with a burst of residential and commercial construction. During the war, citizens found work in the manufacture of arms and equipment. War Bond and scrap metal drives replaced soup kitchens.

The post-war years brought prosperity, as evidenced by the 1955 construction of the Village Shopping Center, Iowa's first strip-shopping center. New hotels and motels went up to meet the needs of leisure and business travelers. In the '60s and '70s, manufacturing plants for Caterpillar and Deere & Co. claimed north Davenport cornfields. Citizens enjoyed fat paychecks, a stable workforce, and security.

In more recent times, Davenport has faced some of its biggest challenges. The agricultural crisis of the 1980s closed down farm implement plants and pushed the unemployment rate into the double digits.These fundamental changes in agriculture forced the city to rebuild its economy. Restructuring efforts resulted in a major hotel-office project downtown, a focus on riverfront improvement, and other innovative ventures, such as the nation's first floating casinos.

Davenport bounced back in the 1990s with a more diversified economy, a burst of downtown improvement projects, and a retailing boom in the northeast suburban area. More excitement looms on the horizon. Planning is underway for a glistening glass art gallery in the downtown, an IMAX theater at an expanded Putnam Museum of History and Natural Science, and a renovated John O'Donnell Stadium.

Davenport is marching into the millennium with a renewed sense of purpose. It has made unity and cooperation its watchwords as it joins its neighbors—Bettendorf in Iowa, and Moline and Rock Island in Illinois—in forging a stronger Quad-City area. A description of Davenport contained in a 1910 brochure promoting the downtown's new Putnam Building is still apt today: "It is delightfully located on the banks and bluffs of the Mississippi River."

One

The Frontier Days

Mississippi River waters flow,
Wind blows, rippling prairie grass.
Pioneers, their cottages rising on the banks and bluff
Lay claim to lands once wild.

Winter whiteness covers the prairie
as scarlet-blanketed Sauk warriors urge their steeds on towards home.
Settlers prepare to celebrate another year's bountiful harvest.
Fiddling, dancing, and praise accompany the new town's birth.

Davenport, dreamed by Antoine LeClaire,
At first home to few,
Flounders, finds its feet, and grows as new inhabitants pour in.
Village gives way to town, then town to city.

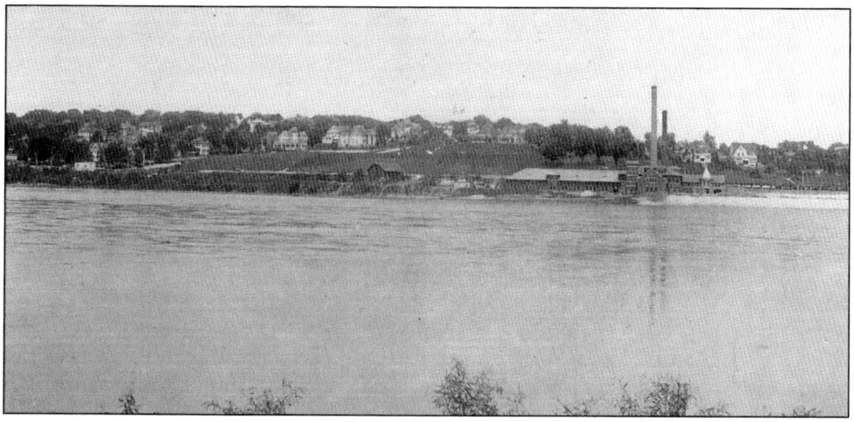

Innovation, hard work, and a steady stream of settlers sparked the young city's rapid growth along the Mississippi River shoreline. Most early businesses depended upon water transportation, while business leaders dreamed of the day train engines would whistle into town. This photograph of Davenport from Arsenal Island reflects a sign of residential growth and business development taking place. Newcomers arrived daily, and many of those intending to head west decided to settle in the Mississippi Valley. "When we set out from Vermont, my Pa was determined to go farther west," wrote Katherine Brock in her diary in 1840. "But when he saw this area, he lost all desire to travel further."

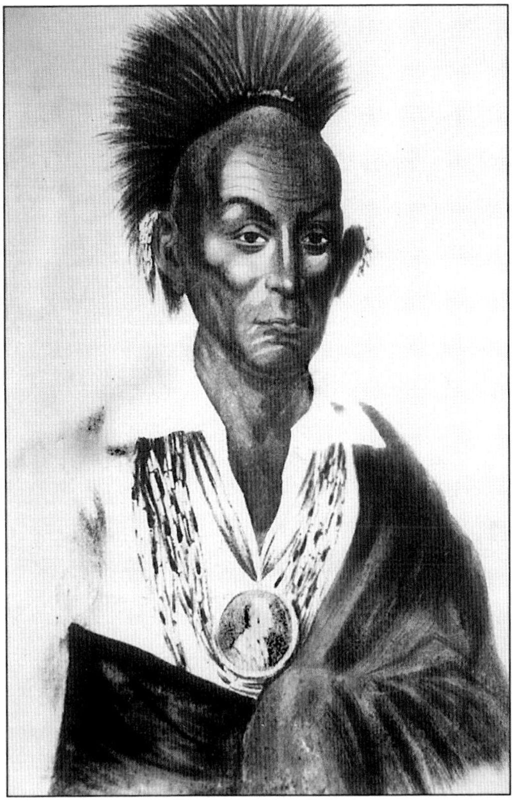

Few individuals in American history shared both the image of warrior and peacemaker as did Black Hawk, leader of the Sauk/Fox, who called the Mississippi Valley their home before the arrival of the pioneers. Feeling his people were swindled out of land rightfully theirs, he led the fight to regain it. Captured and taken to Washington D.C., Black Hawk pleaded his case before President Andrew Jackson. Black Hawk was sent back to his people, and before he died, he wrote a powerful and sensitive autobiography. Many area landmarks and businesses carry his name.

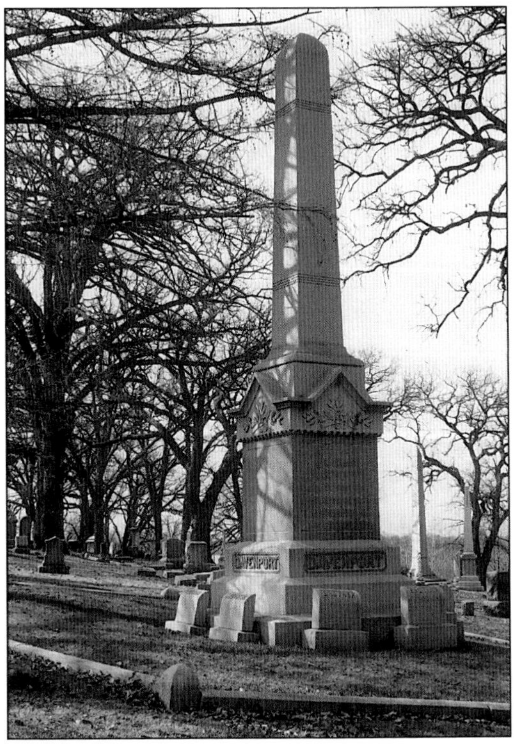

They lie in a quiet place now, the earthly remains of George Davenport and his descendants. The finger branches of trees offer a lacy surrounding; barren and empty in the wintertime, yet plush with green during the spring and summer. The tombstone name, Davenport, stands in proud serenity, not designed in ornate gingerbread like so many markers of the time, but simply strong and solemn. The individual markers of the family that gave the city its name are huddled around the towering sphere.

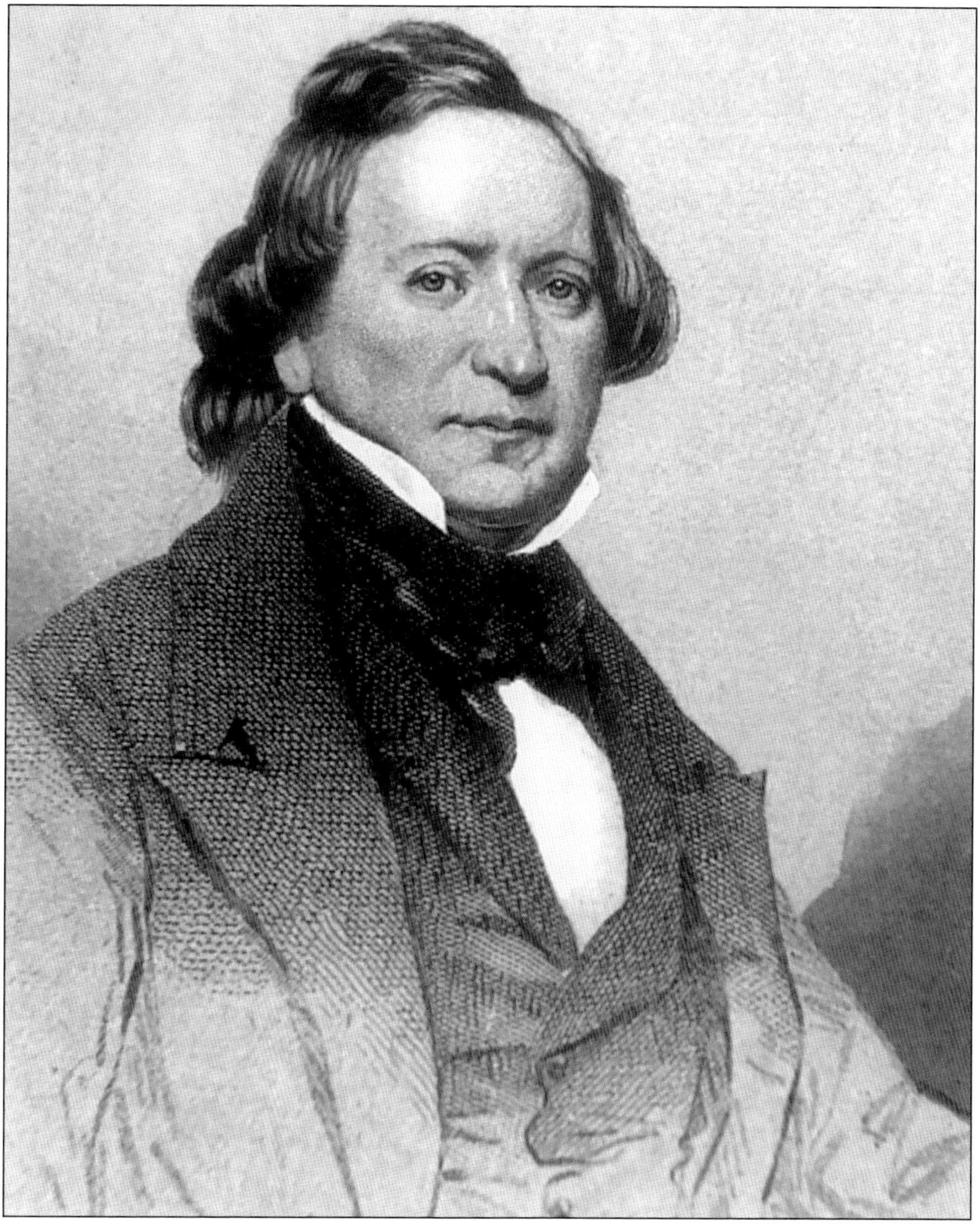

Born in Lincolnshire, England, George Davenport (1783–1845) arrived at Fort Armstrong in 1816. He took care of food and provisions required by the 8th U.S. Infantry Regiment quartered at the frontier outpost along the Mississippi River. He also operated a fur-trading business in Iowa, Illinois, and Wisconsin. He lived with his family in a log cabin on Arsenal Island. During the Black Hawk War, Davenport served as a colonel and quartermaster for the Illinois militia. Military reports label him as "trustworthy, competent, and respected by all." In 1833, he supervised the building of a grand family home. He helped extensively in the platting of the city, named Davenport in his honor. "And a more worthy name the city could not have," observed another area leader, Antoine LeClaire. On the 4th of July, 1845, thieves broke into his home and murdered George Davenport. He was 62.

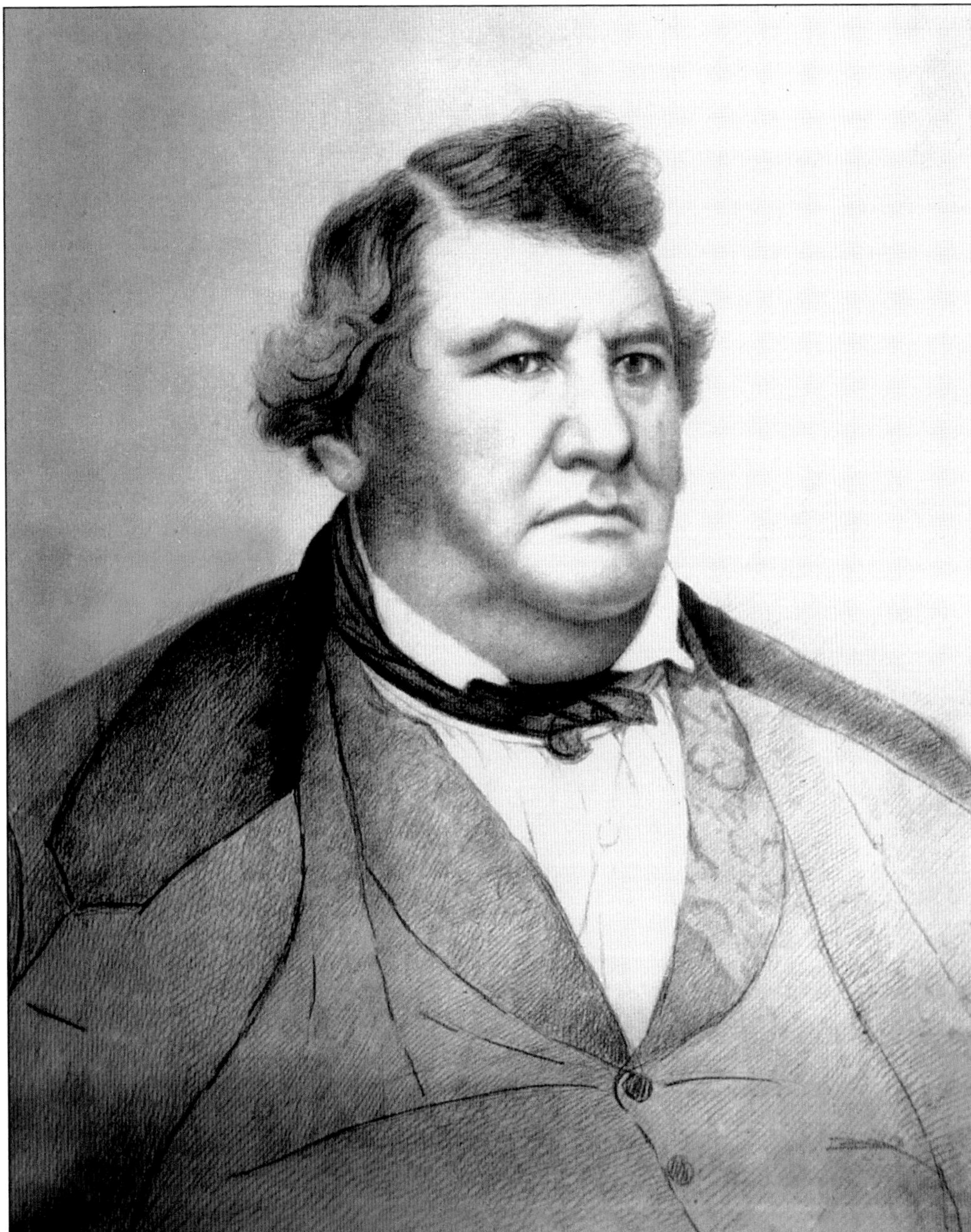

Antoine LeClaire (1797–1861) was a big man, his body eventually carrying over 300 pounds on a 5 foot, 10-inch frame. Yet his ample girth did not diminish his ability to dream, innovate, and accomplish. Arriving at Fort Armstrong as a translator in 1818, LeClaire recognized the potential of the surrounding area and bought up much land. With six other men, he planned and platted the town that eventually became Davenport, named after LeClaire's close friend Colonel George Davenport, an English trader and ferryman. Credited with establishing Davenport's first hotel, ferry, and foundry, LeClaire was also the town's first postmaster, using his pockets for mailbags. The first three months of delivering the mail netted LeClaire the grand sum of six bits, or 75¢.

The new house on West Second was going to be the home for Dr. John Emerson and his bride. Emerson first came to the Davenport area in 1833, when he was stationed at Fort Armstrong on Rock Island. At that time he brought a slave with him, Dred Scott. Later transferred to Fort Snelling, Emerson bought a female slave as a wife for Scott and sent them back to St. Louis. Emerson joined them later. When Emerson and his wife returned to live in Davenport in 1843, this new house was erected. Emerson never lived long enough to reside in the home, dying of consumption. He died at the LeClaire House and was buried in the city's earliest cemetery, located at Sixth and LeClaire Street.

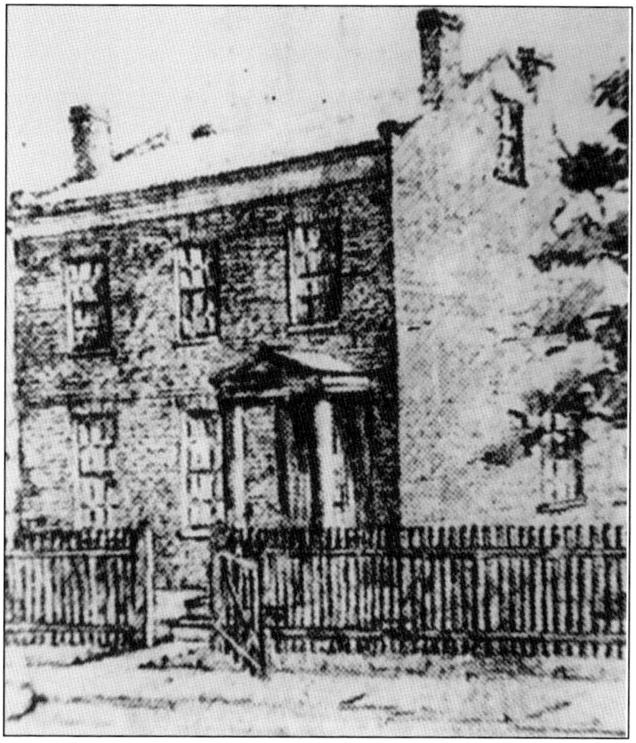

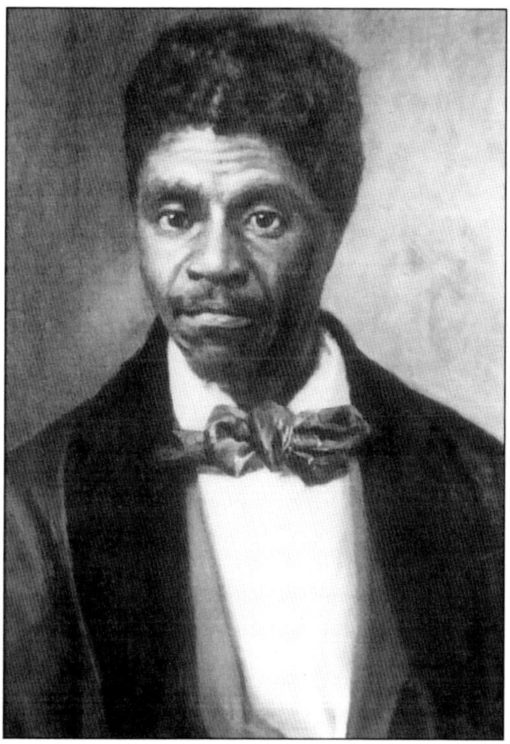

His name was Dred Scott, and in the middle of the 19th century he became known around the country. As a slave to Dr. John Emerson, Scott lived in various free states until he was sent back to St. Louis. Emerson decreed on his deathbed in Davenport that his slaves should be disposed of by his wife. Dred Scott sued, contending that his previous residence in free states made him free. Not so, said the U.S. Supreme Court in a matter to be called "The Dred Scott Decision." The judges contended that Negroes were not citizens, and therefore could not sue in federal courts. Furthermore, states could not take legal property, including slaves, held in other states.

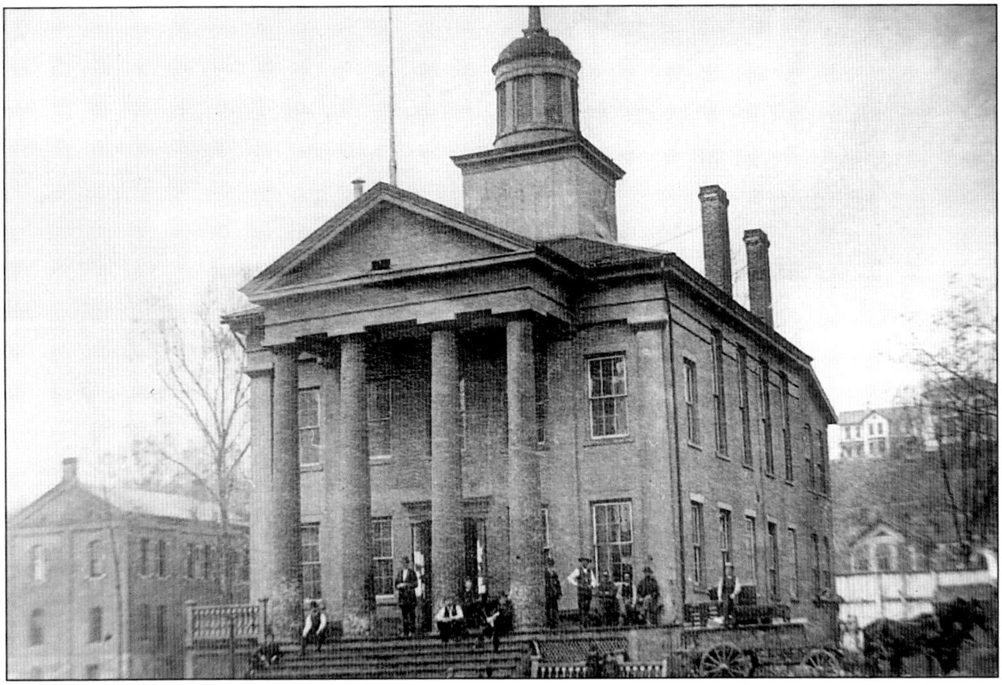

A five-year battle of words raged before this $20,000 county courthouse was built in 1842 on Bolivar Square. Both the residents of Rockingham, a town adjoining the present Davenport, and residents of Davenport wanted their town to be designated as the county seat. Three elections were held before Davenport claimed victory, largely with the help of Antoine LeClaire's endorsement and his $3,000 financial contribution.

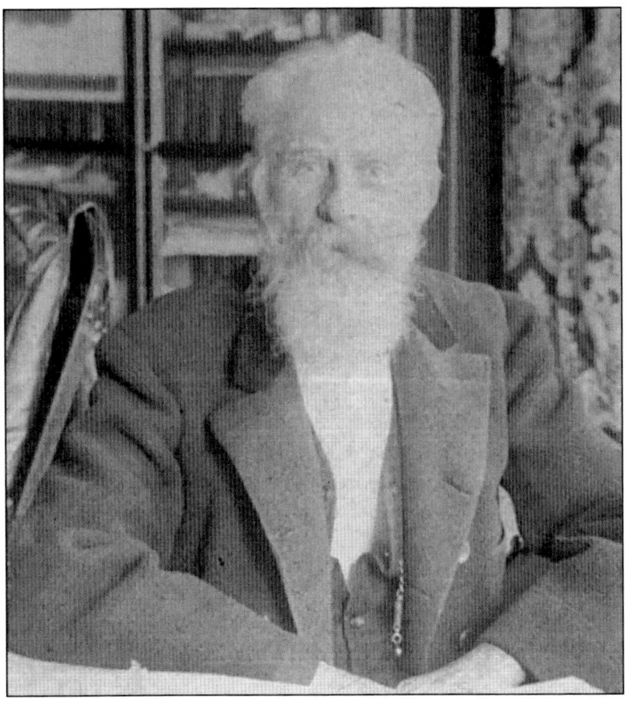

No, it's not someone interviewing to be Santa Claus for the Davenport Chamber of Commerce, or trying out for Kris Kringle in "A Miracle on Thirty-Fourth Street." The gentleman is Nicholas Fejervary, who came to Davenport with other Hungarians when his country underwent a revolution in 1848. Considered quite a philosopher, he invested in area farmland and real estate. He also led in the construction of the Civil War Soldier's Monument. He returned to Hungary after peace was established in that country. Following his death, Fejervary's family donated his land to the city. Say, maybe he was kind of a Santa Claus!

Two

Boomtown and a Dash of Culture

Frontier reels and fiddlers give way
To polished shoe, manners, and glide.
Swish of billowing hoop skirt and dark-clad soldier arms tighten.
"This is our last waltz, my love."
From the side, toe-tapping German Mutter and Vater look on.

Growth continues through the years.
The burgeoning city dons houses of note, church steeples, businesses, and riverfront industry.

"Culture. Davenport needs culture,"
Second and third generation Davenporters declare.
Schuetzen Park, Kimball House, academies of learning, and more strive to
Inspire knowledge and rhetoric as folks ponder the coming century.

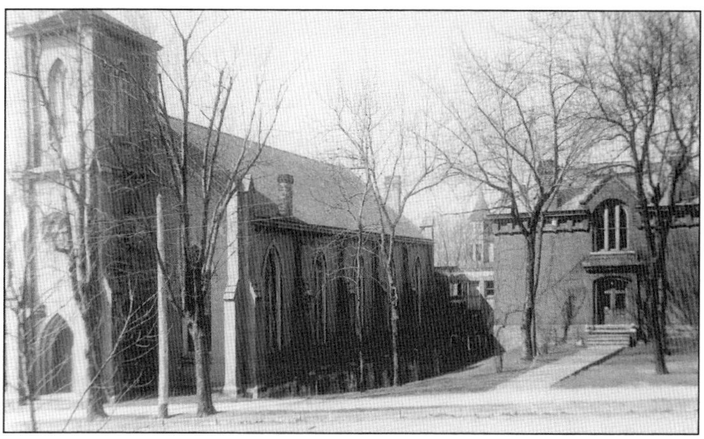

The Davenport Academy and Science Hall, a forerunner to the Putnam Museum, was founded in 1867. It sat next to the Presbyterian Church. Andrew Johnson was president, after taking office following the assassination of Abraham Lincoln in 1865. A variety of programs, most related to some form of science, were offered to community residents by the academy. In August of 1869, members photographed a solar eclipse using the latest photographic equipment available. "Amazing!" declared one Davenport resident, Henry Brecht.

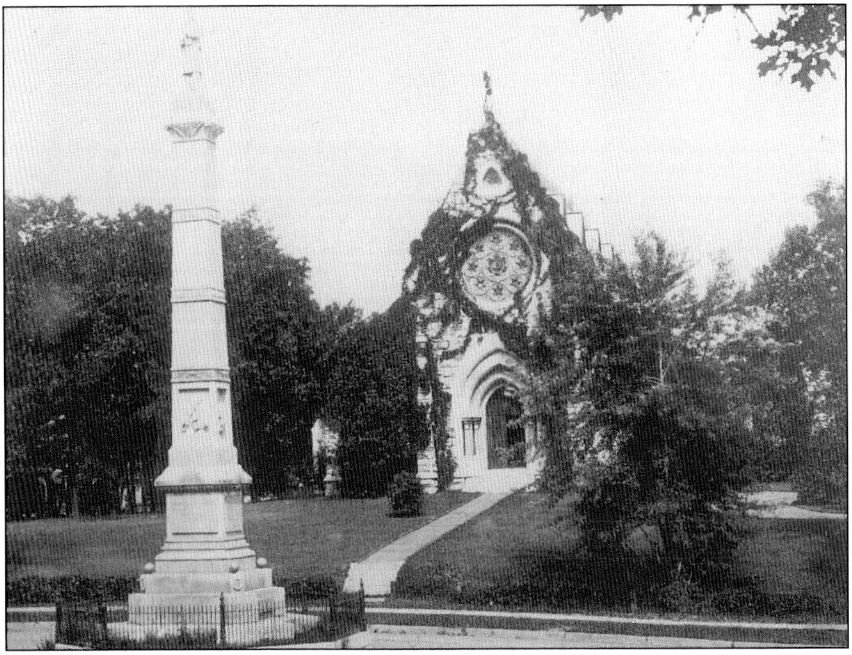

During the Civil War years, Davenport residents knew well the human and financial cost of fighting. Over 12,000 Confederate soldiers were housed in the Rock Island Prison, where they filled 84 barrack buildings. Of the scores of city residents who signed up for the Union forces, few returned whole in body and mind. Others returned forever scarred in body or sanity by the demands of the War Between the States. Some returned in wooden boxes. In honor of those who made the supreme sacrifice, this Soldier's Monument was erected. The elegant Grace Episcopal Church can be seen in the background. "Let us hope this will be the only time the blood of soldiers must be shed for our nation," said the dedication speaker. Sadly enough, his hopes were not realized.

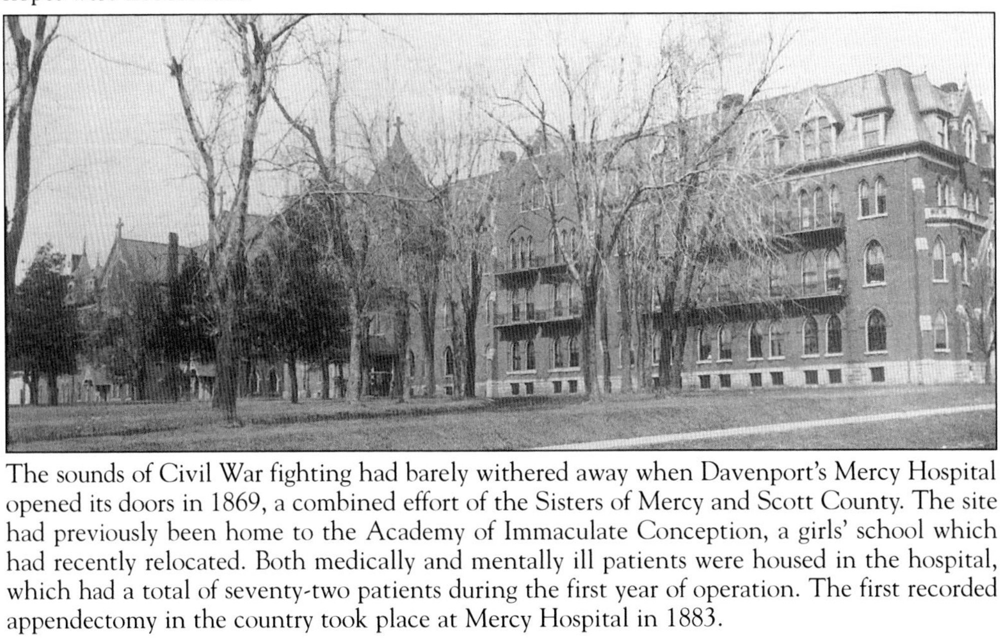

The sounds of Civil War fighting had barely withered away when Davenport's Mercy Hospital opened its doors in 1869, a combined effort of the Sisters of Mercy and Scott County. The site had previously been home to the Academy of Immaculate Conception, a girls' school which had recently relocated. Both medically and mentally ill patients were housed in the hospital, which had a total of seventy-two patients during the first year of operation. The first recorded appendectomy in the country took place at Mercy Hospital in 1883.

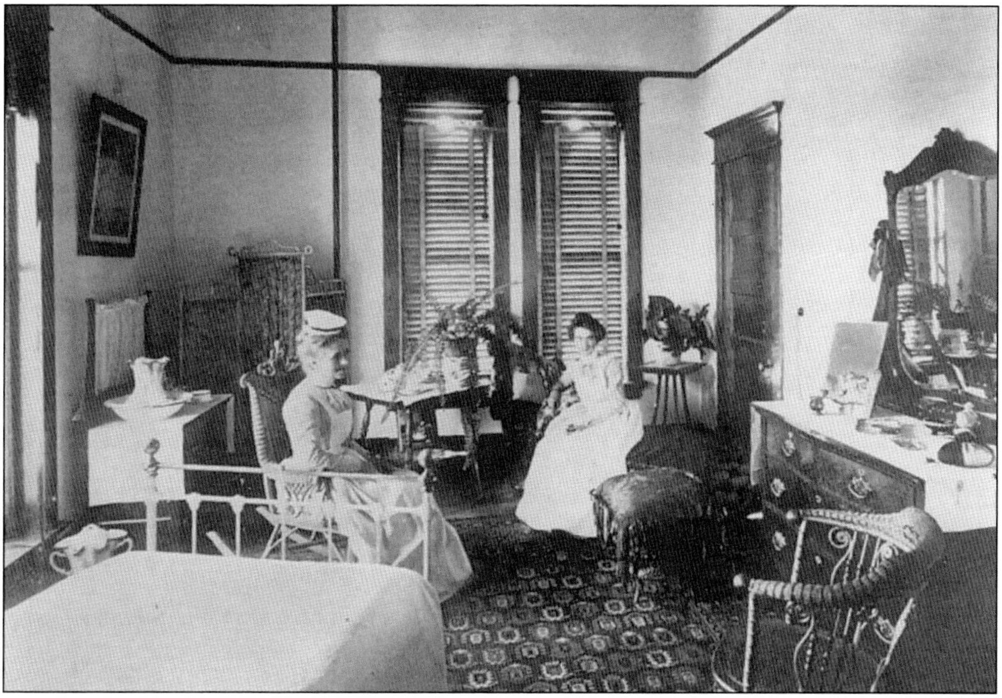

By 1901, Mercy Hospital established a glowing reputation in the Midwest as a fine medical and care center. A fire damaged the facility in 1890, but the Sisters of Mercy quickly restored the hospital to smooth running order. Private rooms, like the one pictured here, afforded colorful carpeting, comfortable furniture for both patients and guests, and richly toned woodwork. The surgery unit underwent constant change in an effort to provide the latest equipment. Early 20th century improvements included new-fangled electrical wiring, and a x-ray machine that was installed in 1904.

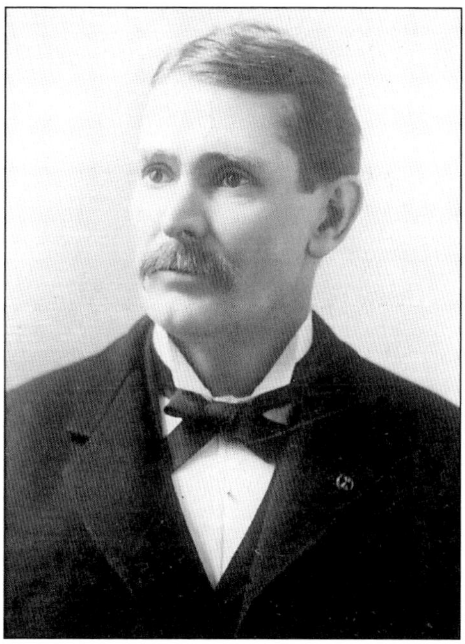

"We better talk to Mayor McClelland about this. He'll know what to do." Such was the buzz in Davenport during the 1870s, and the city's chief executive had more than his share of problems to handle. Bicycles became popular, and kids were always riding them into the river. Saloon patrons with a few too many beverages in them also liked settling their skirmishes in the Mississippi. Often, the river would rise without warning, and Davenport residents would find their businesses and homes under water. "If there's a problem, come and get me," the mayor ordered. Many times, that's what happened!

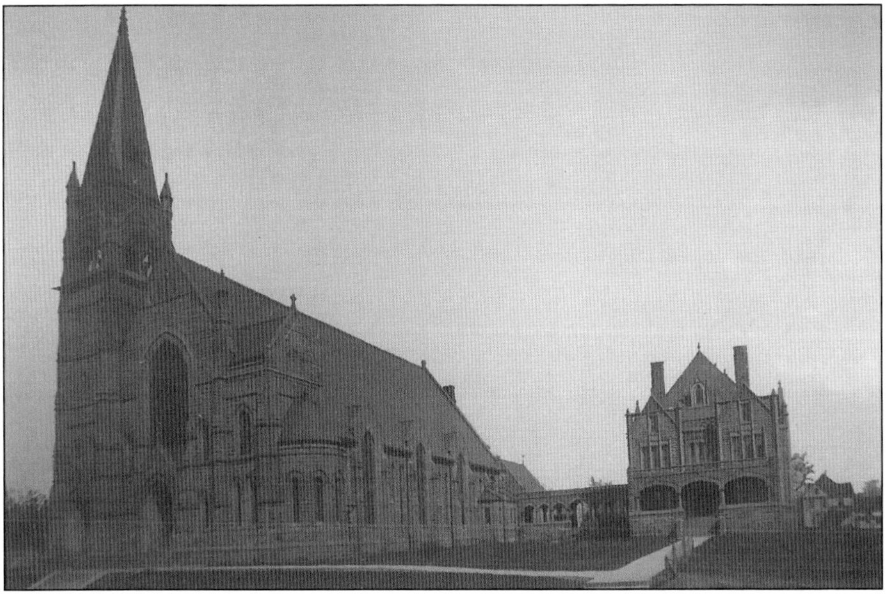

The steady growth of the Roman Catholic population necessitated the establishment of a Davenport Diocese in 1882. A cathedral was needed to serve as the bishop's seat. A fund drive by the faithful quickly raised $100,000 for construction. Begun in 1889, the structure was completed and dedicated as Sacred Heart in 1891. Irish churchgoers in the neighborhood nicknamed the cathedral "Cork Hill." Future additions to the complex included a rectory, convent, and school. "It reminds me of the grand churches we visited in Europe," observes Jason Moskowitz, a Quad-Citian who graduated from Notre Dame and now resides in Chicago.

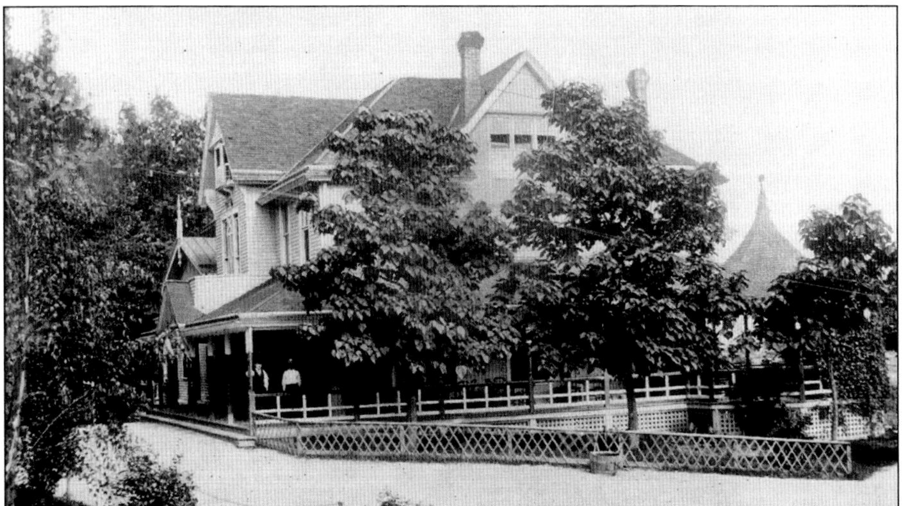

Ja! For German Americans living in Davenport in the 1880s and 1890s, Schuetzen Park was the place to go for *gut* band music, food, beverages, and bowling. Most of all, Sunday afternoon promenades gave *volkes* the chance to exchange stories and gossip. Streetcars brought guests almost to the doorstep. Anti-German sentiments during World War I prompted a name change to Forest Park, but old-timers clung to the original label. The facility became Forest Park Sanitarium in 1923, a chiropractic mental hospital. In the 1960s it became The Good Samaritan, a home for the elderly.

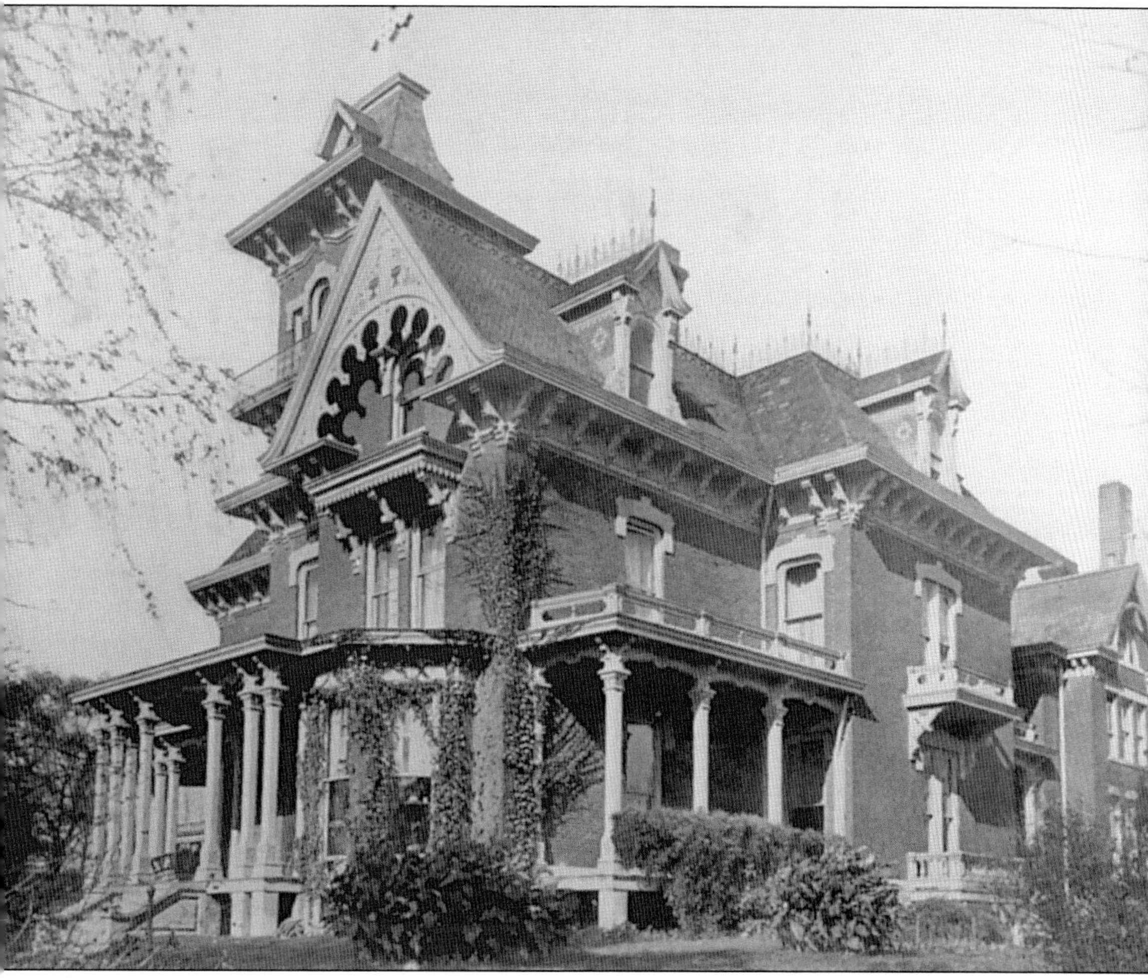

Ah, wouldn't Nancy Drew enjoy exploring this place? Once the residence of John L. Davies, this stately mansion with its gingerbread trim became a school for young ladies called "Cambria Place" in 1884. It was established by the Episcopal Diocese, and the girls attending quickly began calling it St. Katherine's. An annex was soon added and in 1902, a chapel and gymnasium followed. The acquisition of the Renwick mansion and the McCandless property later expanded the school. Longtime resident Carolina Schmidt recalls "the wonderful stories my grandmother would tell us about old St. Katherine's. Secretly, some of the girls referred to it as St. Kit's, but those were the most daring girls. Refinement and etiquette were as important as subject matter. Girls practiced how to walk and stand, and how to appear to be interested when not. It was a special time, I think."

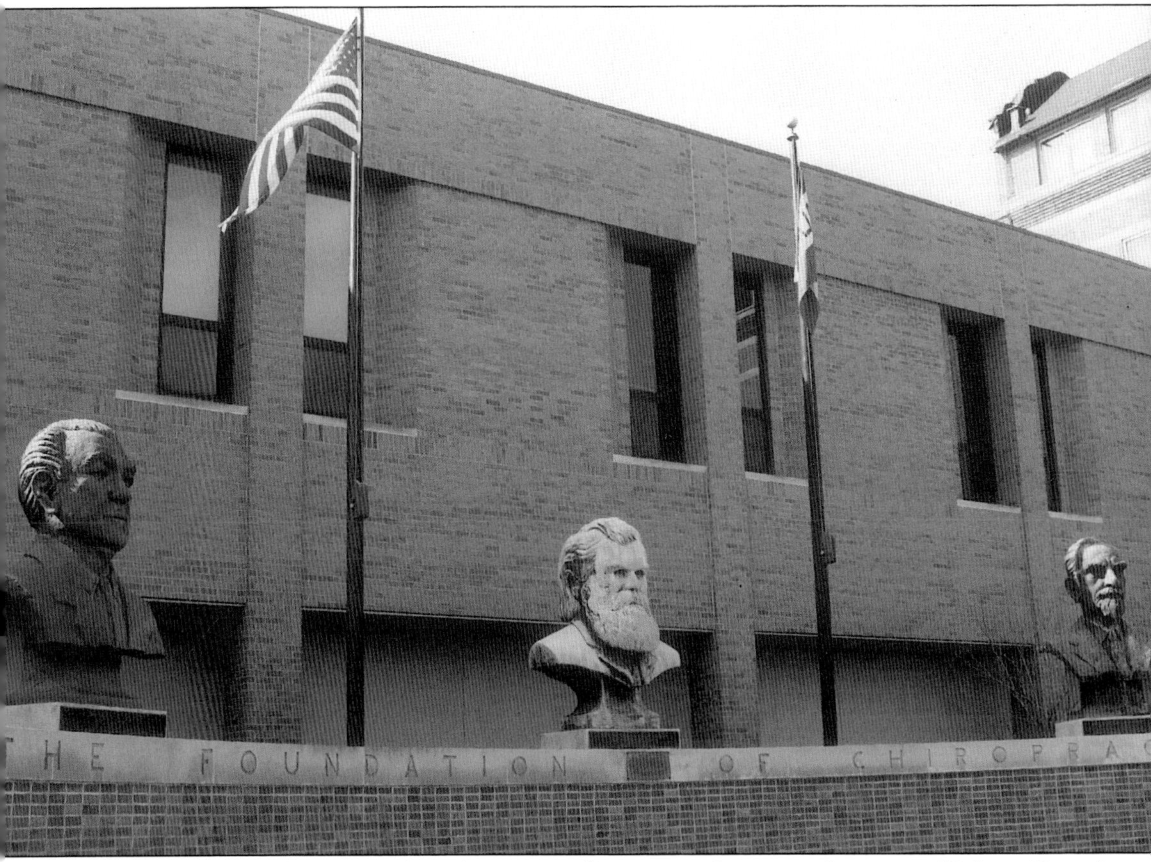

Few names have become such a vibrant part of Davenport history as the name of Palmer. Daniel David Palmer's arrival in the city in 1885 went virtually unnoticed at the time, but by the turn of the century, he had made himself well known to many. His "chiropractic" (Greek, meaning "done by hand") manner of healing aches and pains was sworn to by many, and sworn at by others. The healing treatment focused on the spine, and Daniel David's son, B.J., followed in his father's teaching footsteps. Considerably more flamboyant, B.J. was a world traveler who brought souvenirs of his trips back to Davenport. Palmer's collection of artwork and sculpture brought countless visitors to 805 Brady Street to admire his own "Little Bit o' Heaven." B.J. Palmer's main interest was the College of Chiropractic, a school whose student body climbed into the thousands. Despite the attacks of the medical community on chiropractic medicine ("It's unscientific!"), the healing method gradually gained widespread support. B.J. Palmer's son, David, lent dignity and a business-like approach to everything connected with the school, and he expanded the family interest into a variety of community projects and programs.

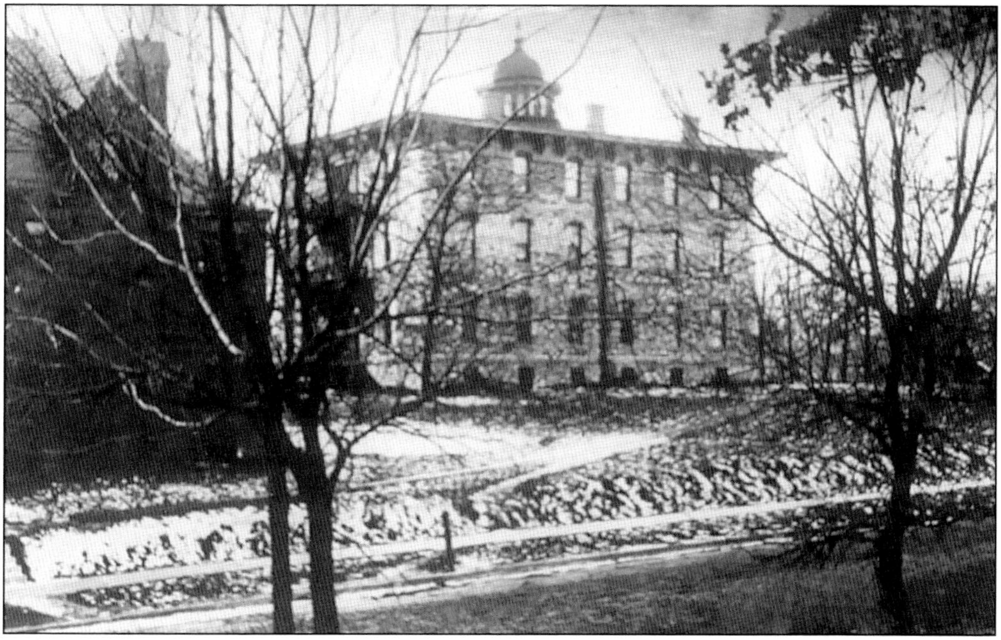

"Oh, we love the halls of ivy…" Davenport's claim to the title of college town dates back long before the days of St. Ambrose and Marycrest. Wolfe Hall was known as Iowa College before the Congregational institution relocated to Grinnell, Iowa, in the middle 1800s. Wolfe Hall then became one of several buildings forming Griswold College, operated into the 1900s by the Episcopalian Diocese of Iowa.

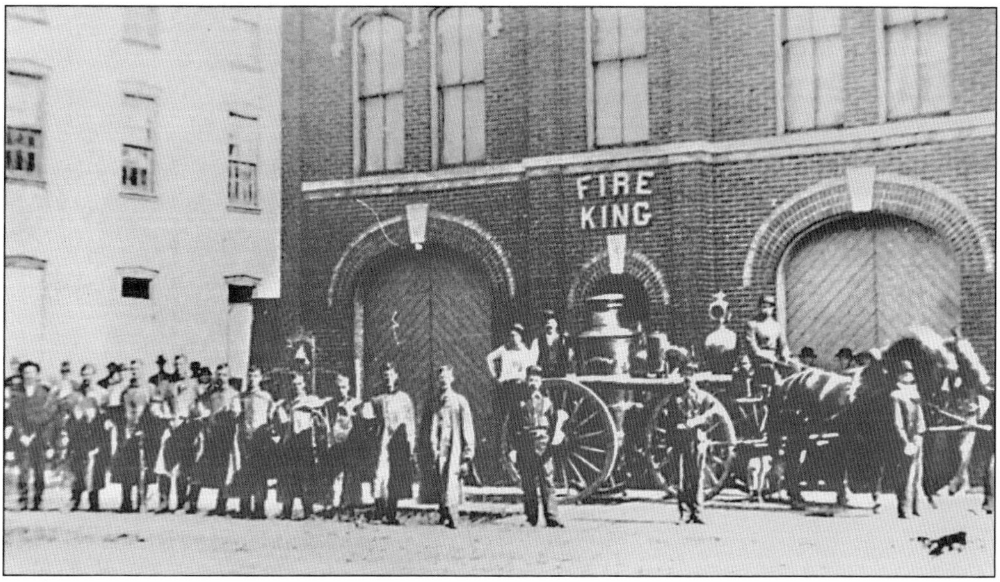

In the 1880s, Davenport relied on volunteers to maintain its fire department, and from most accounts, the citizens were well served. Horses, kept in prime shape, pulled the fire wagons, and efforts were made to keep all equipment in top condition. The transition from horses to motorized engines took place between 1916 and 1918, and by that time firefighters were paid employees of the city. Few fires traumatized the city more than the St. Elizabeth's Hospital blaze on January 7, 1950, when forty mental patients and one nurse lost their lives.

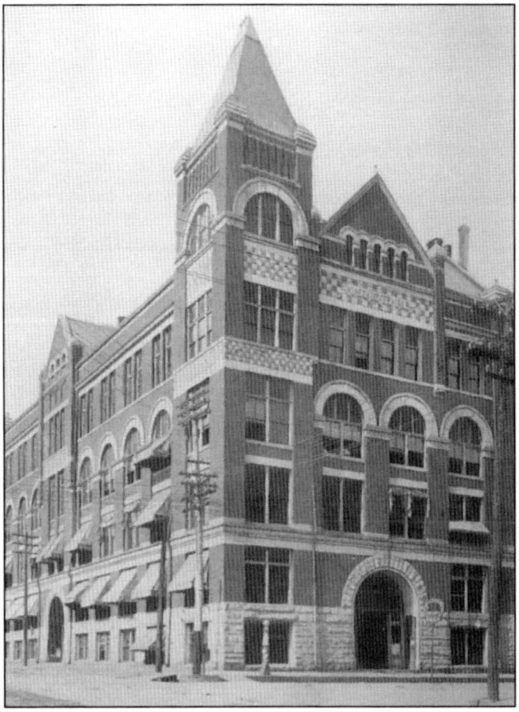

Following the Civil War, secret societies and lodges—over 60 in all—sprang up all over Davenport. Some stemmed from religion, others from work origins, and still others from ethnic backgrounds. Most featured a variety of recreational and social activities. Five Mason lodges pooled their financial resources to build this Masonic Temple at the northeast corner of Third and Main. It was completed in 1887 at a cost of $60,000.

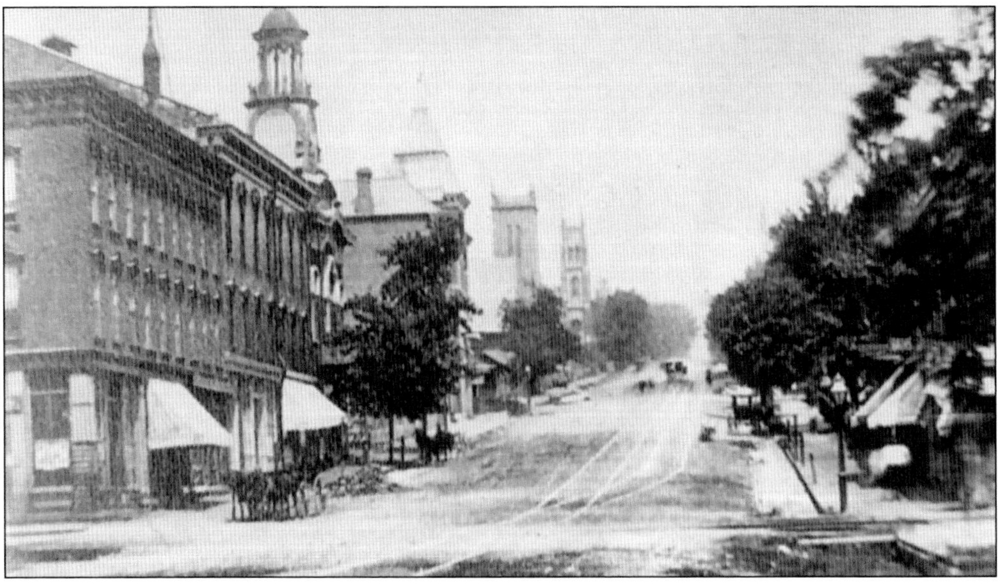

Does this street look familiar? Actually, the photo was taken in 1884. Chester A. Arthur was occupying the White House at the time, while a Mississippi River man from down south in Hannibal, Missouri, had recently won national attention with his latest bestseller, *Huckleberry Finn*. His name was Mark Twain (Samuel Clemens). During this time, Davenport's own Octave Thanet, also known as Alice French, was fast becoming the best-known short story magazine writer in the country. If you need a hint about the picture here, imagine standing at Fifth Street and gazing north up the hillside. If you identified the street as Brady, go collect your million from Regis Philbin, or lace up your Nikes for a Bix 7-style dash up the hillside.

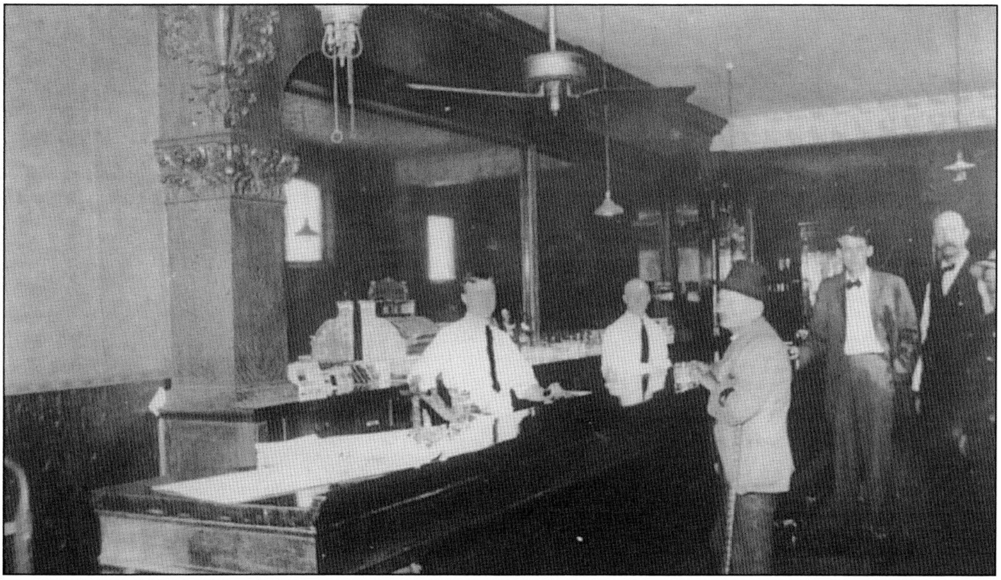

Flash back to 1894. President Grover Cleveland occupied the White House. Unemployment was rising, and wheat sold for 49¢ a bushel after averaging over a dollar between 1865 and 1873. Fire at the Chicago World's Fair caused $2 million in damage. But inside the doors of Frick's Tavern in Davenport, life meandered along cheerfully, with everybody knowing your name, and some generous soul always willing to buy a round for the house. Cheers!

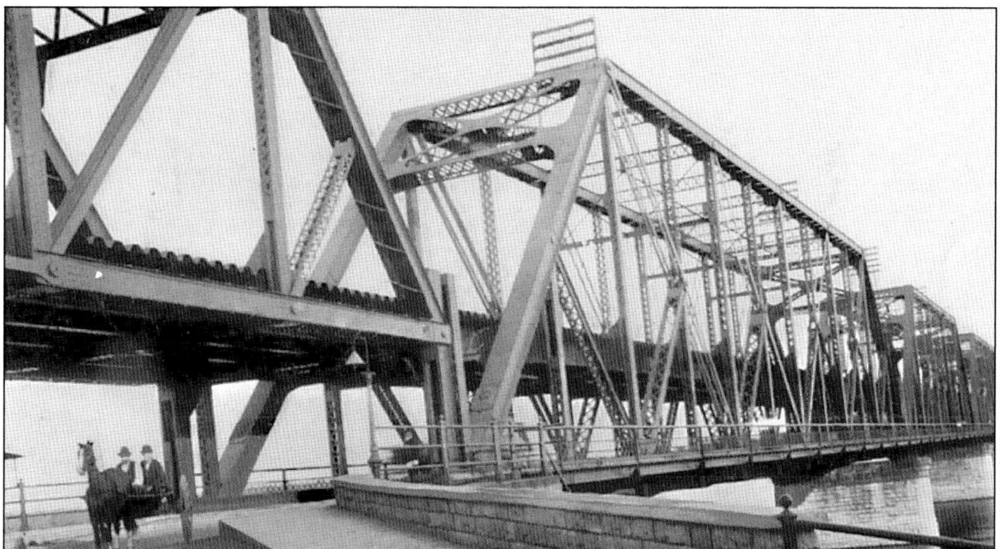

"London Bridge is falling down, falling down, falling down…" Children during the latter part of the 1800s sang this rhythmic melody, nonsensical as it was. But along the Mississippi River, construction crews ensured the Government Bridge would stand strong. Completed in 1895, the span included a double track above, a double lane below, and thanks to an innovative fellow named Thomas Edison, electric lights. Five years later the Crescent Railroad Bridge was completed downstream, adding to the reputation of the area as a transportation mecca. Still used a century later, motorized vehicles bear Davenport residents to work and home along these bridges.

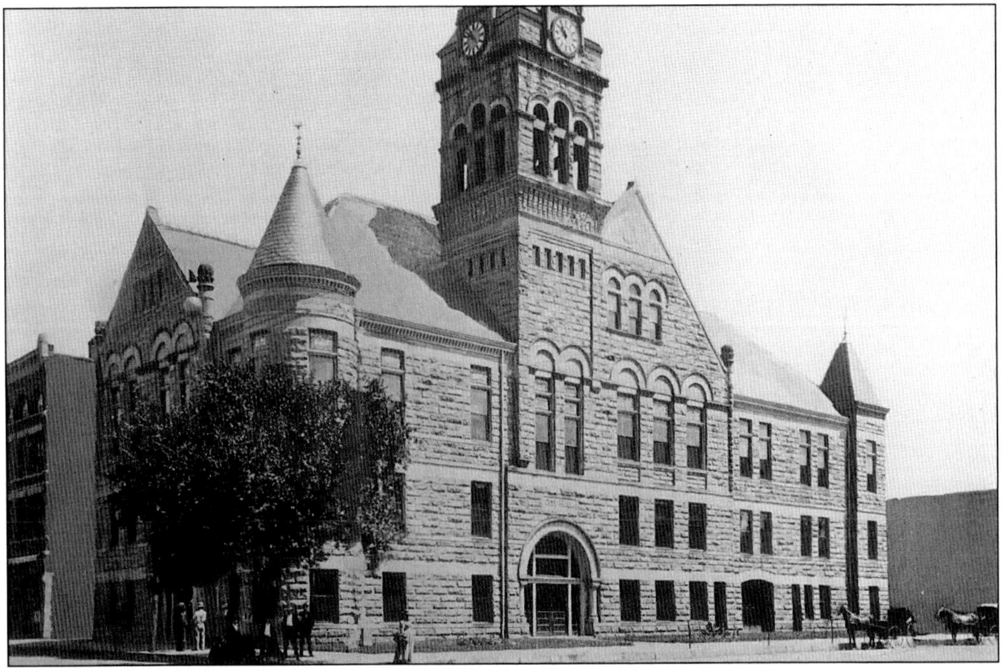

Eighteen ninety-five was a major year for construction in Davenport. On the riverfront, the Government Bridge was in the final stages of completion. In the city itself, the Davenport City Hall was finished. Plans for the structure came from a national design contest, ensuring people all over the country knew of the project. Many scoffed at "tightwad" Davenport city leaders for only spending $100,000 for the materials and construction. Costs of fixing up the interior of the building were considerable during the next few years, and ridding it of soot deposits, due to its proximity to the railway stations, remained a constant problem.

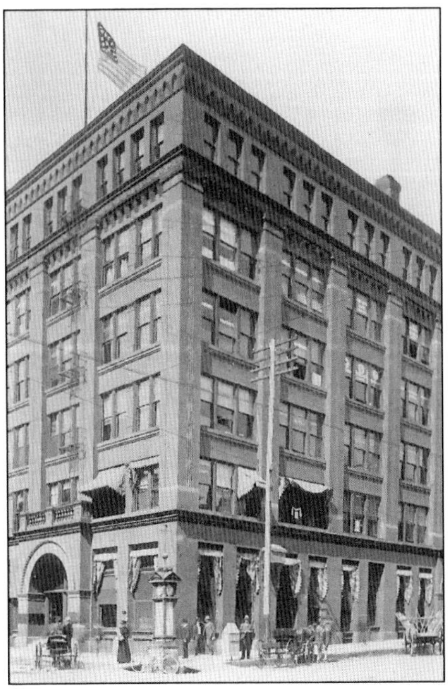

Davenport's McManus Building housed numerous attorneys and businessmen during the late 1800s, and it was a popular corner on which to pause and exchange the news and gossip of the day. The country was still growing, as evidenced by the new stars in the waving flag overhead. Early in the 1900s, the corner would take on unasked-for fame when it became the scene of a shoot-out. The shoot-out occurred when a Davenport man spotted his wife sitting in the buggy of a stranger. For many years, people spoke of the crime as the "McManus Murder" in reference to the site of the tragedy.

Three

TURN OF THE CENTURY AND THE 1900'S FIRST CHALLENGE

"Great Progress Expected in the 20th Century!" Davenport newspapers predict,
As close-clasped couples whirl in the New Year.
Wonders abound in coming years, horseless carriages driving over paved streets.
Weary homemakers rejoice when receiving a Voss washing machine.

Gold stars fill too many Davenport windows following the war to end all wars.
Dancing slippers gather dust in wardrobe cupboards.

Speakeasies fill up and sheiks and shebas charleston the night away.
Bix's cornet blows sweet and sad—not long enough.
Black Thursday blows in, banks close, and lives crash.

War comes again and Davenport sons and daughters head out.
Most come home: not all.

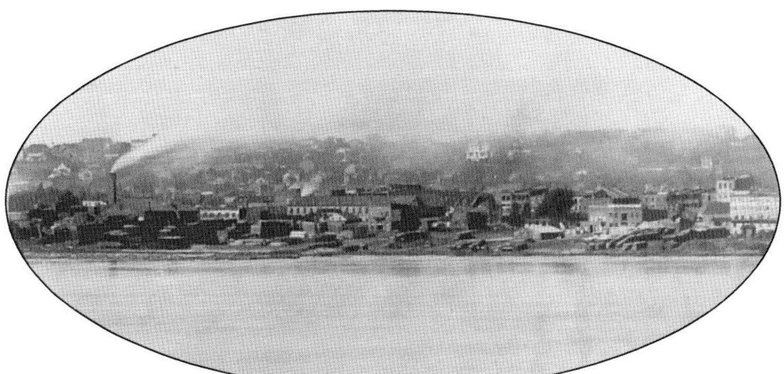

In the waning years of the 19th century, Ulysses S. Grant—hero of the Union forces during the Civil War—grappled with the intricacies and multiple duties of serving as the nation's president. The first Kentucky Derby was held in Churchill Downs, Kentucky, the winner receiving $2,850, and Luther Burbank developed new strains of berries, fruits, and vegetables. On a trip along the Mississippi River, sightseers could gaze over at the quickly growing city. The population stood at 21,184, and steadily increased with the birth of new businesses and industries.

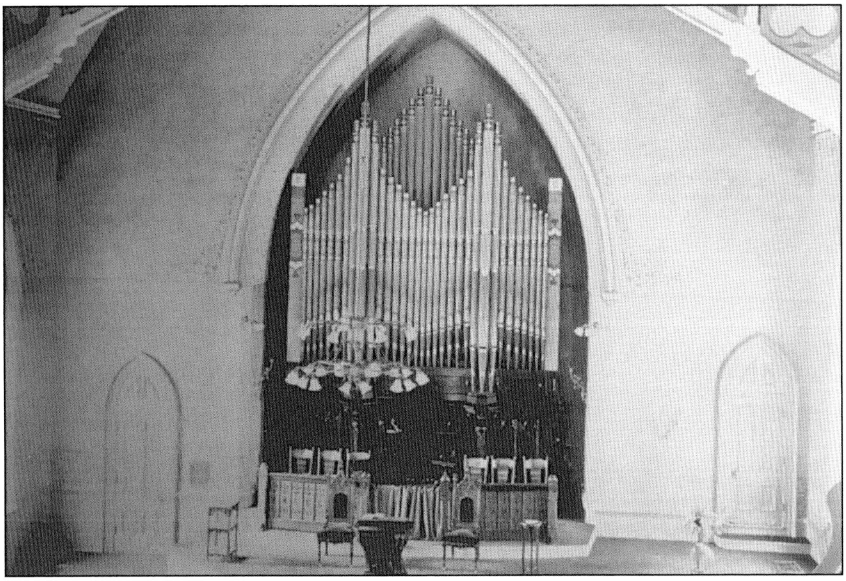

As the 1800s bid adieu and the 1900s entered, Davenport boasted of 23 churches scattered throughout the city. Their congregations worked together to bolster a respectable moral climate, but the individuals reigning at the pulpits had to admonish attendees to "worship God not only on Sunday, but every day of the week, in thought and in action." Most of the exteriors of the places of worship were of gray and brown stone, while the interiors varied. This 1901 photograph was taken from the balcony of the Edwards Congregational Church looking down at the altar.

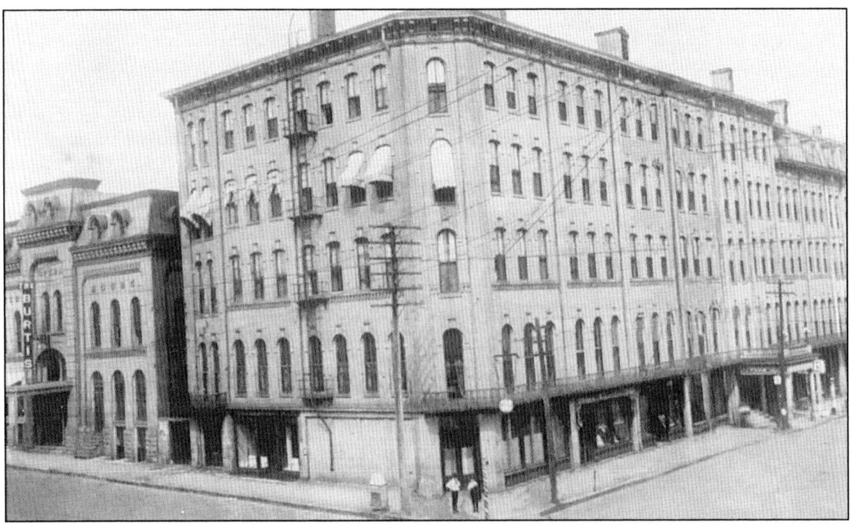

"Iowa's Finest Hotel!" It wasn't just Davenport residents who called it that, but many out-of-towners who stayed at the then luxurious accommodation. First called the Burtis-Kimball House, the structure opened in the 1870s. Amenities included gas lighting, running water, telegraph service, and elevators. Guests in the hotel's 150 rooms raved about the building's facilities. In 1880, the place became known as just the Kimball House, honoring a railroad superintendent. The hotel declined in quality and reputation, and a 1907 major fix-up did not help. When the Hotel Davenport opened in 1908, the Kimball House was divided into apartments.

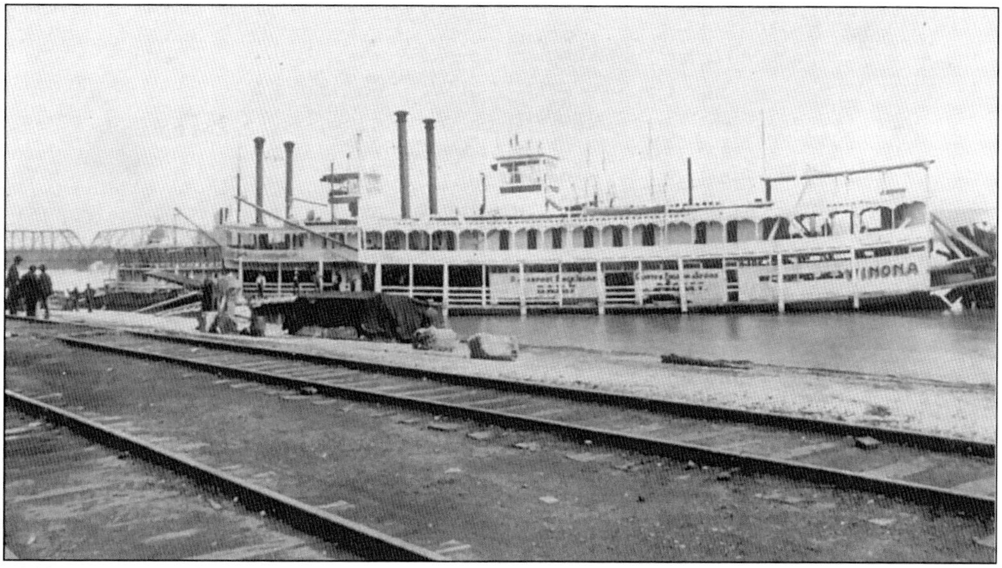

"Old Man River, that Old Man River..." It's interesting that the Mississippi is usually thought of as being masculine in gender, while the boats that sail on its waters are given the feminine gender. One thing is certain: people of both sexes are responsible for creating the strong community known as Davenport. This photo, snapped in 1901, catches the steamboat *Winona* arriving at the levee. The *Winona* was a cruise vessel. Passengers enjoyed fine dining and sights and sat down at night to listen to the ship's band play entertaining music. If the *Winona* was tied up for the night, locals might also come aboard and enjoy the concert.

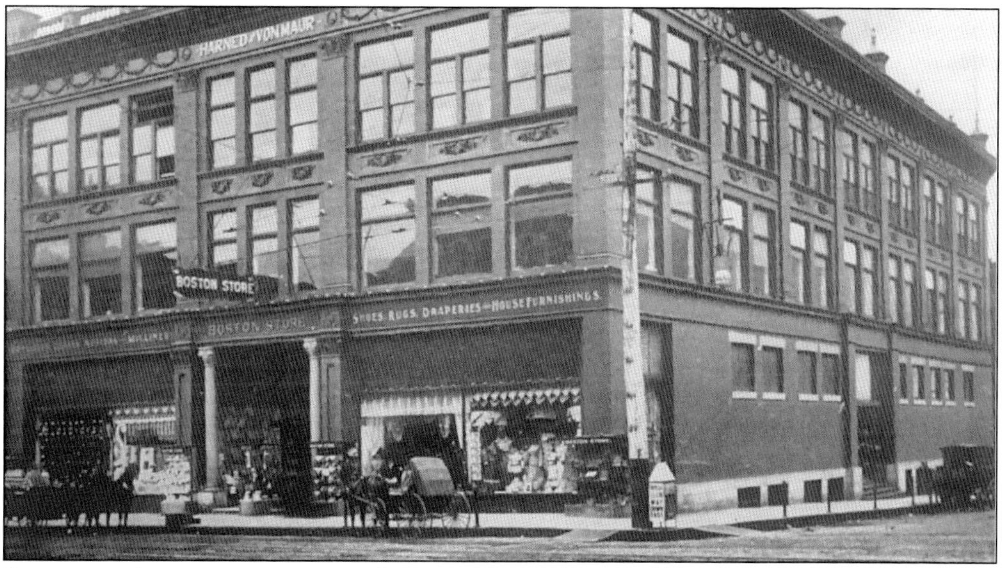

Davenport shops were not quite as busy in 1901 as they would be during the upcoming years' Dollar Day specials, but buggies and electric cars, conveying customers to the Boston Store, pulled up regularly. From draperies to hardware, housewares to millinery, buyers got their choice of quality brands that were transported via railroad cars or river craft. Streetcar tracks can be seen in front of the store, and executives fought to keep them on schedule. Notice the lightning rods, built into the architecture of the structure to maintain aesthetic composition and meet safety concerns.

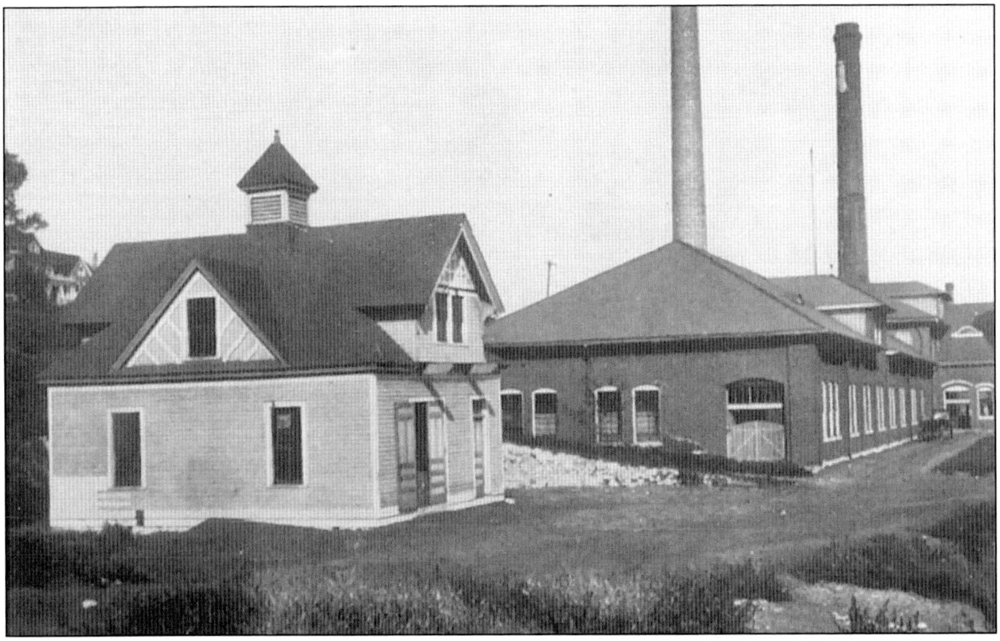

This 1902 picture is captioned "Plant of the Davenport Water Works: the Most Complete Water Plant in the World." Is that hyperbole? Hey, why couldn't it be? The city's relationship to the grand and glorious Mississippi River has always been put to good use, so let us cast away skepticism and modestly accept recognition: past, present, and future. Today, the water needs of Davenport and its neighboring communities are refreshed by the Iowa American Water Company.

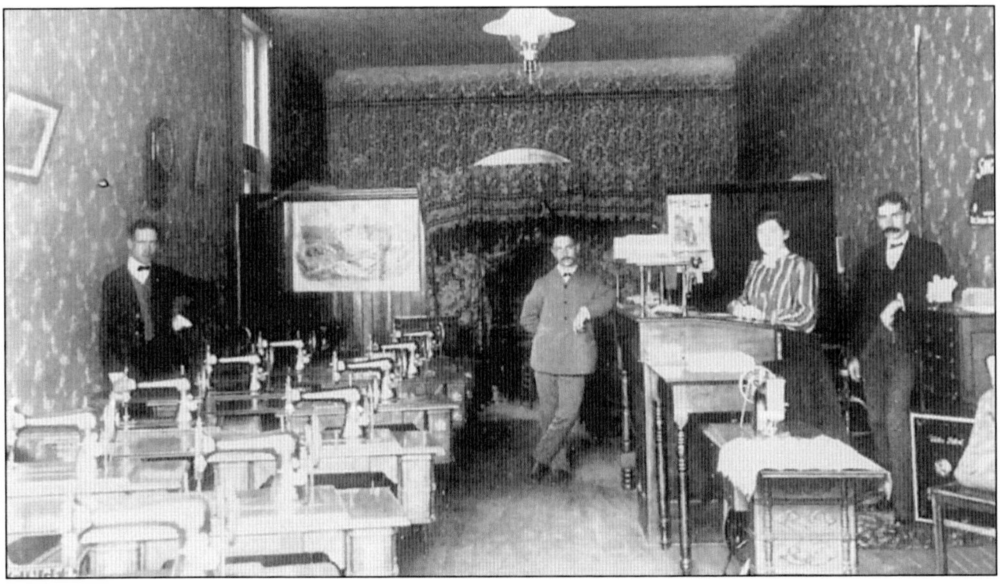

"No one sings like Caruso," reads a newspaper ad from the late 1890s, "and nothing sews like a Singer." The Singer Sewing Machine Store in downtown Davenport did a brisk business, and hatted and gloved female customers were willing to wait for the only lady among the staff to help them. Local artists displayed their offerings too, and people could purchase a machine to mend their rips and tears while taking home an original watercolor as well.

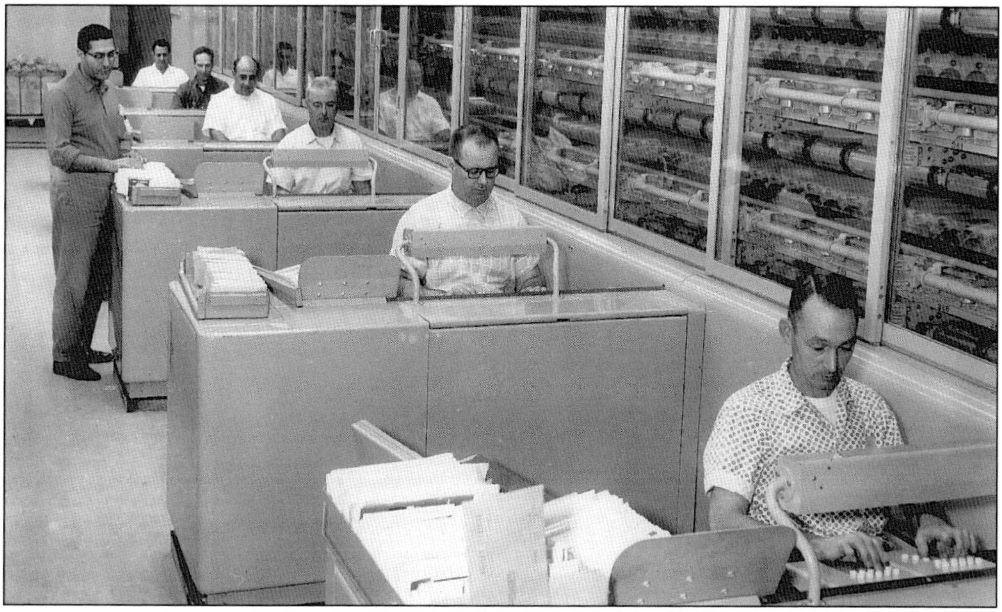

Local history identifies Davenport's first mail carrier as no less than Antoine LeClaire, who carried letters in his generously sized coat pockets. By 1886, nine mail carriers maintained routes, delivering around 1,500 pieces of mail each on a daily basis. They received approximately $600 yearly. The United States Post Office was the first federal building erected in Davenport in 1892 and stood 41 years until being razed in 1933. This 1960 picture catches postal workers busy in the present post office downtown.

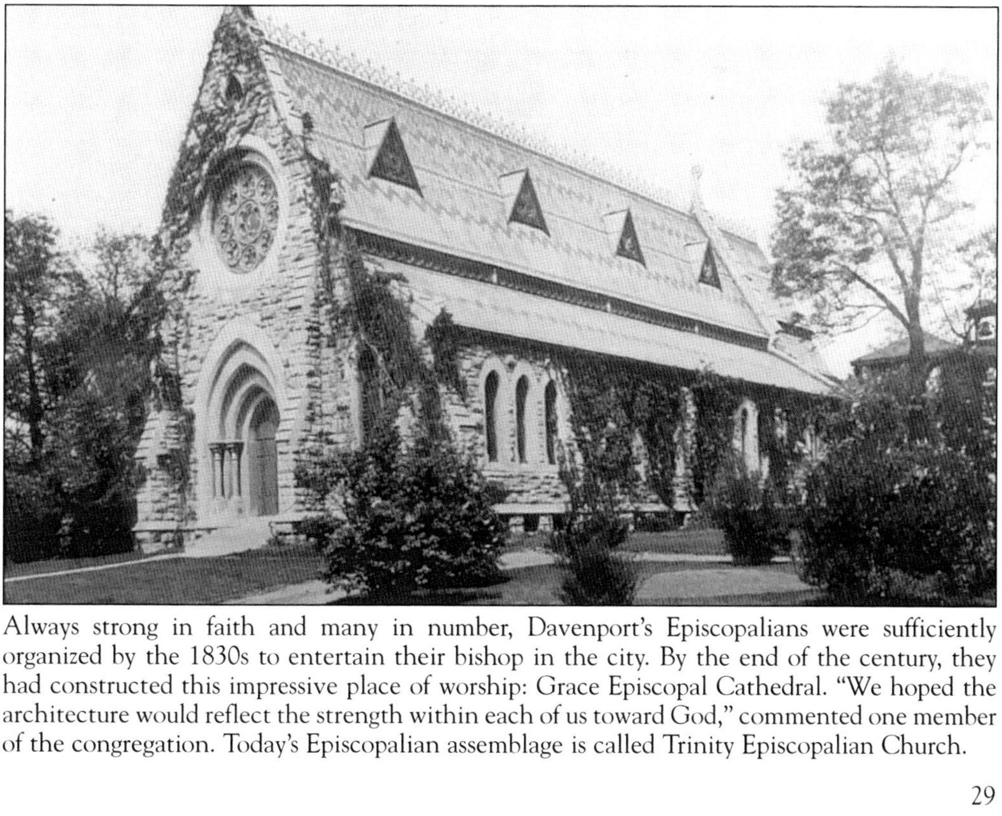

Always strong in faith and many in number, Davenport's Episcopalians were sufficiently organized by the 1830s to entertain their bishop in the city. By the end of the century, they had constructed this impressive place of worship: Grace Episcopal Cathedral. "We hoped the architecture would reflect the strength within each of us toward God," commented one member of the congregation. Today's Episcopalian assemblage is called Trinity Episcopalian Church.

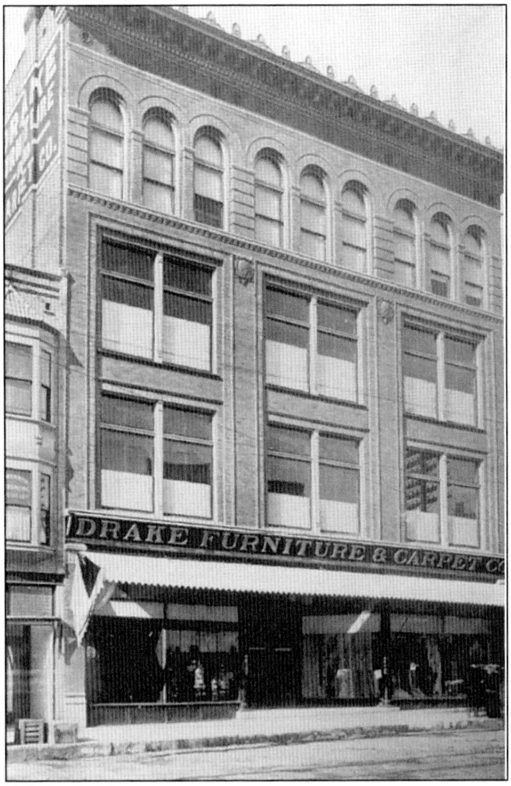

"Sofas and chairs and the carpeting on your floor—When you buy from Drake, you always get more!" The slogan used by Drake Furniture & Carpet Company in 1901 attracted many customers to downtown Davenport. "Drake's was a fine, reputable business," noted Francis Connors, a city resident whose family came to Davenport from Chicago in 1902. "We bought almost everything we owned from Drake's, and they even had an agreement to send potential customers to our home to show off their offerings. My grandfather received a small commission when the people bought from Drake's."

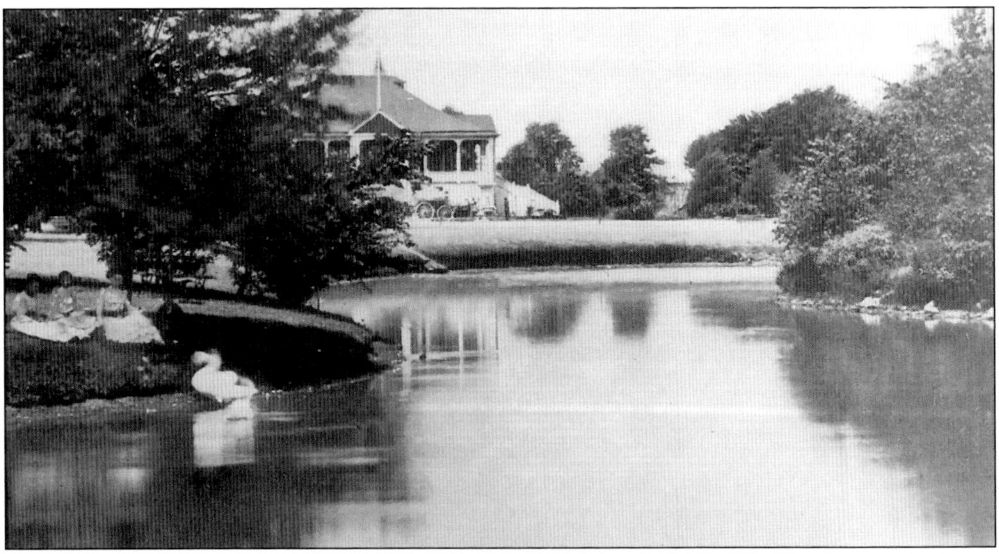

Well, if New York can have a Central Park, why can't Davenport? No reason at all, and the latter park has always been far safer than the former. Laid out on the old Scott County fairgrounds, Davenport's Central Park attracted immediate attention in the late 1800s. Streetcars conveyed visitors up Brady Street, letting them off to enjoy the fountains, conservatory, and music pavilion. Some preferred quiet walks along the pathways and across wooden bridges. Eventually, the park was renamed Vander Veer Park, in honor of a former park board member.

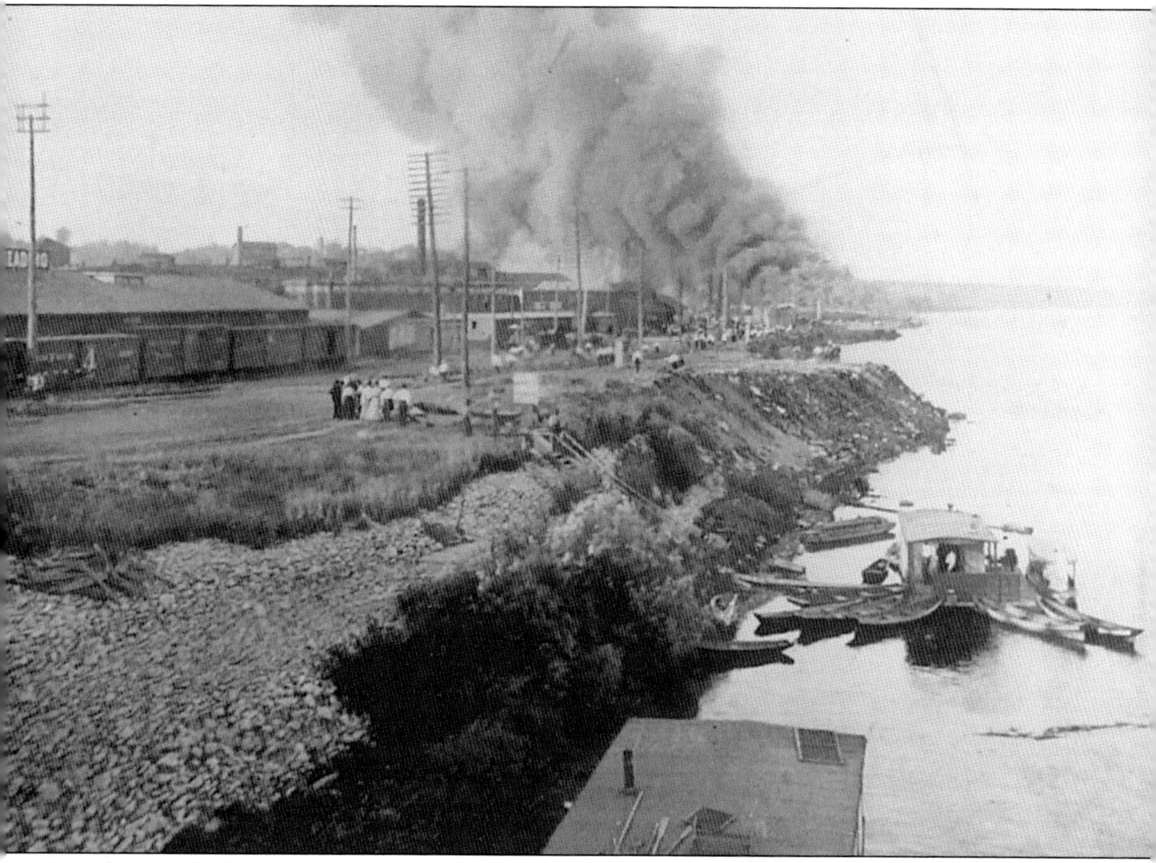

"In the good old summertime, in the good old summertime..." Before the days of air conditioning, Iowa summer days could get pretty muggy. Usually, dips into the Mississippi offered folks a chance to cool off. However, on the afternoon of July 25, 1901, the river shoreline became the scene of a blaze that first started at the Riverside Flour Inn. The fire then scorched a pathway to the Weyerhaeuser and Denkmann lumberyard. Firefighters arrived from Davenport, Rock Island, and Moline, but their combined and sweaty efforts failed to quell the raging flames. Even hoses exploded from the heat, alongside buckling streetcar and train tracks. The spectacular blaze brought spectators to the area, especially at the base of Tremont Avenue. Too late, those watching the fire realized they were in danger and fled from the scene, flames licking at their heels. For hours, the blaze raged on, until finally burning itself out. The community immediately threw itself into helping those who were directly affected. Eight blocks of buildings burned down, at a cost of over $1 million. Sympathetic sisters from the Academy of Immaculate Conception offered free housing to those who had lost their homes, while thousands of dollars rolled in for relief aid. Firefighters were never able to pinpoint the cause of the blaze.

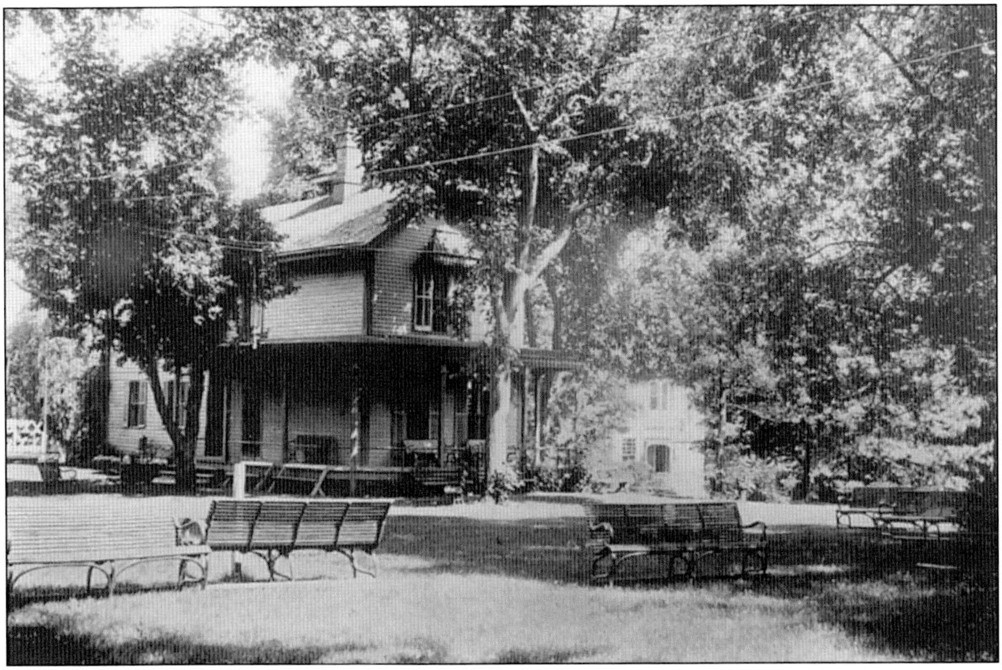

"Our kids need a safe, clean place to socialize." Such was the sentiment expressed by many Davenport residents during the 1890s. An agreement between Dr. A.M. Judy, a Unitarian minister, and other congregational leaders, led to this original clubhouse and to the construction of a handsome building in the early 20th century. The Outing Club offered facilities for bowling, lawn tennis, billiards, and cotillions. Today, the elegant and stately mansion maintains an active calendar of events that attracts members and guests alike.

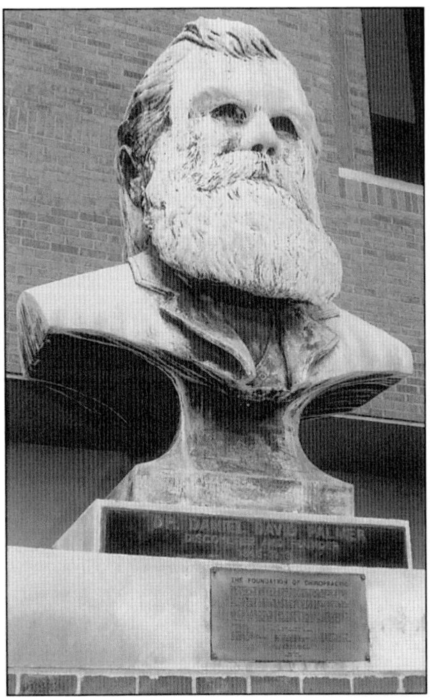

It all began with this fellow. Actually, it all began with the first person who moaned, "Oh, my aching back." Daniel David Palmer was born near Toronto, Canada in 1845. He developed a form of magnetic healing and settled in Burlington, Iowa, in 1893. In 1895, he moved to Davenport where he further explored the system of adjusting joints, especially in the spine, by manual manipulation to heal disease and injury. He opened the Palmer School of Chiropractic in 1898, which was taken over by his son, Bartlett Joshua ("B.J.") in 1903.

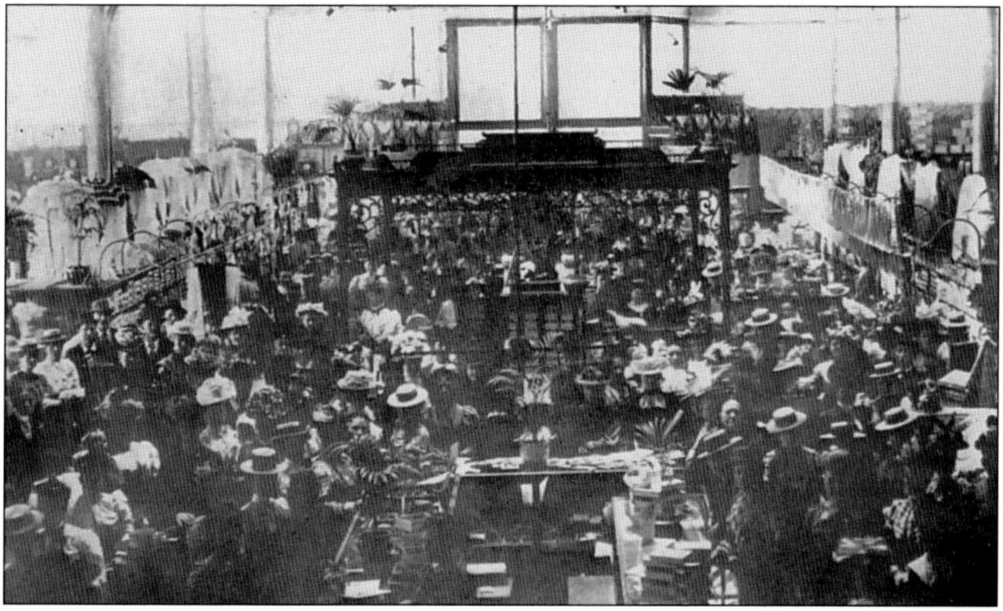

Major department stores competed for business in downtown Davenport in the late 1800s. Customers stood elbow to elbow in the aisles of the Boston Store as evidenced here, a scene that resembles today's floor of the New York Stock Exchange. The idea of being able to purchase every type of home furnishing or tool under one roof was a popular one, stemming from the country store idea of the Old Wild West.

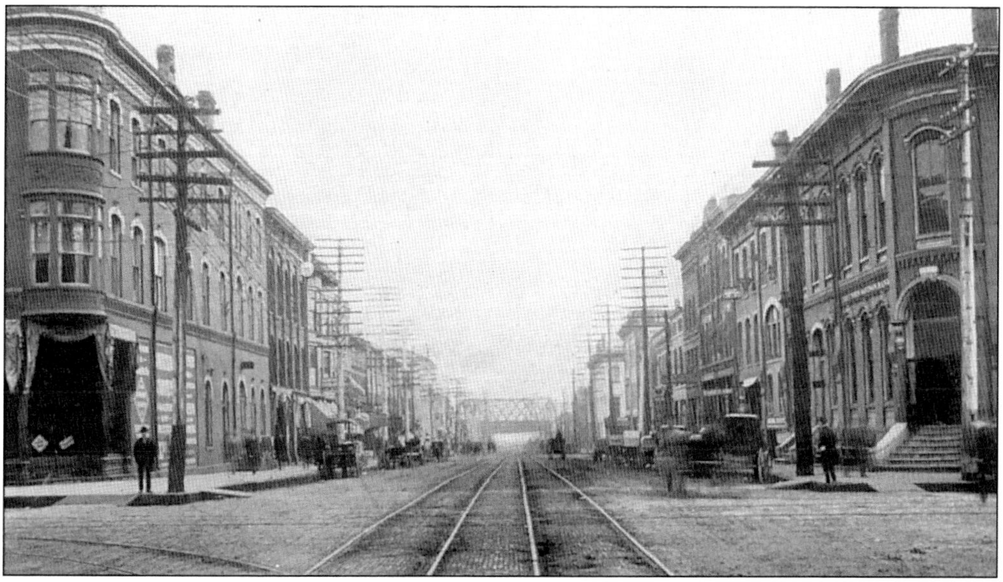

Here's an idea for the curious and adventuresome, especially for those who enjoy making comparisons and contrasts. This photograph was taken on Third Street, looking east from Brady, in the year 1900. If you go to that location today, you will see what a difference a century can make. Imagine what the same spot might look like in 2100. Time passes so quickly, yet Davenport still enjoys some of that riverside atmosphere, so long a part of its river heritage. We who live here take the Mississippi so much for granted, yet those who visit from far away often want to make it the first sight they see.

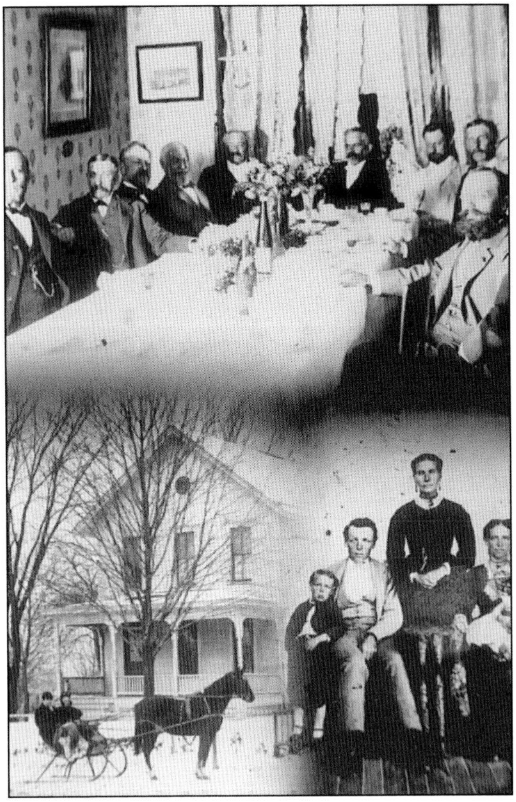

Today, the Christmas letter is an annual project for many Davenport residents, but at the end of the 1800s, some families had photographs taken to be included with special holiday mailings. Whether it was a meeting of menfolk enjoying an after-dinner discussion and cigars, a couple out for a sleigh ride, or a posed family portrait, there is no doubt that the family and friends of those pictured here appreciated receiving such greetings. One can't help but wonder why no one is smiling. Hey, everybody! Say cheese!

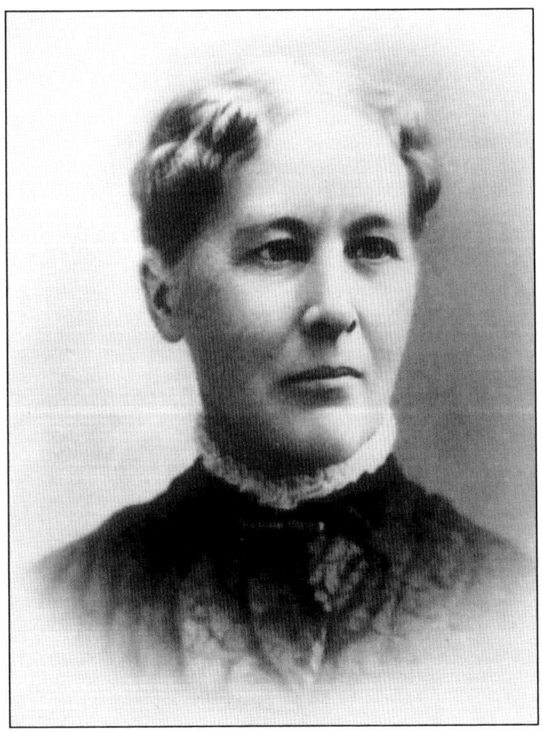

"Pick up your slates, please, and copy down the following spelling words." Now here is the look of a professional schoolmarm! Phebe Sudlow was born in Poughkeepsie, New York, in 1831, and began teaching in the newly organized Davenport School District in 1858. She became principal of the high school in 1872—the first woman in the nation to hold such a position. Two years later, the school board selected her to become Superintendent of Schools, another national first. She left Davenport to become a professor at the University of Iowa.

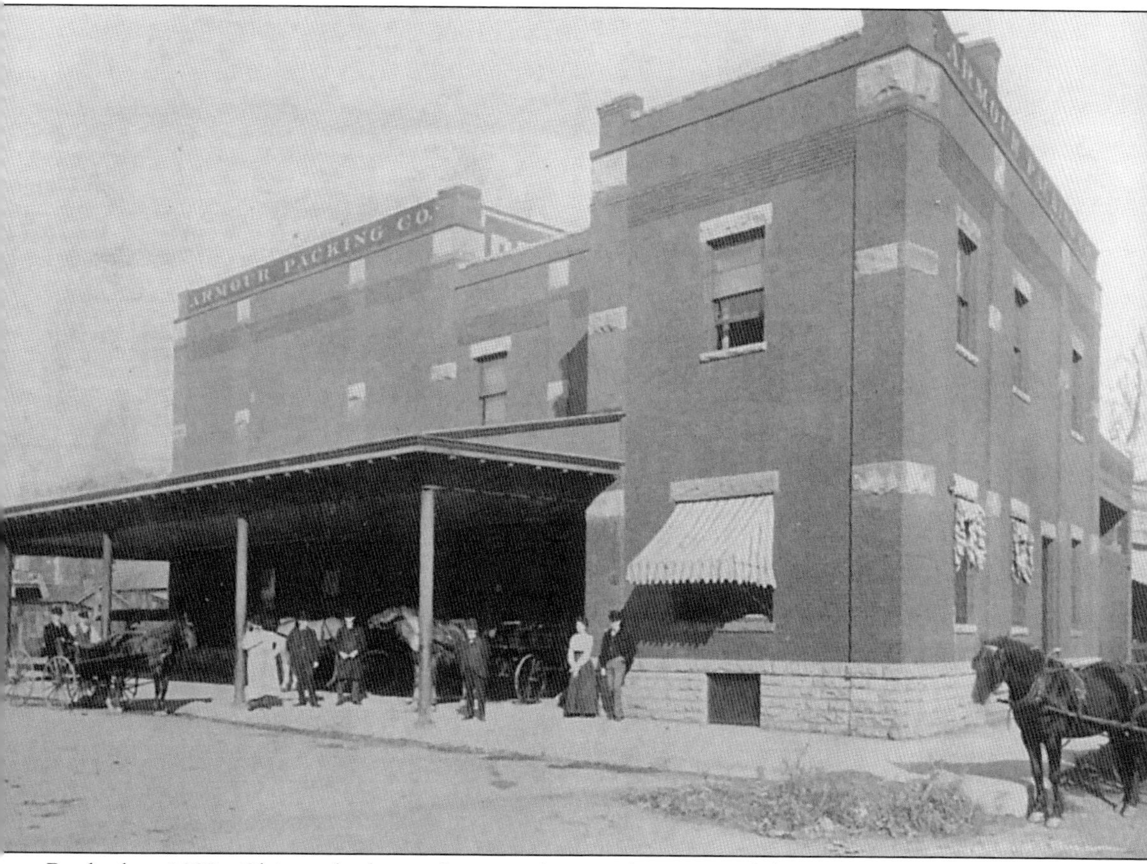

By the late 1800s, Chicago had carved out its claim as the center of the meat-packing industry. Most allowed the heartland city that distinction, but throughout the Midwest were scattered branch houses of the major companies. In Davenport, that was the Armour concern. The buggy traffic was brisk as grocers regularly made their calls to load up, and some customers dealt directly with the branch in order to get their meat as fresh as possible. There were occasional complaints by neighbors of the Armour branch in Davenport, but city leaders recognized the value of the meat business, and turned a deaf ear to those who thought the business was "smelly" and brought too much traffic. There are many who fondly recall the days of the neighborhood meat market and grocery store. "Folks in some of the supermarkets try to be friendly," observes Gladys Meyer, a long-time city resident, " but some of the local grocers used to let you run a tab if money was hard to come by. Can you imagine that happening today?"

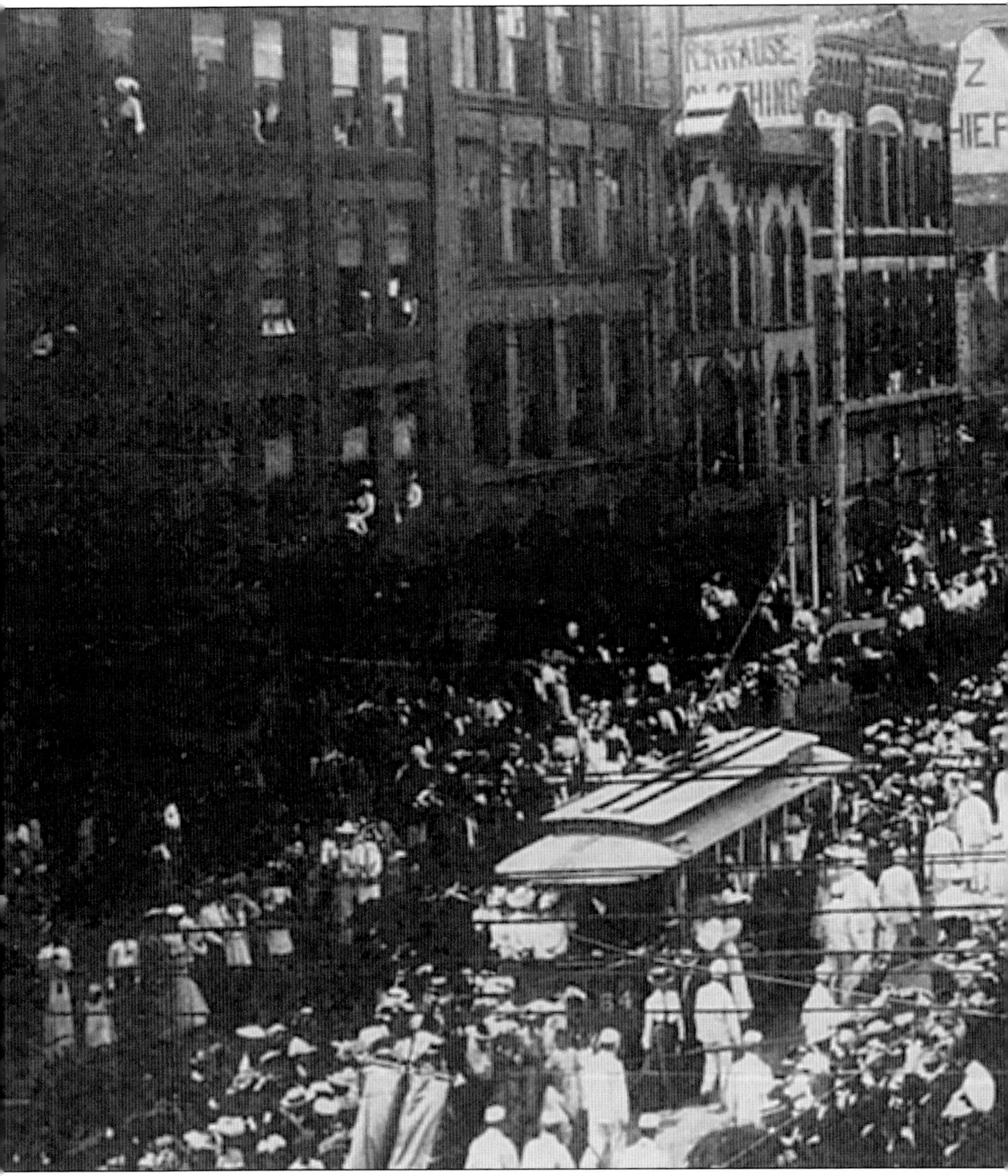

Is it New York City's Fifth Avenue on Easter? Could it be Chicago's State Street on St. Patrick's Day? Let's try one more. Any chance it could be downtown Davenport on Labor Day? If you guessed the latter, you're right on target! Actually, Labor Day as a holiday was a mere eight years old when this photo captured the parade route. It became an official holiday in 1894 during the administration of President Grover Cleveland. This photo was snapped in 1902, only a year after Theodore Roosevelt became president, following the assassination of William McKinley. How did the typical Davenporter observe this special holiday? Often, no work meant sleeping

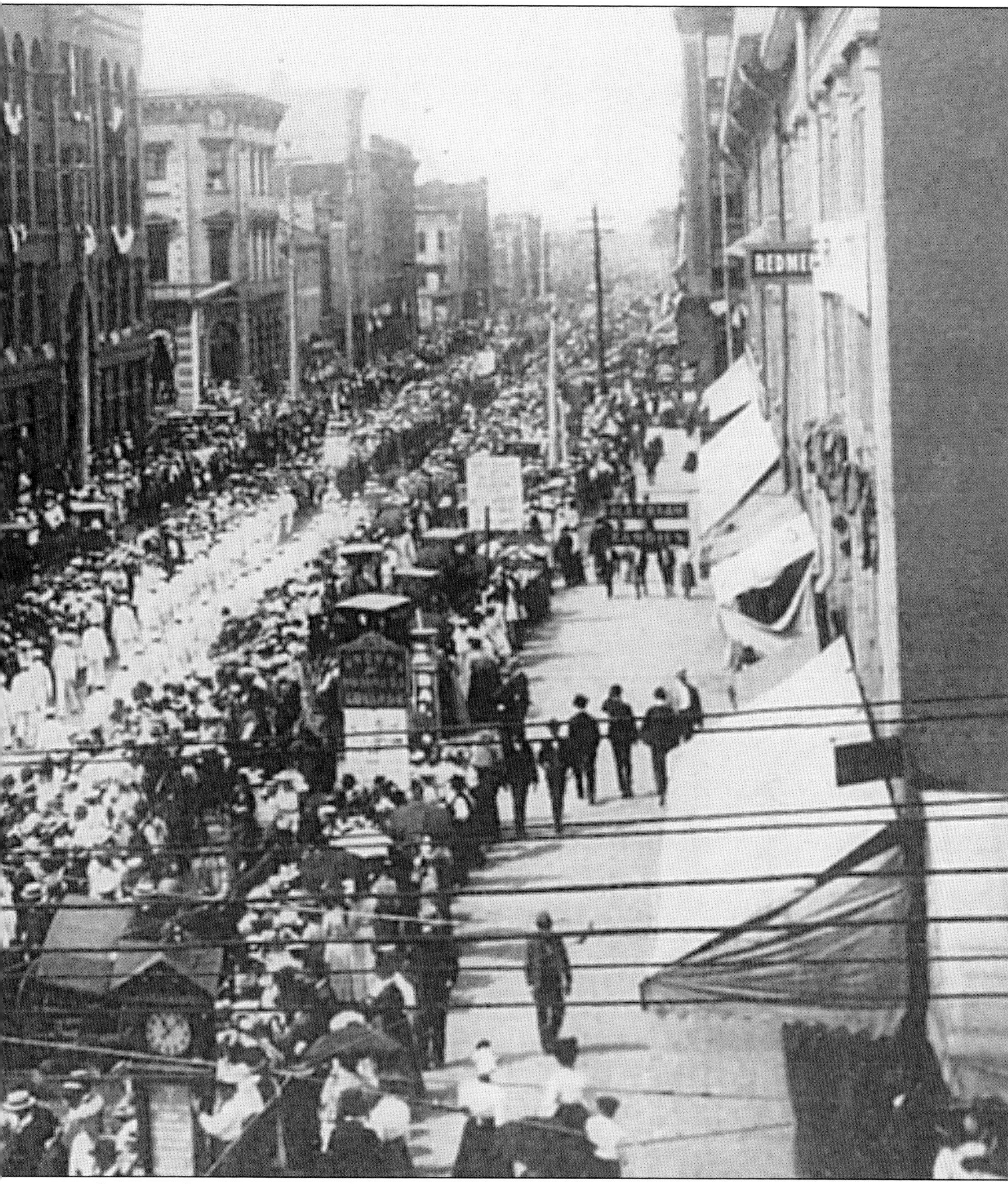

in, and sitting down to a major dinner at noon with invited family and friends. Then, it was time to head for the downtown parade, where they enjoyed band music, decorated vehicles, and floats. Early 20th century evening pursuits included playing a spirited game of cards, euchre being a favorite of many. Someone in the family could usually "tickle the ivories" for a grand singing spree, and before anyone knew it, it was time for bed. After all, Labor Day only lasted 24 hours, darn it.

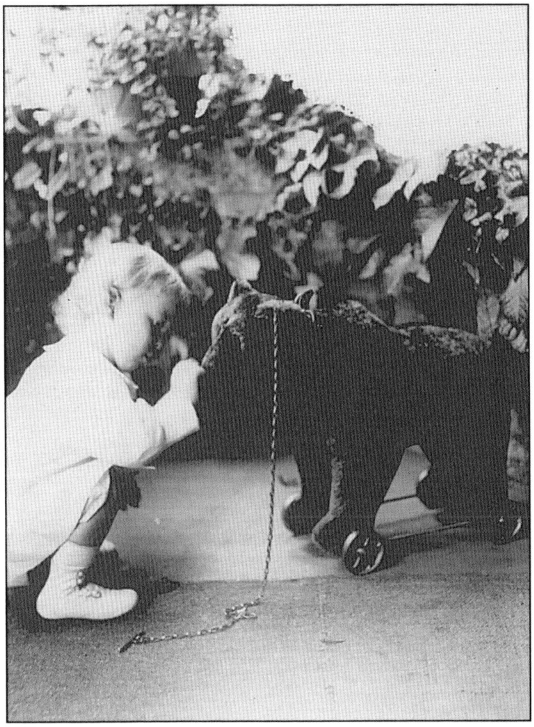

"Now, what would you like to do today? Shall I take you for a walk?" This intense and serious discussion between a boy and his pull-toy in Davenport happened in 1904, but it could have taken place about anywhere in the country. Pull toys were a popular craze at the time. Future toy fads would include Barbie Dolls, G.I. Joes, and Beanie Babies. The boy in this picture is unidentified, but a Mrs. George Cable paid for the photograph from the Hofstettler Studio collection.

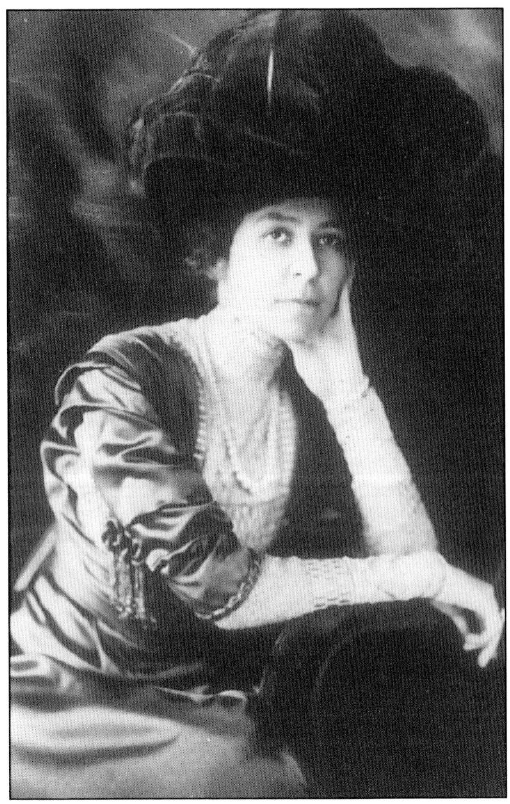

G.W. Delaney might well have assumed the label of "Davenport's Gibson Girl" during the early 1900s. From 1890 until the World War I, women imitated the form and fashions captured by the ink drawings of Charles Dana Gibson, as they appeared in the old humor magazine *Life*. Always immaculately attired, and often with the stylish kind of pearls and gloves that Miss Delaney displays here, the Gibson girl had her effect on men's appearance as well. Males shaved their beards and mustaches in hopes of sliding a smooth cheek against that of the feminine ideal, and spooning.

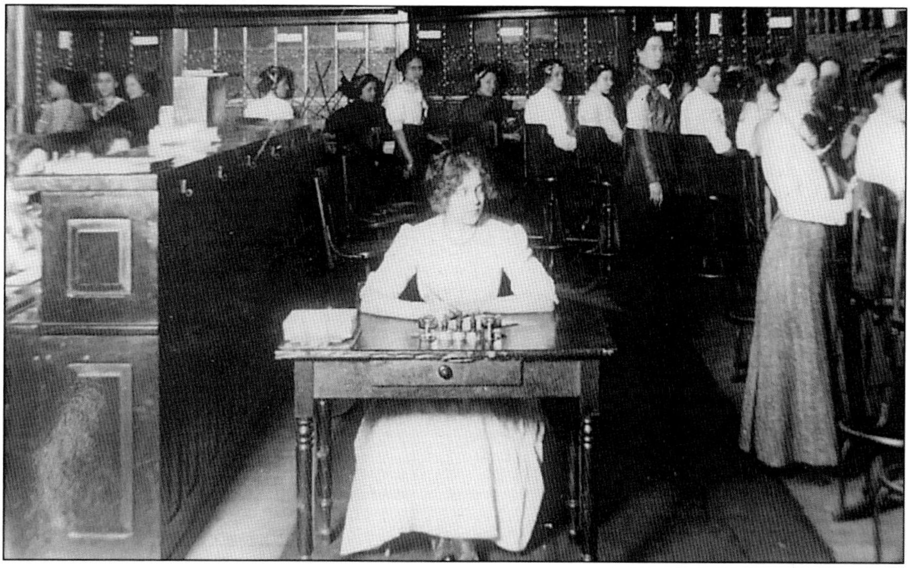

"Number, please?" In this present day of cellular phones, it's hard to imagine a time when telephoning was a manual activity, assisted by live, trained operators. A supervisor, ready to handle special problems, sat in the middle of the telephone exchange to oversee activities of her team of operators. As technology evolved, the need for human operators diminished, and they were replaced by machinery. "There was something reassuring about talking to another person on the end of the line," says long-time Davenport resident Agnes Patterson. "Recorded messages are so impersonal."

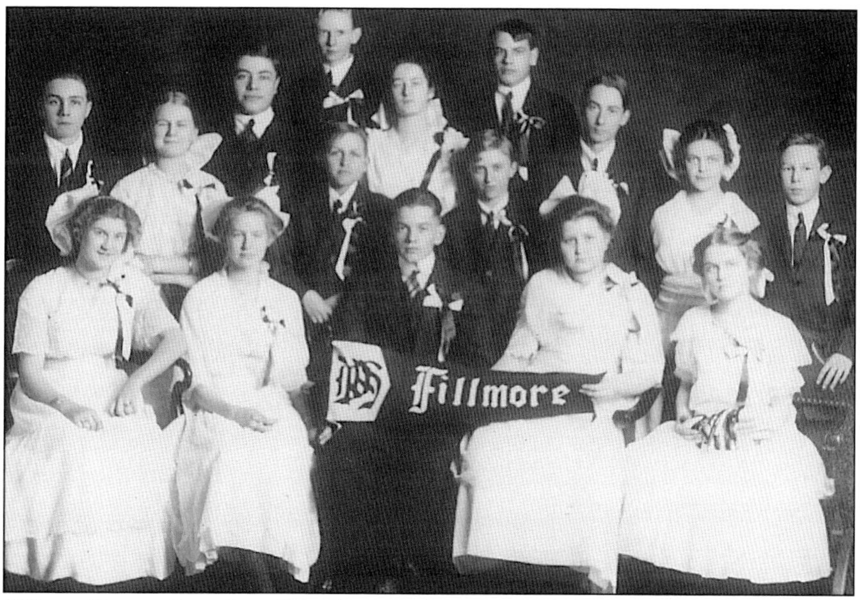

In the White House, President Woodrow Wilson was fighting to keep America out of war, but sadly, that fight would be lost. The year was 1915, and the eighth graders at Davenport's Fillmore School spruced up for their graduation to high school. The young ladies wore white dresses, and the young men wore dark suits and ties. "No one can predict the future," the guest speaker told the Fillmore grads, "but it is imperative that each of you possess a good mind and a sound character to face any situation."

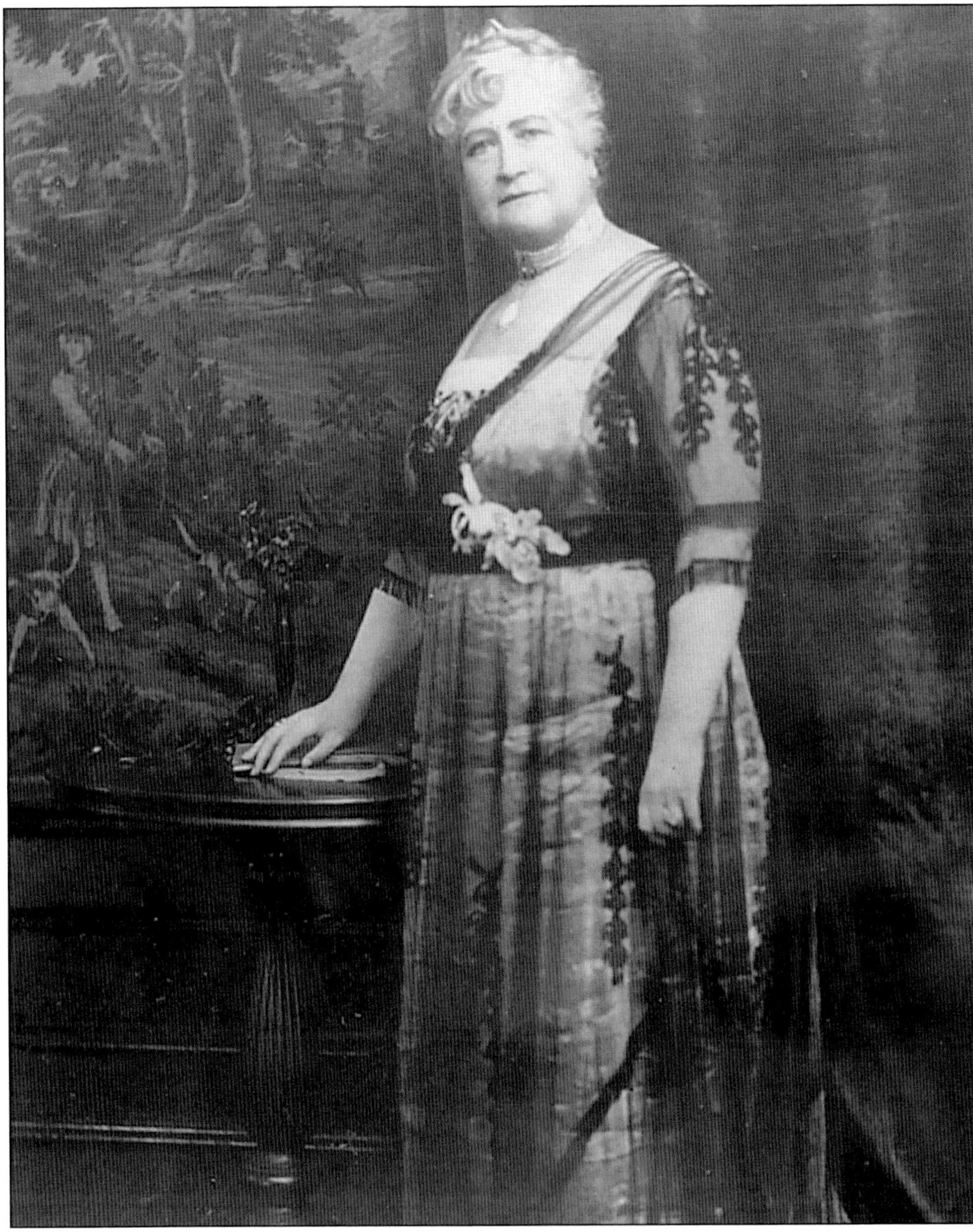

Her bearing was regal, her manners impeccable, and yet neither approached her stature and the position she enjoyed on the national literary scene in the late 19th and early 20th centuries. Her real name was Alice French, and she came from a prominent Davenport family where she was nurtured in Victorian graces and values. However, her readers knew her by the name "Octave Thanet," and they thrilled to her short stories and novels. She used "Fairport" in place of Davenport in her writings, much as Mark Twain (Samuel Clemens) used "St. Petersburg" instead of Hannibal. She was the first of several noted Davenport writers to achieve national prominence, followed by George Cram Cook, Susan Glaspell, Arthur Davison Ficke, and Floyd Dell. Octave Thanet's flowery style lost favor by World War I, and by the time she died in 1934, she was all but forgotten.

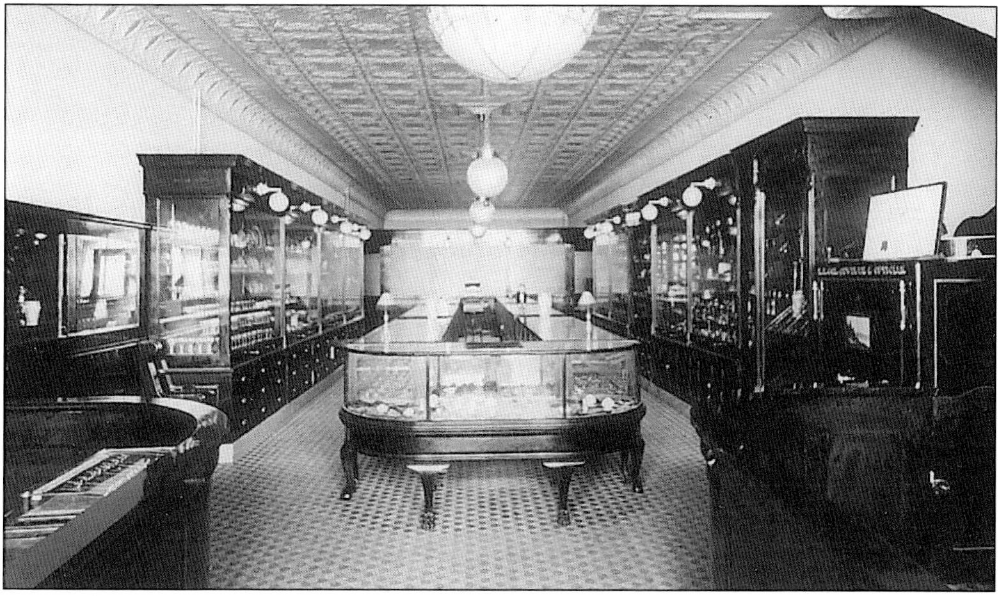

You might enter the establishment searching for a diamond pendant. Or maybe it's a ruby ring you always wanted. Then again, it might be a pair of spectacles to see the world clearly. Whatever the case, H.R. Cox Jewelers and Opticians offered a sparkling store from floor to ceiling, and every glass case in between. "Our customers may come in looking bewildered and unsure," claimed the proprietor, "but they leave smiling." This 1912 photo helps show why.

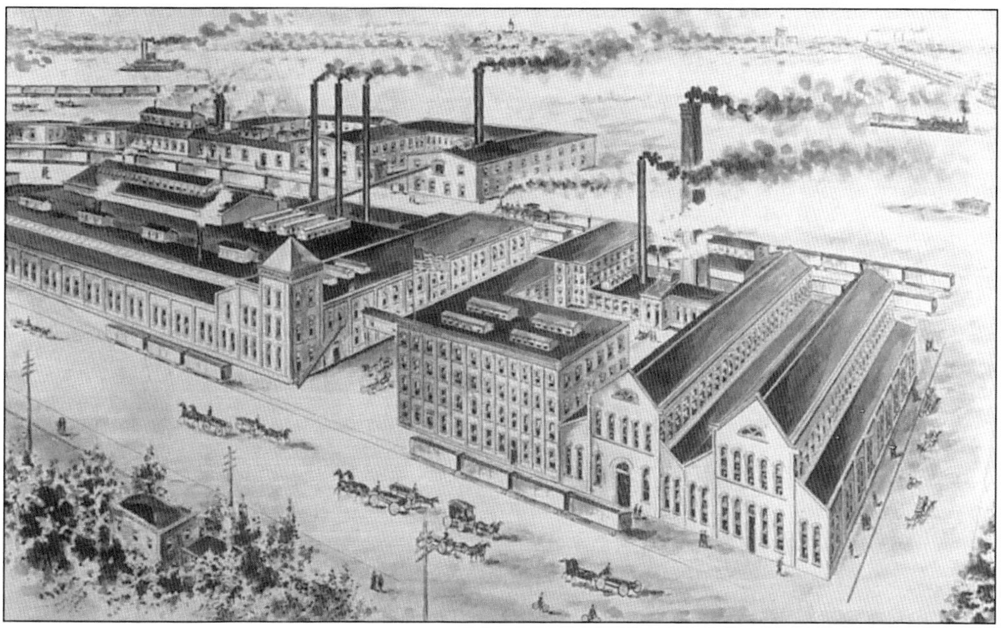

William and Joseph Bettendorf were two uniquely matched brothers who set up their Bettendorf company in Davenport. While William proved the inventor, his brother Joseph took care of the financial matters. Unfortunately, neither had a nose for smelling smoke, and as the 20th century opened, disastrous fires destroyed much of their plant. Offered incentives to rebuild in neighboring Gilbert, the brothers accepted the offer, after which the city was renamed in their honor.

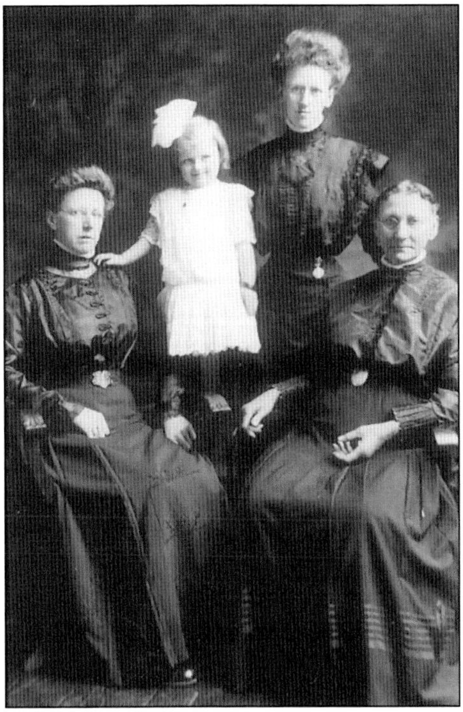

Average lifespans have increased drastically since the early years of the 20th century, yet many early families also laid claim to multiple generations. In 1913, photographers from the Hofstettler Studio of Photography snapped this picture labeled "The Dietz Group." The photo shows four distinguished-looking ladies, striking a pose for the camera. While the older threesome maintain somber and sober expressions, the youngest member of the group reveals a trace of the film great to-be Mary Pickford, showing more than a glint of mischief in her eyes and grin.

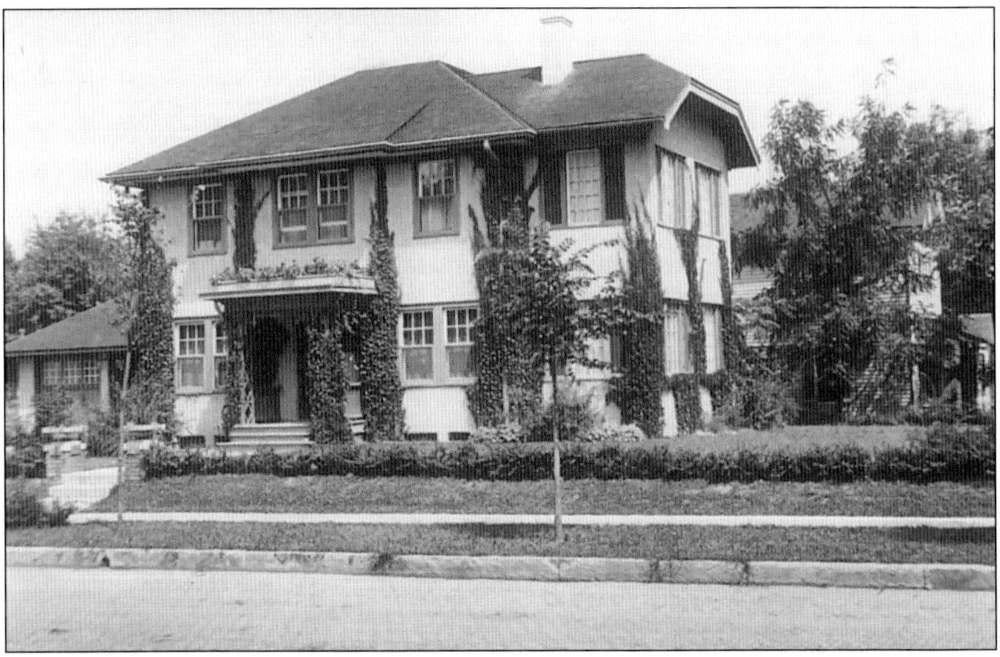

A drive around Davenport reveals a plethora of architectural styles, some imported, and others totally "American homegrown." In the earlier part of the 20th century, greenery adorned many structures and landscapes. The imposing home of Dr. Charles and Blanche Glynn, shown here, won many admiring glances from friends and neighbors. The Glynns moved into the home at 1505 Grand Avenue during the summer of 1914. Surprisingly enough, the well-built structure still looks much the same today.

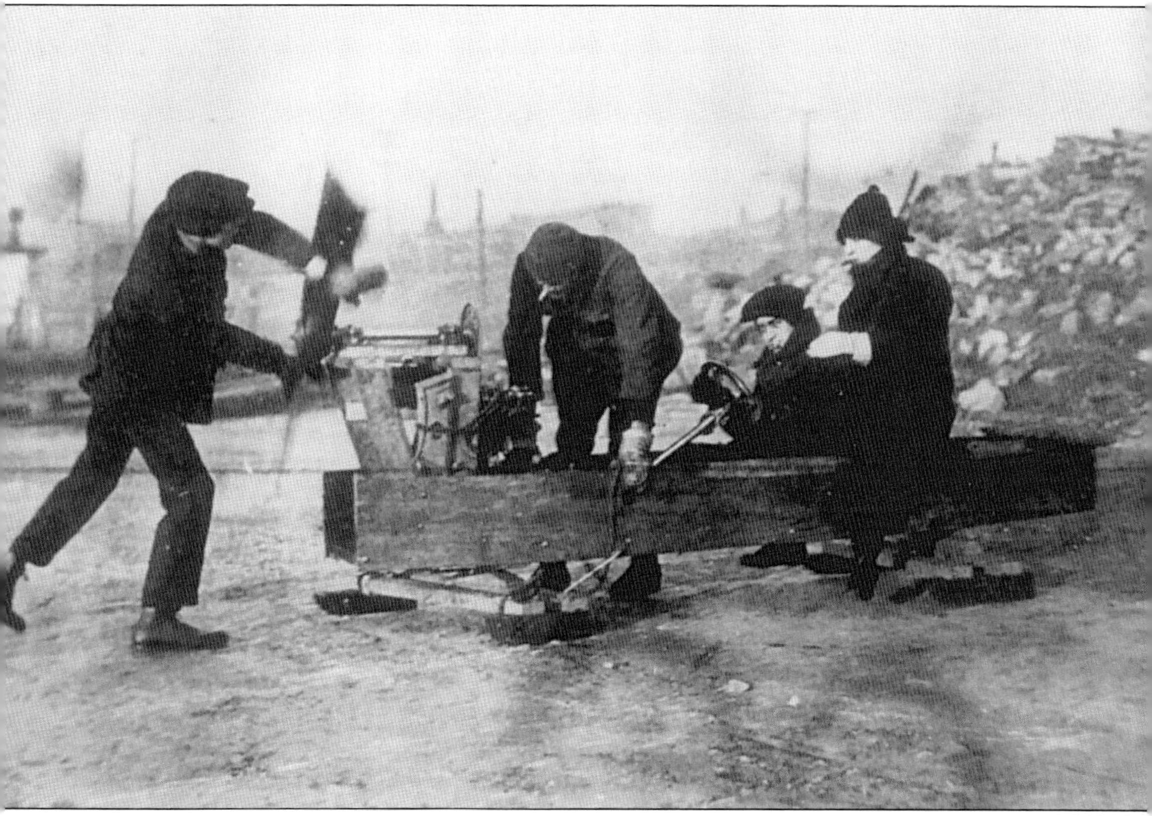

Well, Orville and Wilbur Wright got their start somehow too. The scene here is a boat club at the foot of Davenport's Gaines Street, approximately where the John O'Donnell Stadium now stands. The cast of characters includes Louis J. Mass, William Mass, John N. Mass, and Marta Wesenberg (later to become Mrs. Louis J. Mass). The creative Mass boys put together their own iceboat powered by a motorcycle engine. Sometime between 1912 and 1916, Iowa became a dry state, while Illinois still sold alcohol. The winter in question was exceptionally cold, freezing the Mississippi into nearly 20 inches of snow. The Mass gang made regular trips to the Rock Island side, where they picked up beer in front of the Harms Hotel while spectators looked on and applauded. Then it was back to Davenport. Unfortunately, the iceboat became unstable at high speeds, and would begin spinning uncontrollably. But it was fun while it lasted!

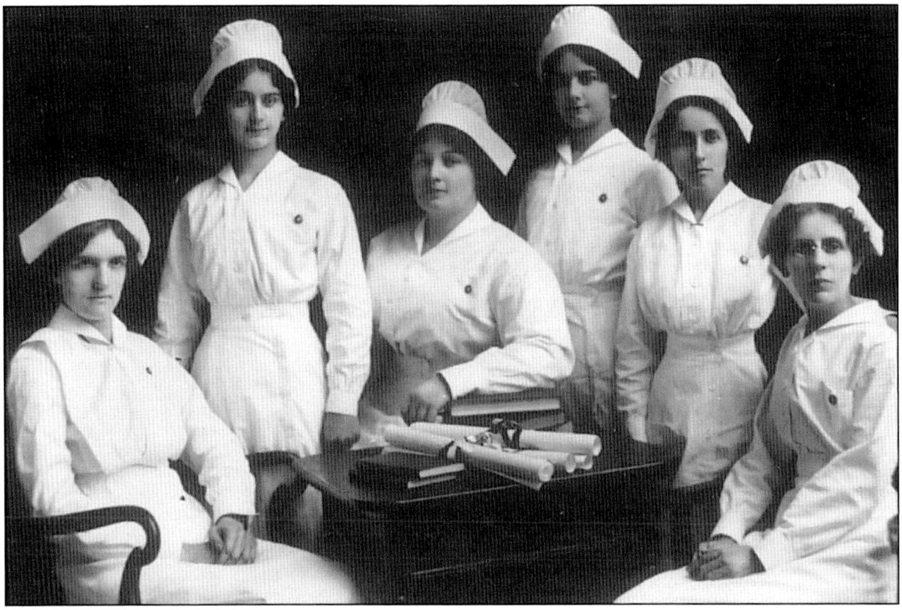

They came from different backgrounds, but these Davenport nurses, Class of 1915, felt a similar purpose: they wanted to assist the sick back to health. The nurses' uniforms were immaculate and crisp, and their nursing pins displayed proudly. None of these nurses knew that there would soon be a "call to arms" that could summon them to share their services far beyond the safe shores of the Mississippi. World War I would change some of their lives, as would deadly influenza outbreaks on the home front. But, for the moment, the women basked in the recognition of their own accomplishments.

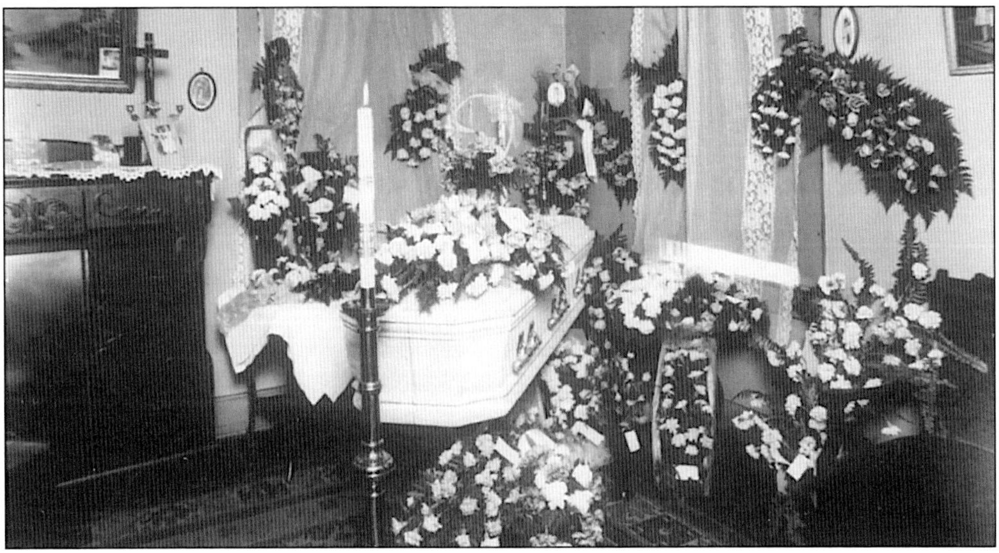

The average life expectancy for men in 1900 was 47.3 years. For women, the average life expectancy in 1900 was one more, 48.3. Major killers were heart attacks, influenza, pneumonia, and tuberculosis. Many families chose to have wakes and funerals in their home, as did the Davenport family of E.E. Jacobs, whose casket is pictured here. Playing the piano was an extra source of income for area musicians. "Beautiful Isle of Somewhere" and "How Great Thou Art" were often requested melodies by the grieving families.

"We have come together to witness the blessed union of ..." In this case, the couple about to be married was Alvina Eichner and Charles Fredricks. The date was January 15, 1905, and the site of the nuptials was the Davenport home of the bride's uncle at 1325 West Third Street. In-home weddings were popular during the early part of the 20th century. Both participants, judging from their expressions, appear most earnest about the vows of matrimony they are about to exchange.

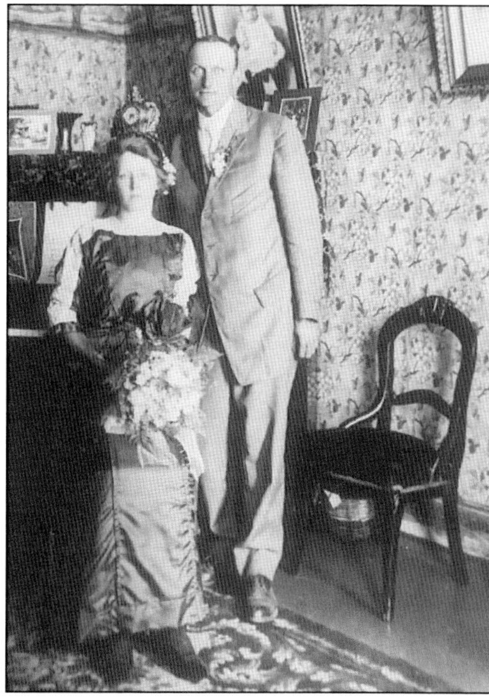

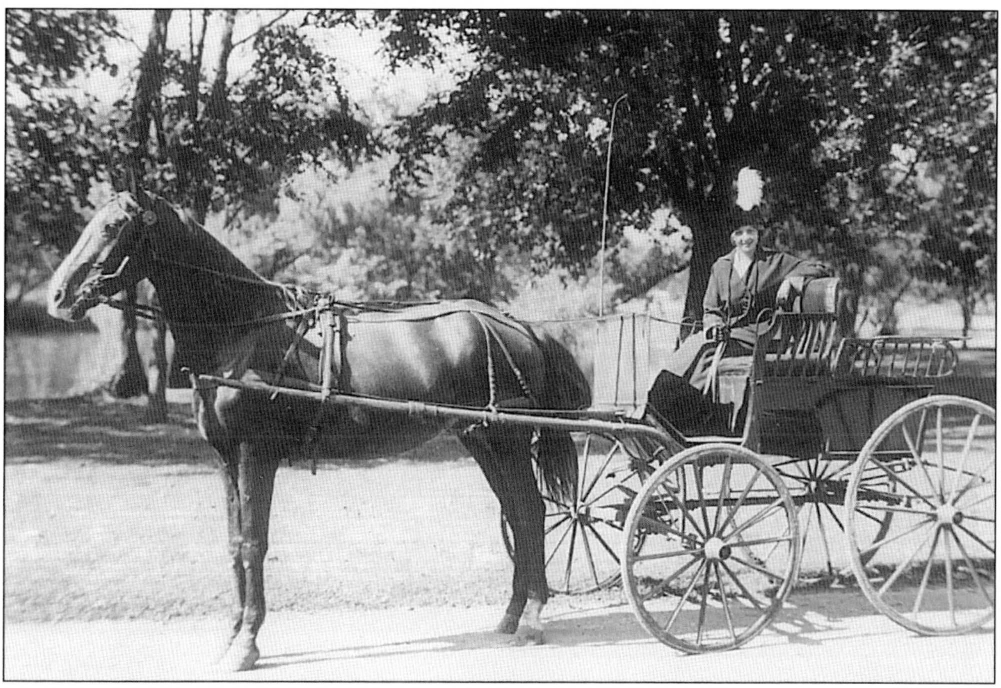

A radiant Hazel Alice Sheeley smiles warmly in her buggy on this autumn morning. It is her wedding day, September 13, 1914, and the sun casts a warm, welcome glow. Her husband-to-be, Aubrey Marshall Horton, is ready to assume his position beside her, and hopefully the couple will ride off into a "happily ever after" future. Sadly enough, it was a dream that did not come true. In October of 1915, Mrs. Horton died, a week after giving birth to a son, Stanford.

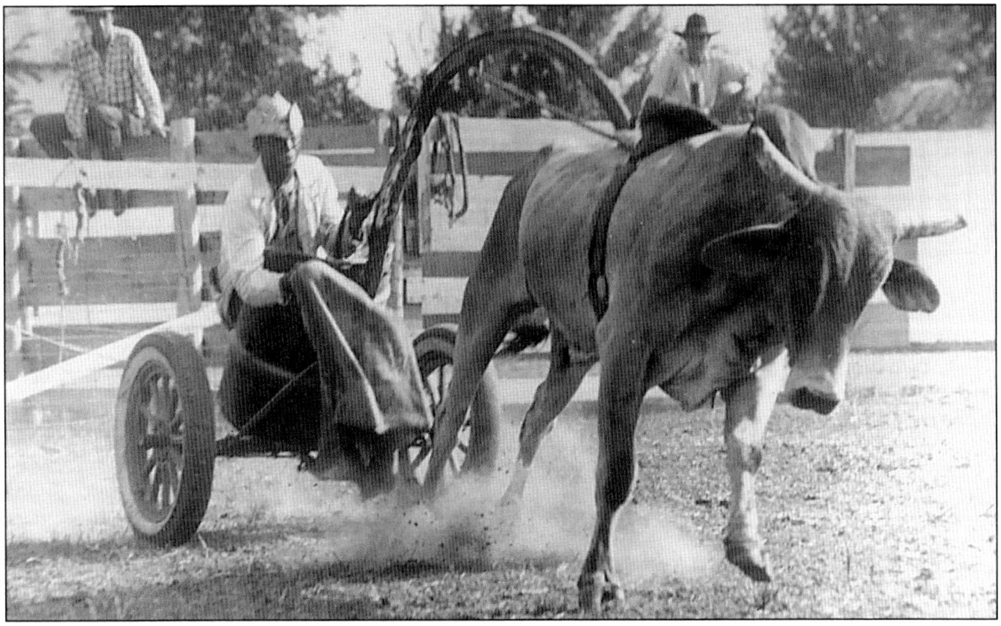

"The sun is a-shining to welcome the day...Heigh Ho! Come to the Fair!"—the Mississippi Valley Fair, that is. Since its opening in August of 1920, the grounds have welcomed millions of spectators—more than 115,000 in its first week! Both automobile races and antics have delighted audiences, while other activities appeal to a variety of tastes. In this photo, "Rodeo Slim" tests his own speed and precision against a bull during a 1950 escapade.

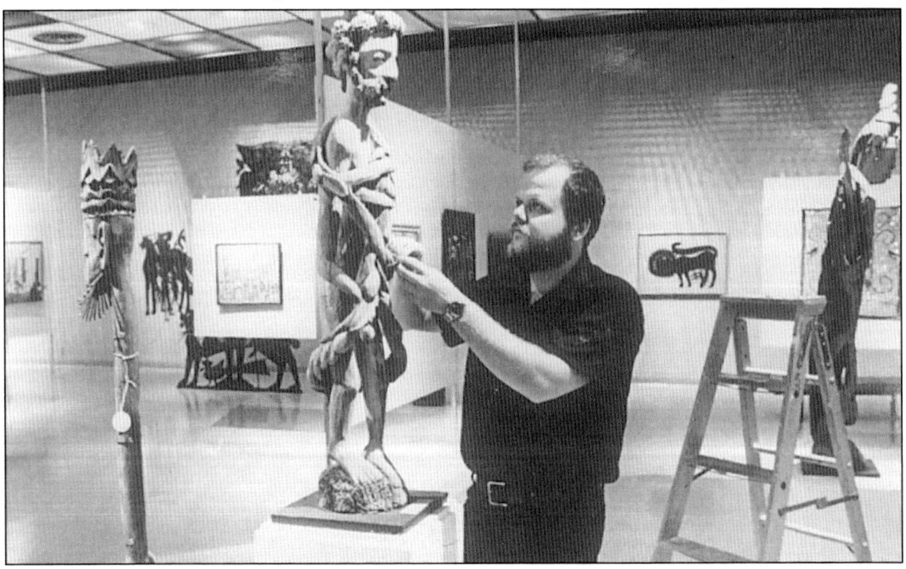

"American Gothic," by Grant Wood, is perhaps the painting most quickly brought to mind when one thinks about Iowa art masterpieces. Yet there are countless other treasures and exhibits featured at the Davenport Museum of Art, as an appreciative Tim Saver, pictured here, could testify. Charles Augusts Ficke, a former mayor and city philanthropist, provided a major impetus for the creation of the Davenport Municipal Art Gallery in the early 1920s, through the donation of his sizable art collection. Present plans call for moving the museum from its 1737 West 12th location to downtown by 2003.

"We're in the money, we're in the money, we've got a lot of what it takes to get along…" Davenport's financial institutions have come and gone, changed names, and changed hands over the years, but their physical presence has always appeared solid and imposing. The Davenport Bank and Safety Deposit, shown here, was taken over by the Union Savings Bank and Trust Company in the 1920s. All seemed well until the fall of 1931, when rumors of financial problems circulated. By the next year, Union Savings closed its doors, leaving many Davenport residents without funds.

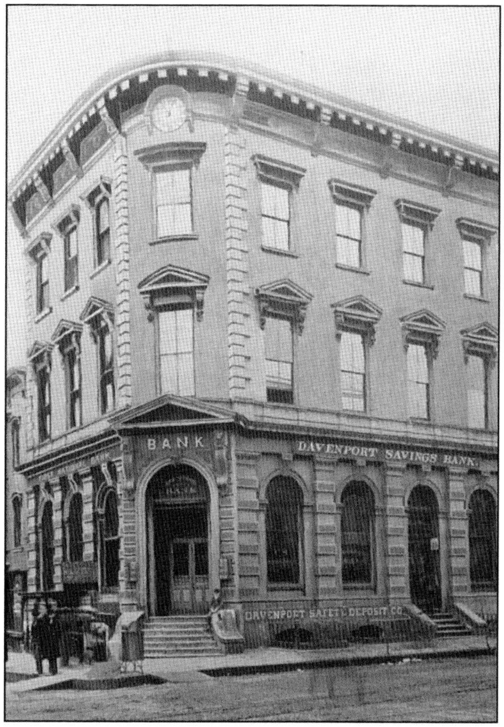

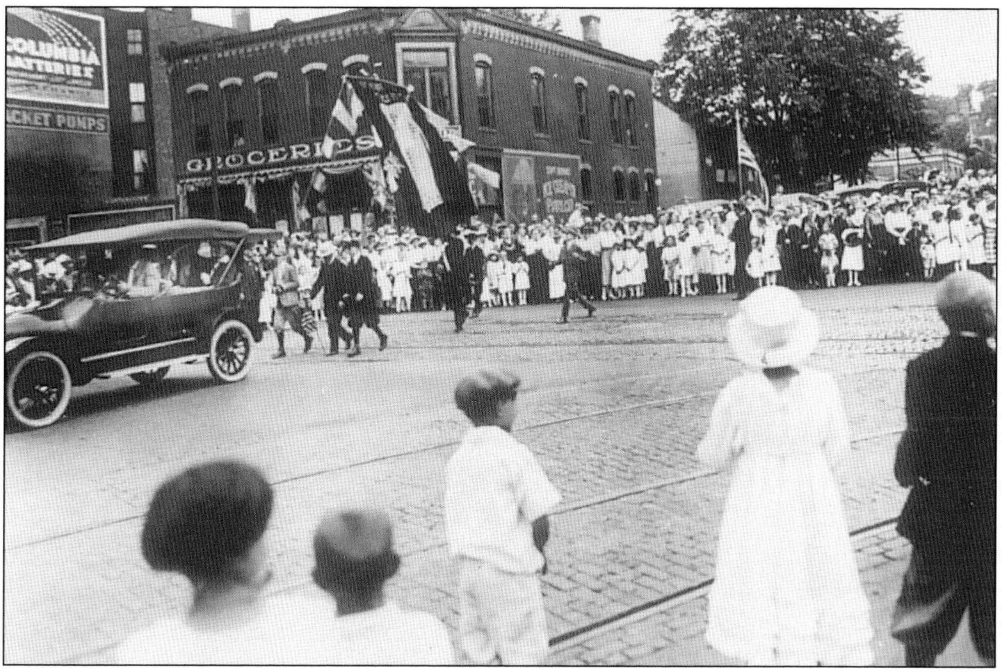

"Strike up the band! Let's have a parade!" As the 1920s roared, Davenporters cheered, this time at the Grotto Week Parade. Note the styles the young people are wearing as they inch forward to get a closer look at the passing groups. Warren Harding was in the White House, and e.e. cummings raised eyebrows with his poetry, which lacked orthodox punctuation and typography. As for Iowans, many grumbled at being residents in the first state to impose a tax on cigarettes.

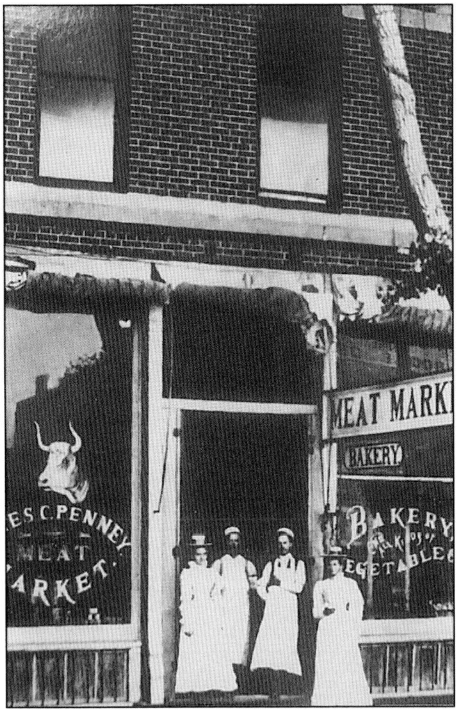

"Hey, I'm going down to J.C. Penney's. Does anyone need any meat or baked goods?" Yes, Davenport could claim a J.C. Penney's all the way back in 1892. You couldn't buy clothes or furniture at the store, yet you could almost get everything else for a full meal. That's no "bum steer" pictured on the window. You could buy vegetables at this place of business too. The apron-clad fellows look ready to wait on patrons, but the immaculate ladies appear more likely to be customers.

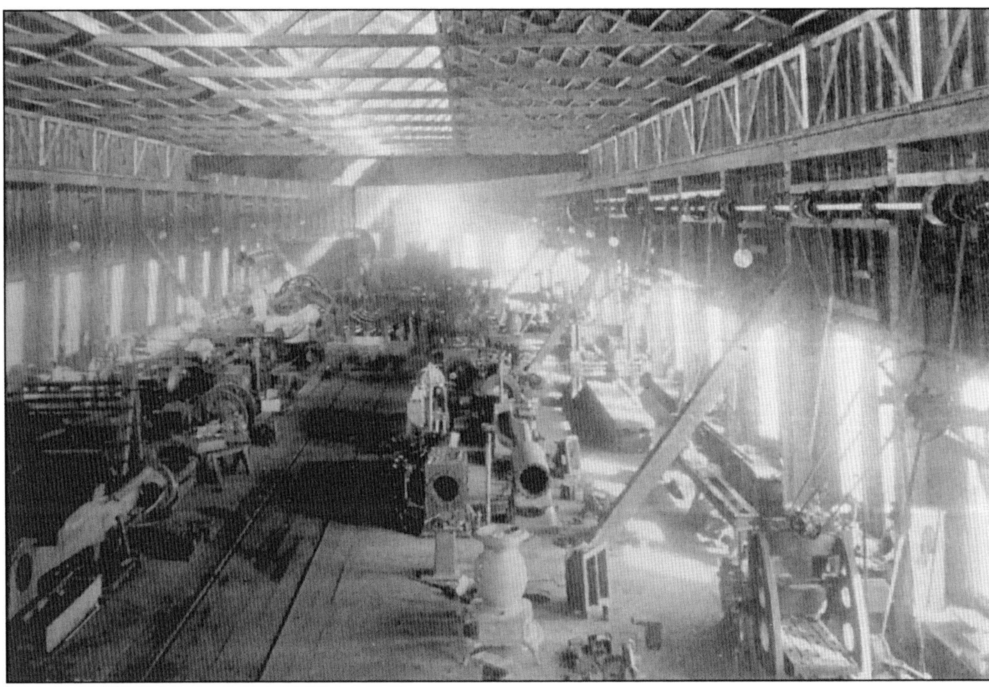

Early in the 20th century, Davenport was a hustling, bustling, manufacturing city where new businesses opened each year. Workers were encouraged to keep their stations clean, and obviously the folks at W.W. Whitehead Company took that suggestion seriously, as shown by the interior shop shown here. Labor groups were well organized, largely through the Workman's Industrial Home Association, and the Tri-Cities Federation of Labor.

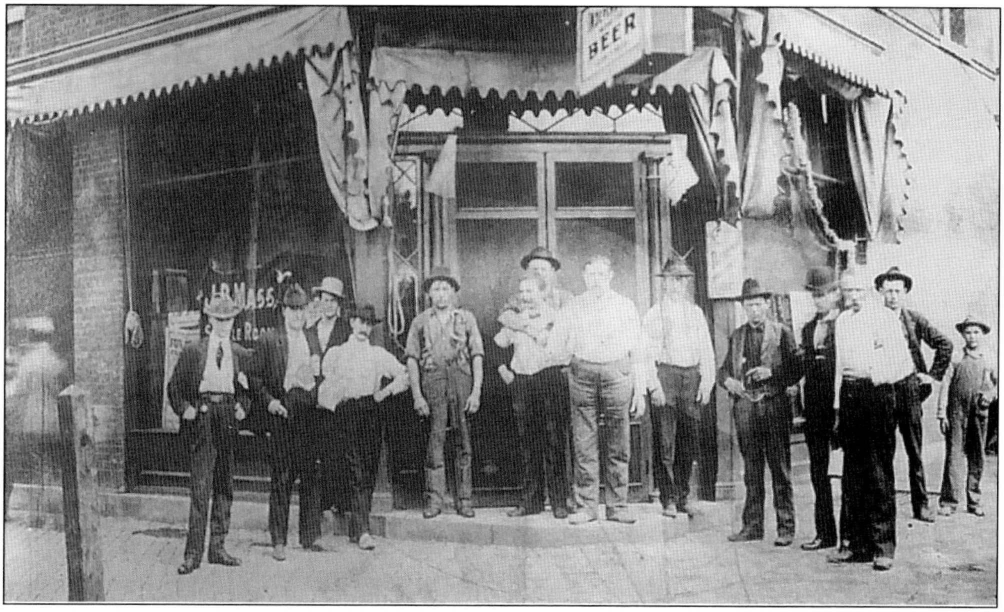

Some things change, and other things remain much the same. Back in 1901, John Petermass built this saloon and apartment house at 702 West Third. The facility was a popular neighborhood social center, yet reports of noise and "rowdyism" were few. "My grandfather visited the saloon every night after work," recalls Davenport resident Florence Hanson. "I think it must have been a place like *Cheers* on television. My grandmother use to complain that he spent too much time at the place, but he always came home sober with good stories to tell."

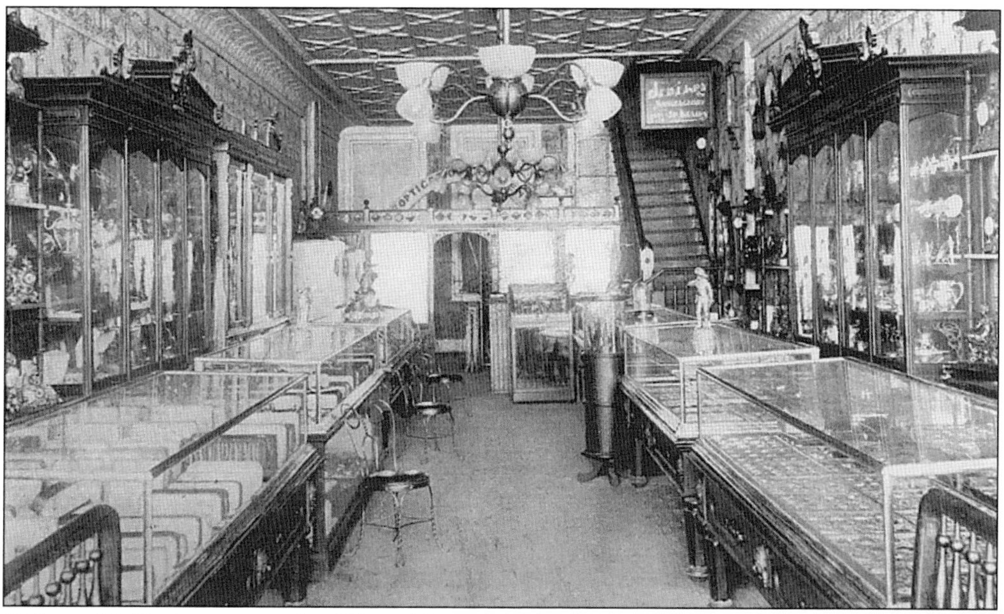

William McKinley was in the White House as (the first president to use the telephone as a campaign device) the deadly Galveston tornado hit, and the first automobile show was held in New York City. The year was 1900, and in downtown Davenport, M.E. Nabstedt & Sons Jewelry Store welcomed customers into a show room that sparkled as much as the jewels within its cases. "A gift from Nabstedt's is a treasure forever," was one of their advertising lures.

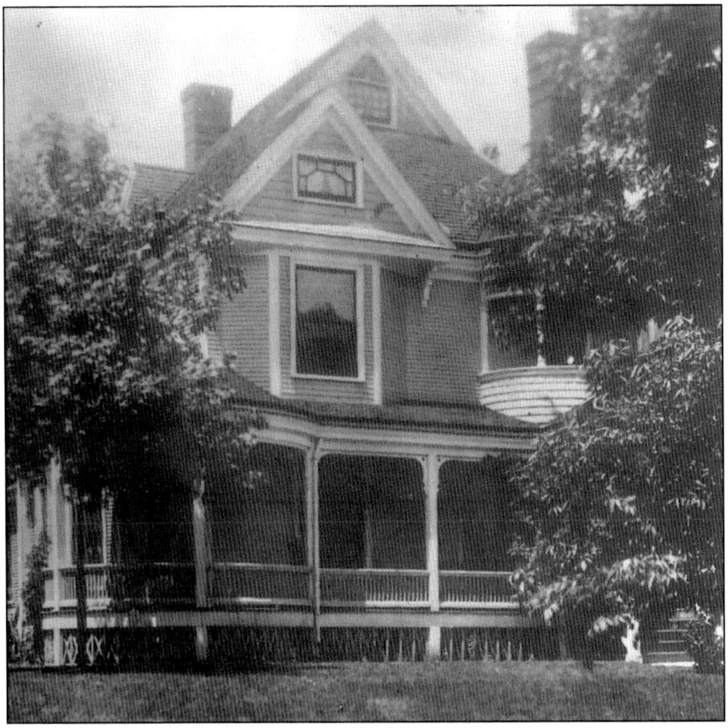

The sprawling structure at 1934 Grand Avenue offered a lengthy wrap-around front porch suitable for kids to race on, and enough nooks and crannies for countless games of hide-and-seek. It was the home of Bismark and Agatha Beiderbecke, plus their three children: Mary Louise, Burnie, and Leon, quickly nicknamed "Bixie" or "Bix." Music drifted from the home often: the piano compositions were performed by Agatha or Bix, and later, Bix offered classy and jazzy cornet tunes.

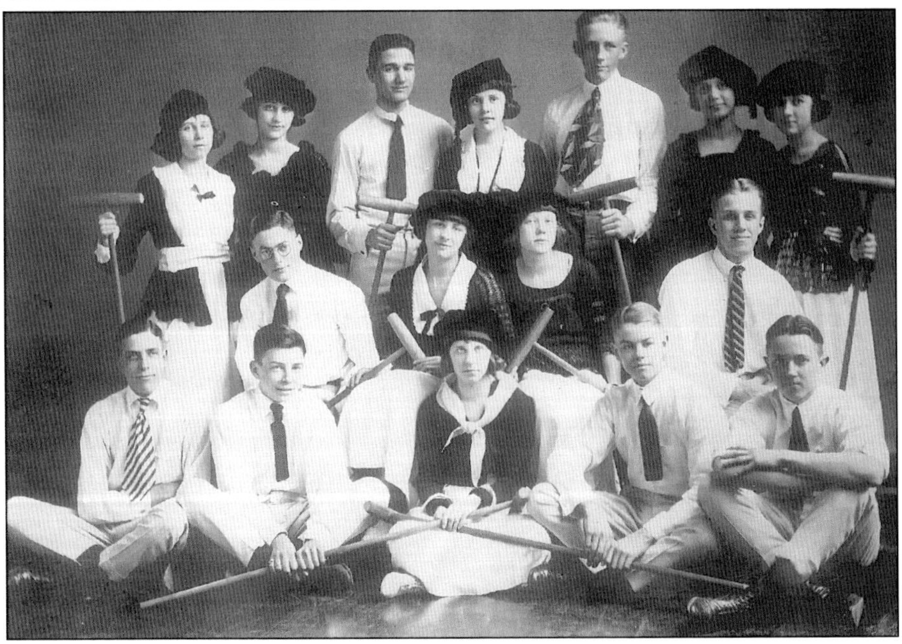

Finding an "A" on young Bix Beiderbecke's report card posed a challenge, but his low grades were caused more by lack of attendance than by lack of intelligence. This Central High yearbook photo shows how Bix spent too many nights playing his horn with fellow musicians. He wanted desperately to please his parents, yet teacher lectures in school classrooms were drowned out by the sounds of music filling his mind. In the fall of 1920, his parents enrolled Bix at Lake Forest Academy outside Chicago.

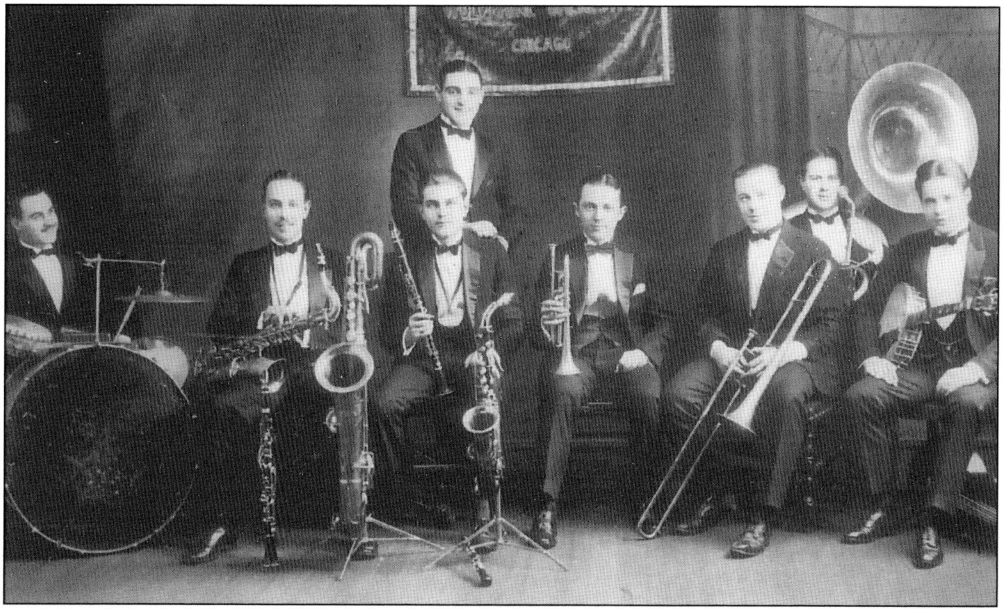

Sporting the latest 1920s hairstyle, the part in the middle, Bix poses here, cornet on his knee, with the other members of The Wolverines ensemble. Bix joined the band in November of 1923, playing lead cornet. The group was especially popular with the college crowd, and news of an appearance by The Wolverines packed ballrooms and gyms across the Midwest. When the orchestra played at Indiana University, Bix made a good friend and musical colleague in the famed Hoagy Carmichael.

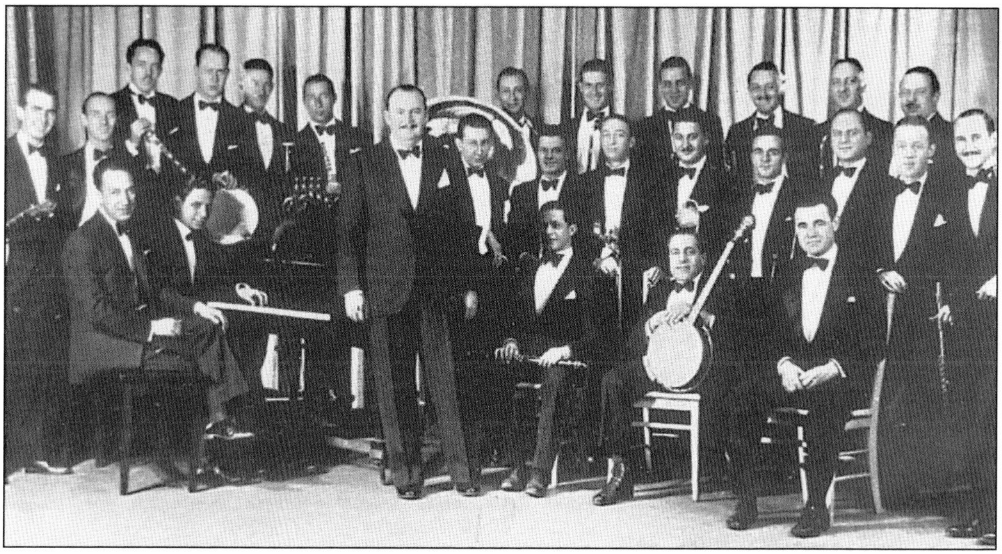

Known as "The King of Jazz," Paul Whiteman assembled a group of the top musicians in the country during the late 1920s. The orchestra leader knew talent, and therefore knew he had to have Bix Beiderbecke playing cornet. Bix is shown here, third from right in the top row, sporting a mustache. Whether playing on record or performing live, Bix received glowing reviews. "Gabriel could not blow a horn better than Bix Beiderbecke," observed one newspaper writer. This August 1928 photo captures Bix at a time when he was already neglecting his health, sleeping too little, and drinking too much. Three years later he would be dead at 28.

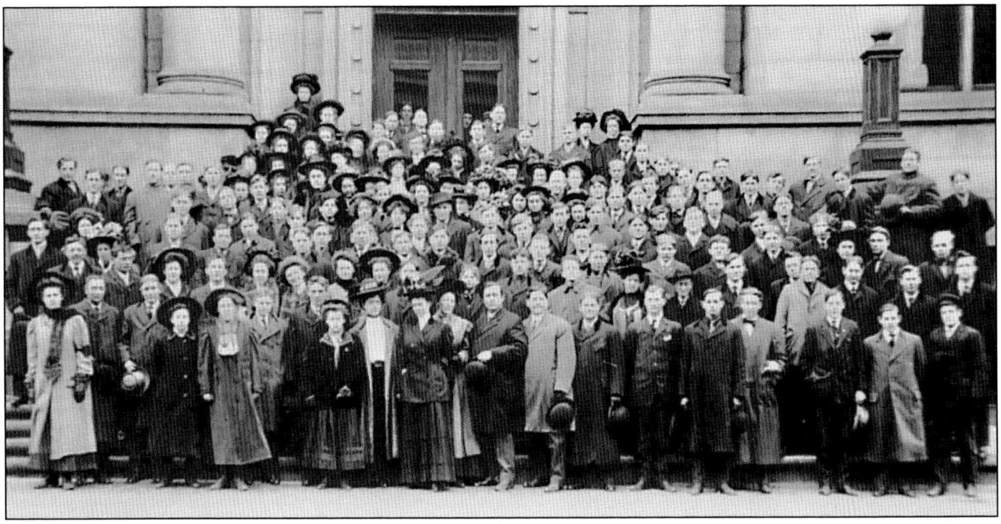

See any business leaders of America in this picture? You just might. Students enrolled in Brown's Business College pause for a picture in June of 1909. Men still outnumbered women at this institution of higher learning, but increasingly, females were enrolled in courses outside the secretarial curriculum. Women did not have the right to vote yet, but the suffrage movement waxed strong, and most could sense that garnering the vote was only years away. Local notables like Claris Cook, Phoebe Sudlow, Annie Wittenmyer, Alice French, and Susan Glaspell had already earned distinctive honors as women.

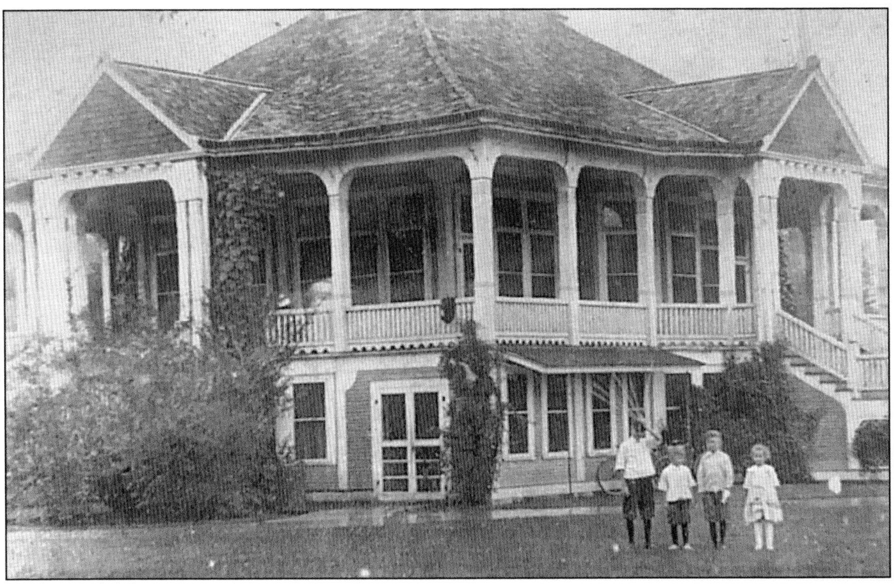

In the early part of the 1900s, this was called Suburban Island. The clubhouse and grounds attracted many area families for Sunday picnics and swimming. In 1918, the name was changed to Credit Island, thanks to public suggestions and voting conducted by the Davenport Board of Park Commissioners. For a brief time during the 'teens, a rough track carved through the woods served as an airstrip for intrepid Davenport aviators. Presently, the grounds are used by golfers. "I can remember playing hide-and-seek among the beautiful trees when it was still Suburban Island," says long-time Davenport resident Agnes White. "There were some fine hiding places there."

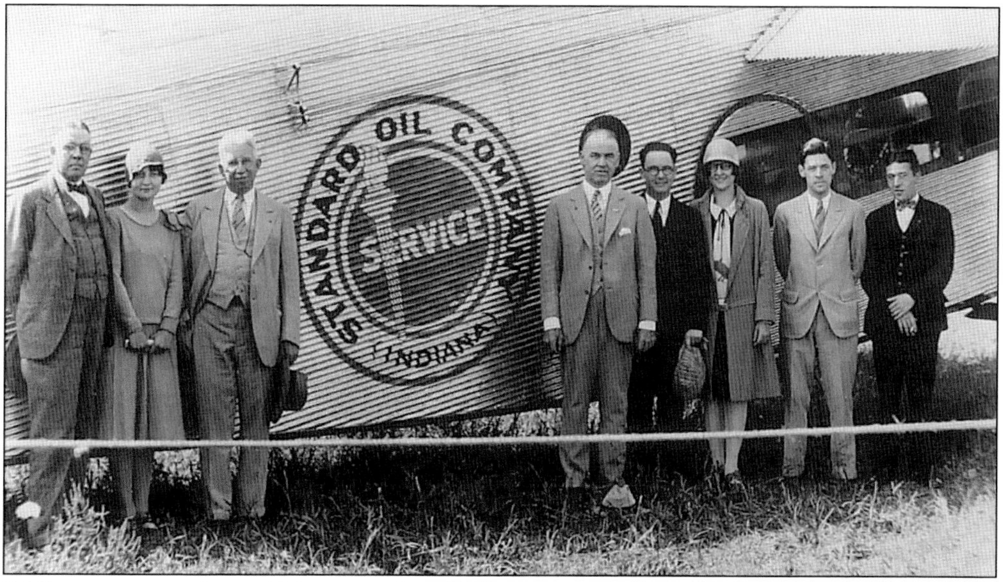

"Off we go, into the wild blue yonder..." That's an excellent flying song, not only during wartime, but in times of peace as well. The 1920s were years of peace, welcomed after the fighting of World War I. Davenport's Cram Field, located on Division Street behind Duck Creek, boasted a constant stream of commercial and recreational airships, such as this one owned by the Standard Oil Company. Among the faces is John O'Donnell, the famed journalist who would later have a stadium named after him. He is second from the right.

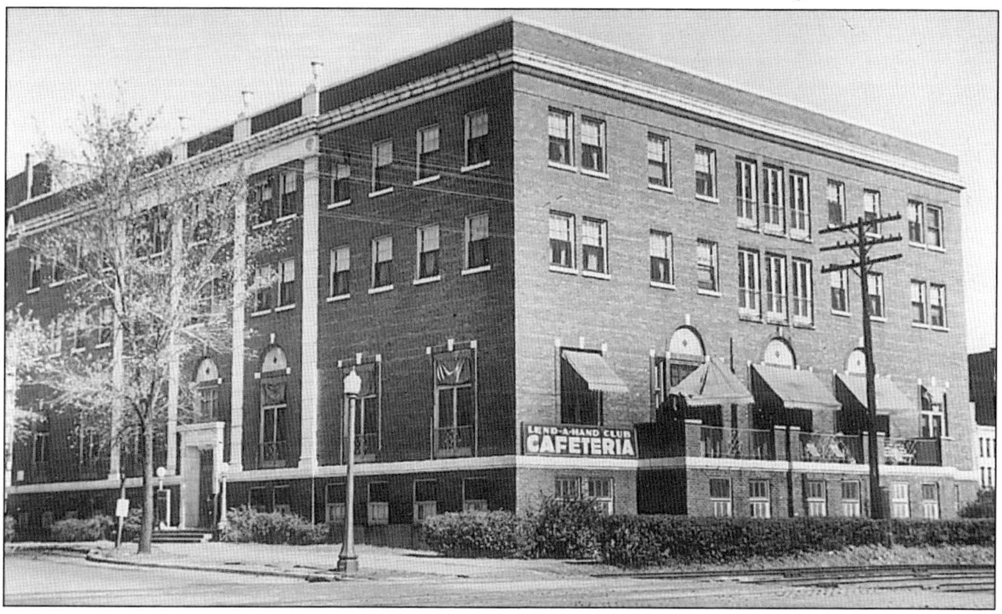

The Lend-A-Hand Club began operating in Davenport in 1887, as a place where women working away from home might enjoy supervised social and educational activities. The club, one of a national chain, moved around in various rented facilities in downtown Davenport until 1923, when a building was erected on South Main Street near the riverfront levee. The facilities within included a swimming pool, rooms, a cafeteria, and a lounge. The Lend-A-Hand closed as a women's facility in the 1960s, later re-opening as a housing unit for senior citizens.

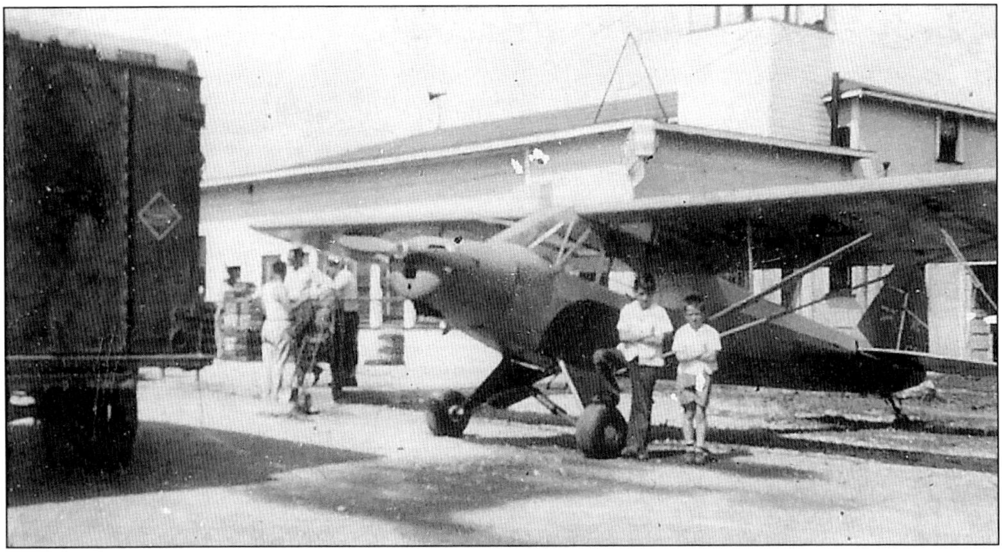

Say, isn't that Sky King and Penny standing near their plane? No, the location is Davenport's Cram Field, an airport planned and constructed during the 1920s, when the economy was booming. The airport complex was named after flight enthusiast and newspaper publisher, Ralph Cram. Located north of Duck Creek along Division Street, Cram maintained an active schedule of both commercial and personal flight services. With the introduction of the larger Mount Joy Airport, Cram Field closed. Later, the Mount Joy site ceded most of its passenger flying service to the Quad-City Airport, retaining private plane services only.

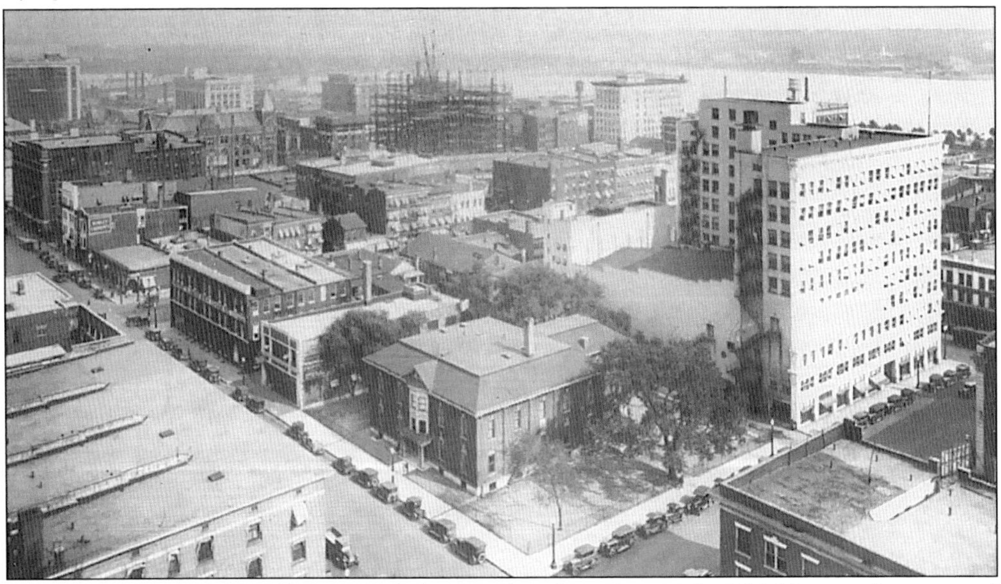

"Say, Mr. Lindbergh, would you mind slowing the plane down a bit? I'd like to take an aerial picture of Davenport. This southeast view from Fourth and Ripley would be a good shot. Yes, the 300 block and West Fourth. Quite a growing city, isn't it? If it looks likes this now, in the 1920s, can you imagine what it will look like in…in the year 2000? Yup, the new president is indeed an Iowan: Herbert Hoover. He hails from a little town called West Branch, just west of here. I must say, Mr. Lindbergh, you sure do know how to navigate an aircraft. You could set it down at Cram Field, if you like…"

Now, just who might this attractive young lady be, her flashing smile illuminating a dark corner of the Mississippi Hotel? Actually, she was just passing through Davenport as part of a national touring dance show. That's one clue: she's a dancer! Here's another: it was the dreary 1930s, and she brightened up the stage with a FANtastic dance routine. One more: _____ McNally. If you managed to guess Sally Rand, the famous fan dancer, you're right on target! (You are also probably over 60, too!)

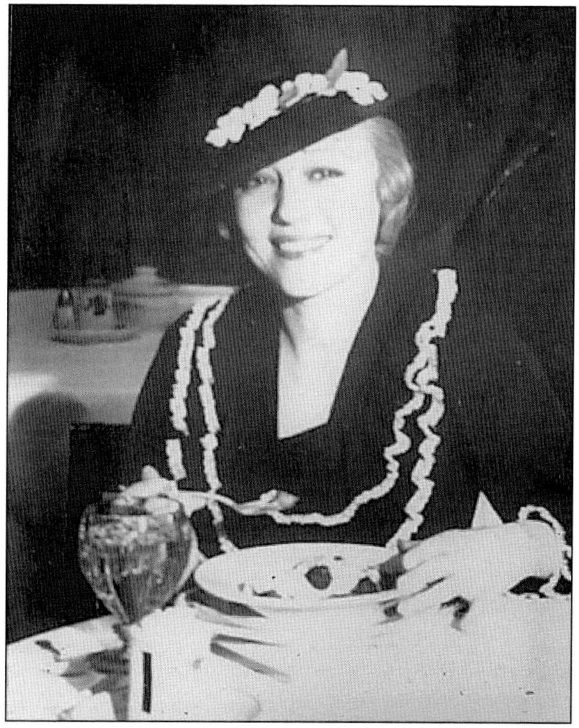

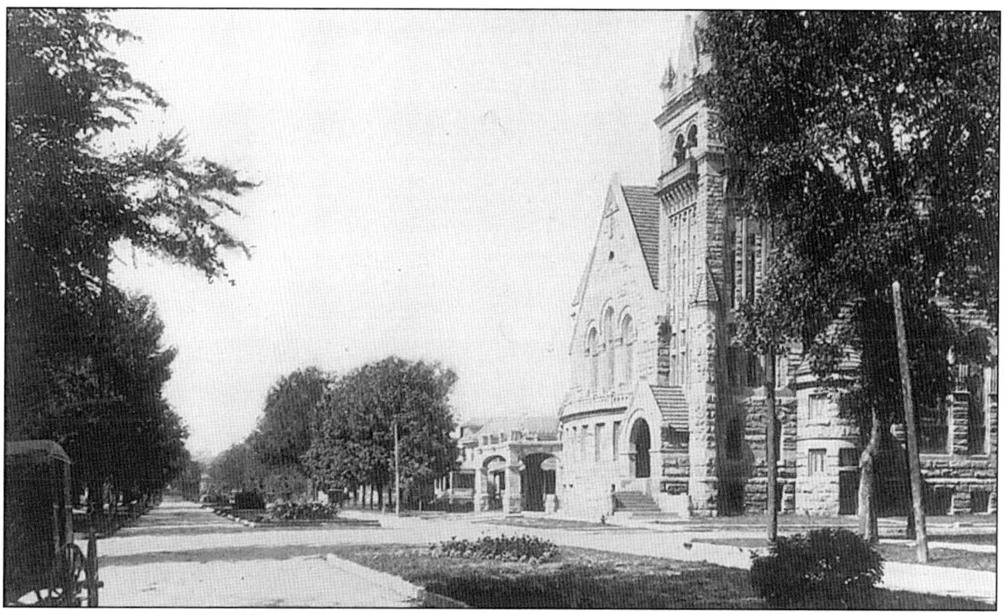

Davenport has claimed many picturesque corners through the years, spots where Norman Rockwell might have settled down and painted a scene from America's heartland. Looking west on Kirkwood Boulevard was just such a spot, with the imposing First Presbyterian Church, whose congregation was the oldest Protestant group in the city. Like many churches of the time, it was created out of brownstone, with a bell tower encasing a rich set of chimes. The green-rimmed trees framed the quiet street in spring and summer, turning to royal autumn tones in the fall, and becoming snow-laden in the winter.

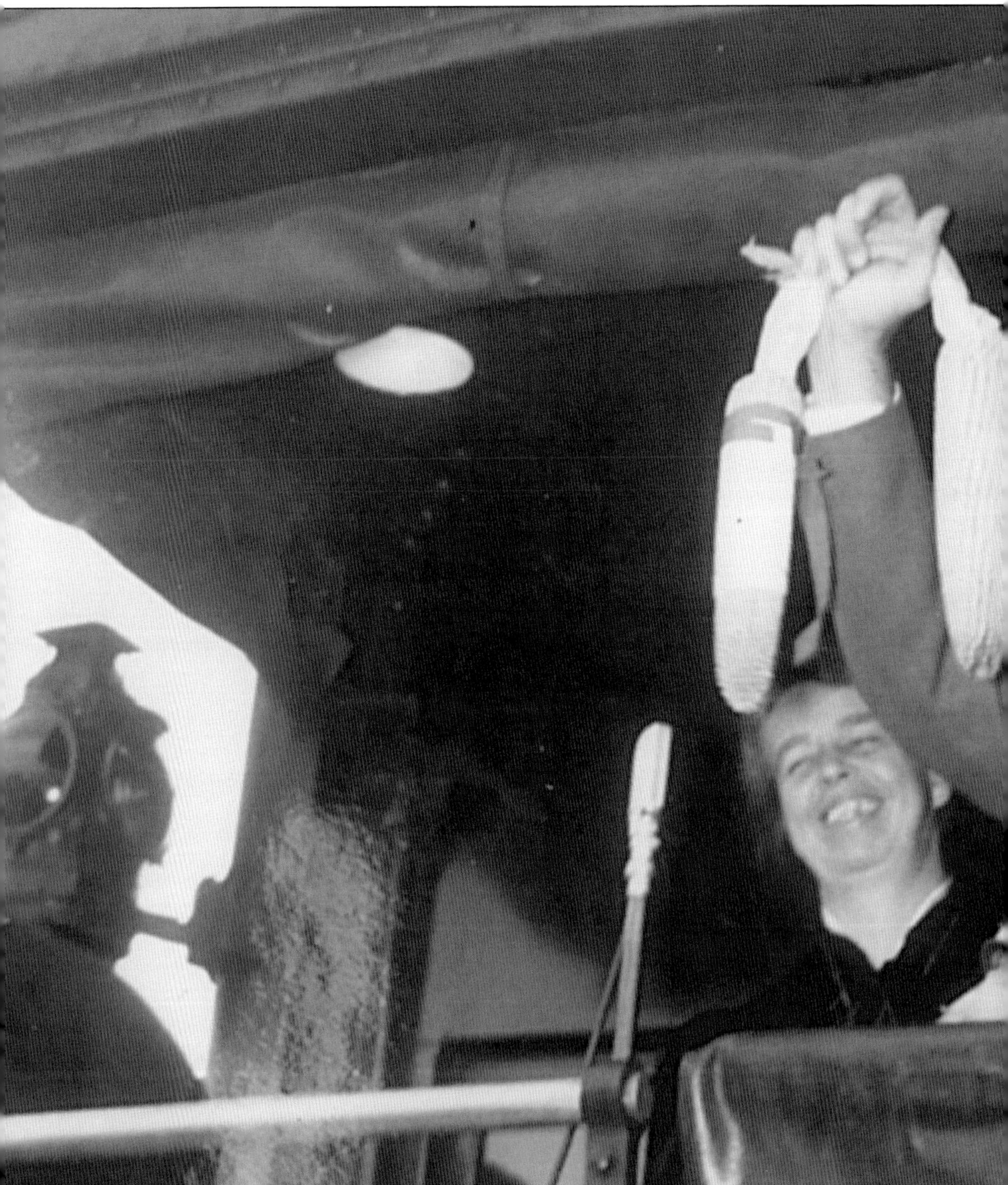

"Happy Days are here again, the skies above are clear again…" With one four-year term under his belt, President Franklin D. Roosevelt was riding the victory train when he arrived in Davenport in the fall of 1936. Spectators who attended spoke of FDR's "infectious smile," and his articulate oratorical skills. The Davenport crowd interrupted Roosevelt's speech 26 times, as he spoke from the rear of the train. Truly, his New Deal programs had won many followers.

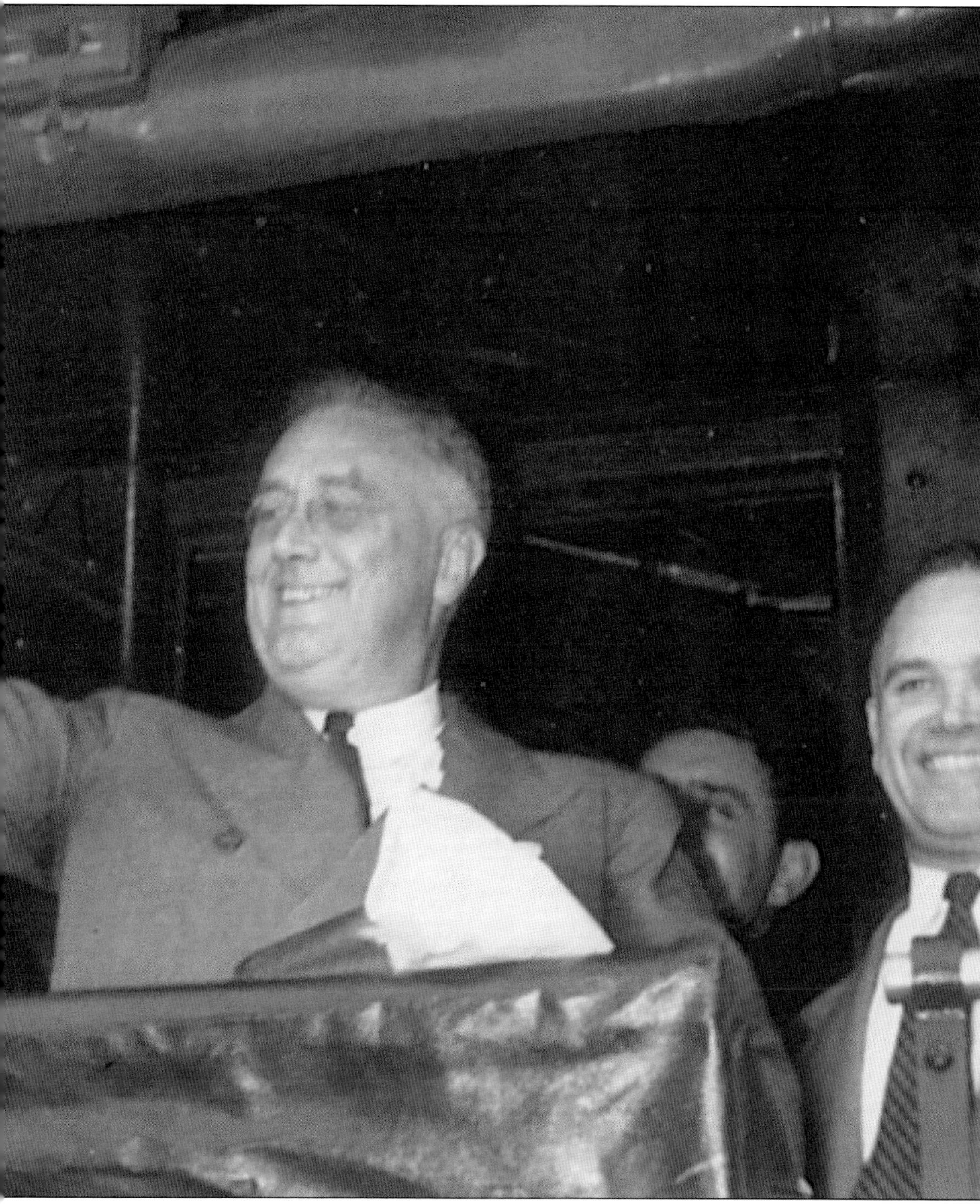

FDR's wife, Eleanor, had already achieved her own place in the spotlight, and would go on to forge a place in history. Not only did FDR win the 1936 presidential election; he went on to win in 1940 and 1944 as well, the only four-term United States president. Roosevelt's unexpected death in April of 1945, plunged the nation into mourning.

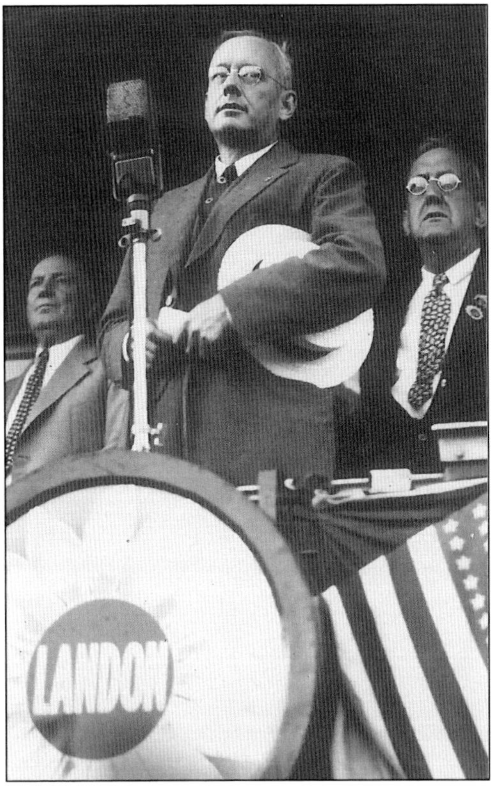

The 1936 Republican presidential candidate chosen to take on the popular incumbent, Franklin Delano Roosevelt, was Alfred Mossman Landon of Kansas. Roosevelt was credited with bringing the nation out of the Depression, and many considered anyone running against him to be a sacrificial lamb. Nonetheless, Landon campaigned with energy and enthusiasm, including at this railway stop in Davenport, where he appealed to "fellow Midwesterners" for votes. Landon carried only two states in the November election: Maine and Vermont.

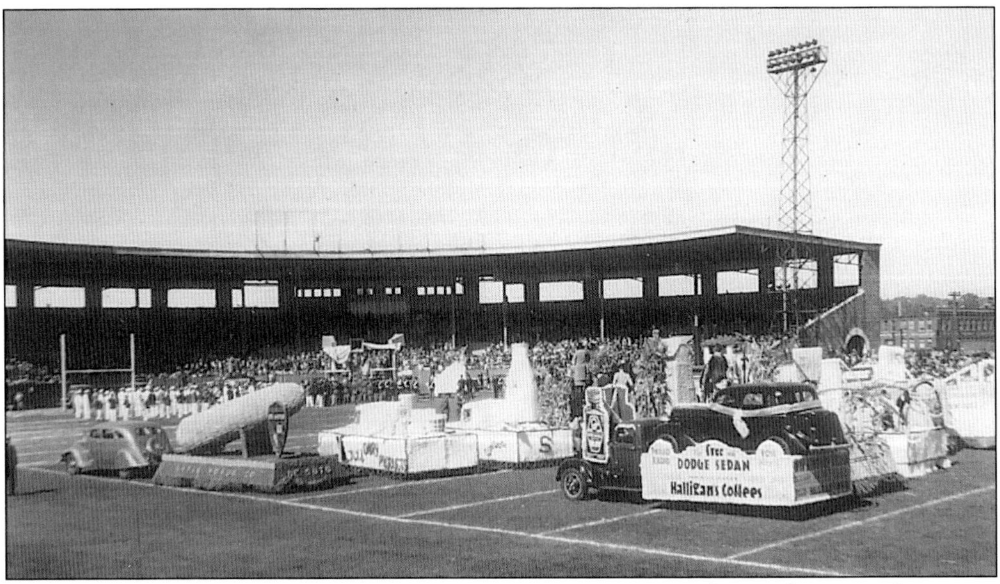

The United States was getting back on its feet in 1936, recovering from a disastrous depression that had put people out of work, caused many businesses and farms to collapse, and cast a gray shadow over countless families. People were reading the bestseller "Gone With the Wind," and setting attendance records at athletic events. Floats rolled into the Davenport Municipal Stadium to the accompaniment of local bands, as folks of the Mississippi Valley celebrated Agricultural Day.

Few families have contributed so much to Davenport as that of the Palmer family. Daniel David, B.J., Mabel, and David: the list of family innovators and contributors is lengthy and impressive. The Palmer School of Chiropractic, "Little Bit o' Heaven," and WOC Communications are only a few of the enterprises associated with the Palmers. Dr. David Palmer, shown here, was instrumental in the development and promotion of WOC Radio and Television during the 1940s, 1950s, and 1960s. "People should give back to their communities in whatever way they can," he often said, and then proceeded to match his word with example.

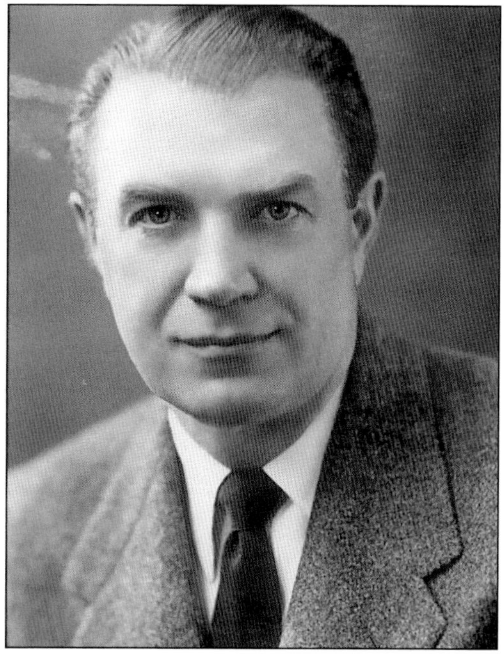

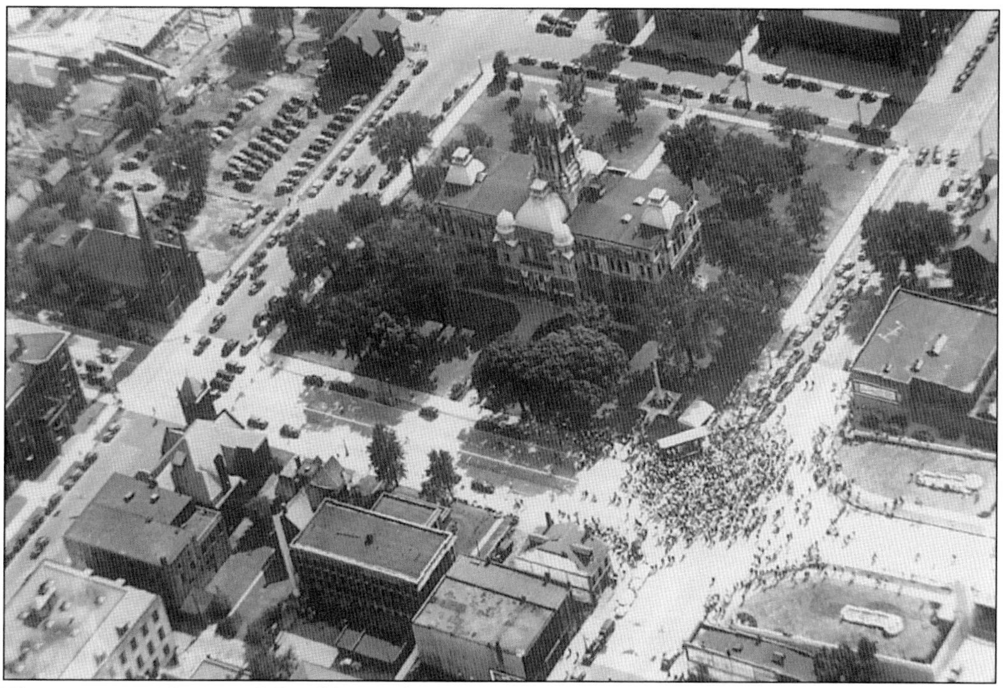

The year was 1941, and Franklin Delano Roosevelt was in his third term as President. War clouds were gathering in many places around the world, but few Americans anticipated the surprise attack on Pearl Harbor that would take place on December 7th. There were other events going on in the country, such as this celebration of the completion of the Centennial Bridge. Davenporters started from the Iowa side and crossed the bridge to Illinois, gathering at the Rock Island County Courthouse as seen here. The annual St. Patrick's Day march across the Centennial is the only two-state affair in the country in observance of the holiday.

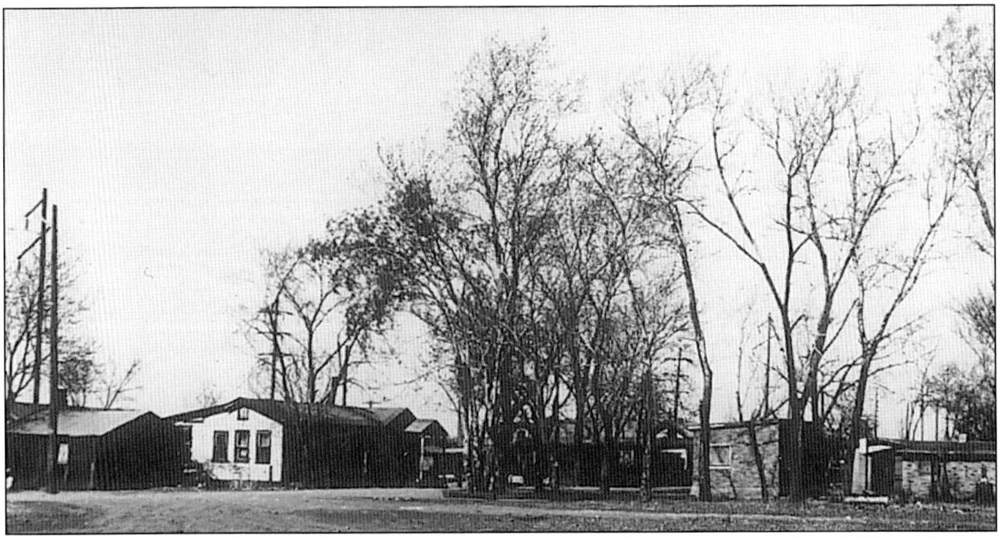

With World War II just past, United States servicemen and servicewomen headed back home, causing a rise in building construction. The area pictured here, Cook's Point, grew swiftly, welcoming Hispanics to Davenport. The residences were modest, the yards small, but the people were proud of their new homes and worked hard. Newcomers eagerly shared their recipes and music among their non-Hispanic neighbors. At school, the youngsters delighted in demonstrating how to put together colorful piñatas, filled to the brim with tasty candies, which would spray the spectators when the piñata was smashed.

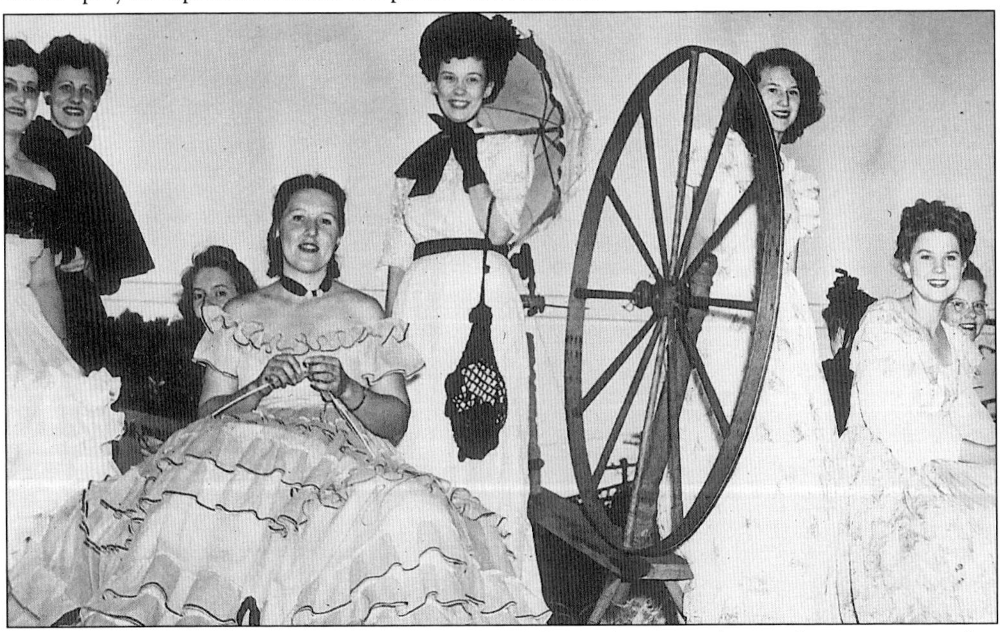

World War II was over, and what better way to celebrate the peace than with patriotic parades, beauty pageants, athletic competitions, beard growing contests, and fireworks. You name it, and Davenport hosted it. For 1,000 days during 1946 to 1948, area residents enjoyed "State of Scott" events. Organized largely through the Davenport Chamber of Commerce, the three-year-long festivities brought new pride and attention to all who participated, including this collection of gals displaying styles of the past and present.

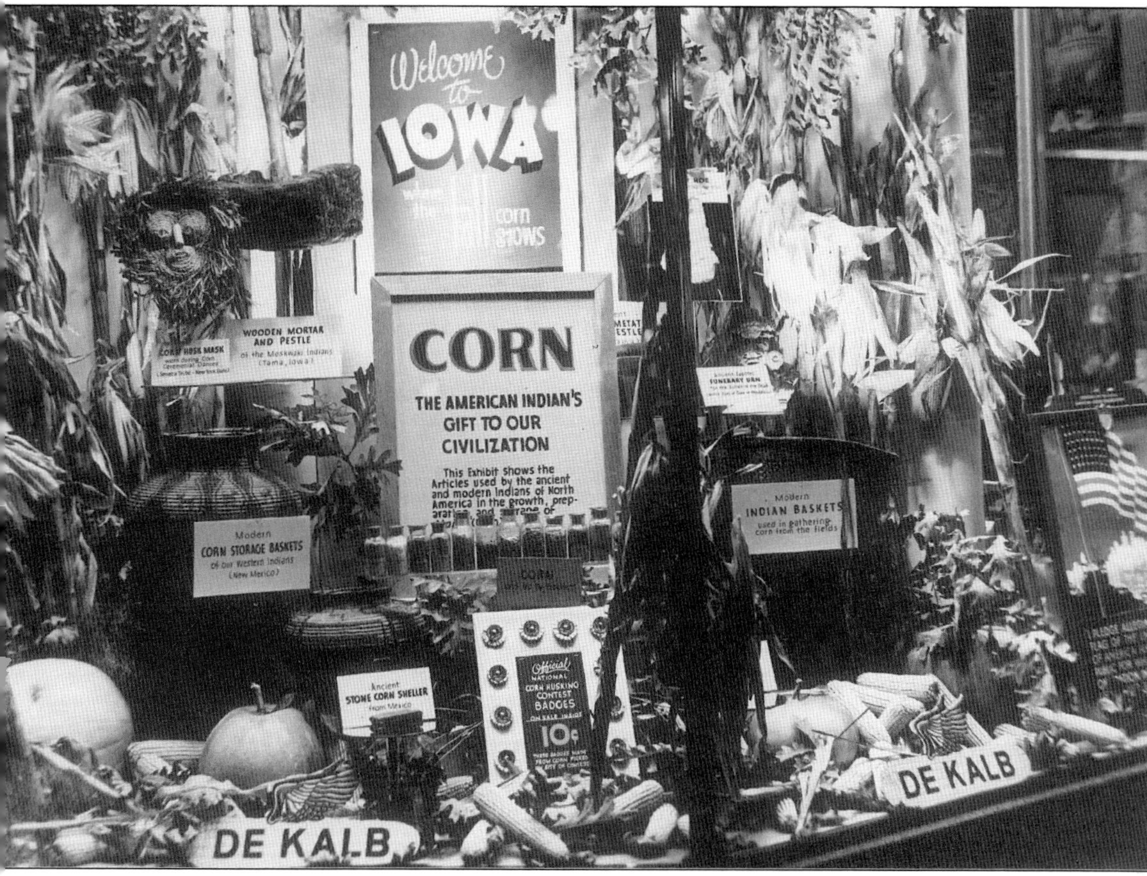

People continued to come to Davenport from all parts of the country—north, south, east, and west—in 1947. The sounds of war were merely an echo in the distance, and new festivals and celebrations were popping up throughout the United States. "Popping" was just the right verb as far as Davenport was concerned. Corn grabbed a major spotlight as visitors thronged the town, ready to take part in the National Corn Husking Contest. Displays like this one, in the W.T. Grant window, were common downtown, welcoming visitors to the city. Competitions were held between families and neighbors as to whom who could eat the most popcorn. More creative popcorn lovers designed popcorn balls and dyed them. Three fraternity fellows from the University of Iowa popped up a heaping bathtub-full of the tasty treat, and then proceeded to eat it all—in only three hours! Go, Hawkeyes!

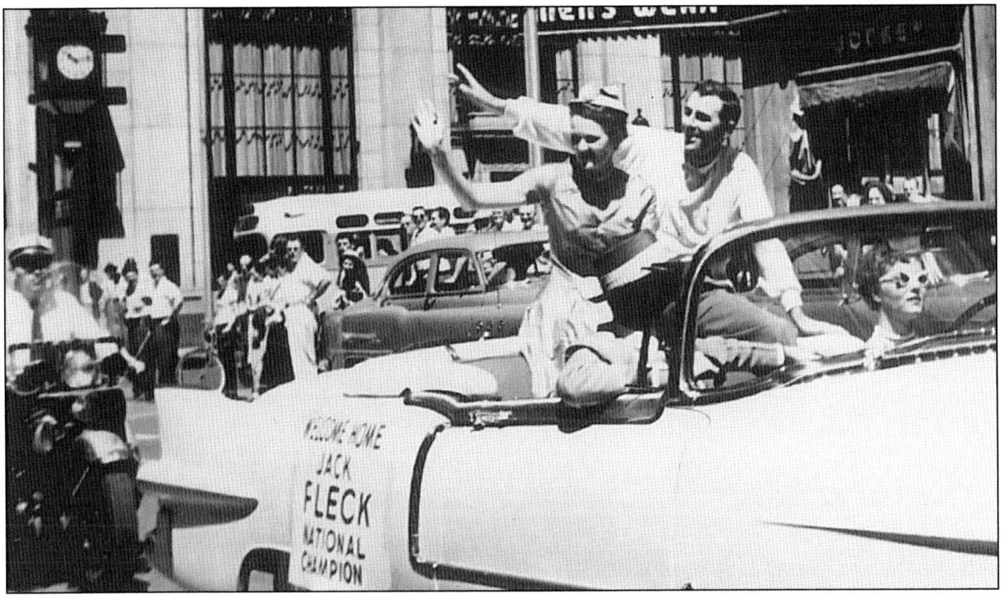

Hail to the conquering hero! A smiling Jack Fleck and his wife enjoy the cheers of the crowds as they weave their way through the streets of downtown Davenport in 1955. Fleck's accomplishment? He had managed to defeat superstar Ben Hogan, and capture the U.S. Open championship at the Olympic Country Club in San Francisco. A former pro at Duck Creek and Credit Island, Fleck proved that nice guys don't always finish last!

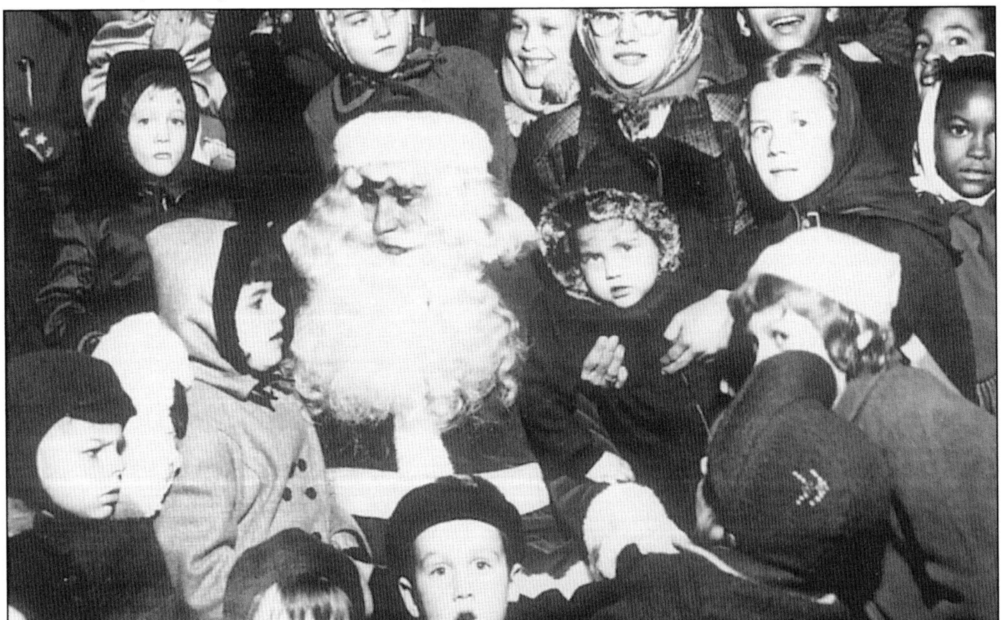

"And what do you want for Christmas, little girl?" The 1940s (before anyone ever heard of a shopping mall) brought countless bargain hunters to downtown Davenport. "Dollar Days" were especially wild. Youngsters besieged the department store Santas, asking wistfully or whinefully for a new toy or sibling. Many Davenport and Quad-Cities adults remember the thrill of viewing the Petersen Harned Von Maur display windows filled with miniature moving figures.

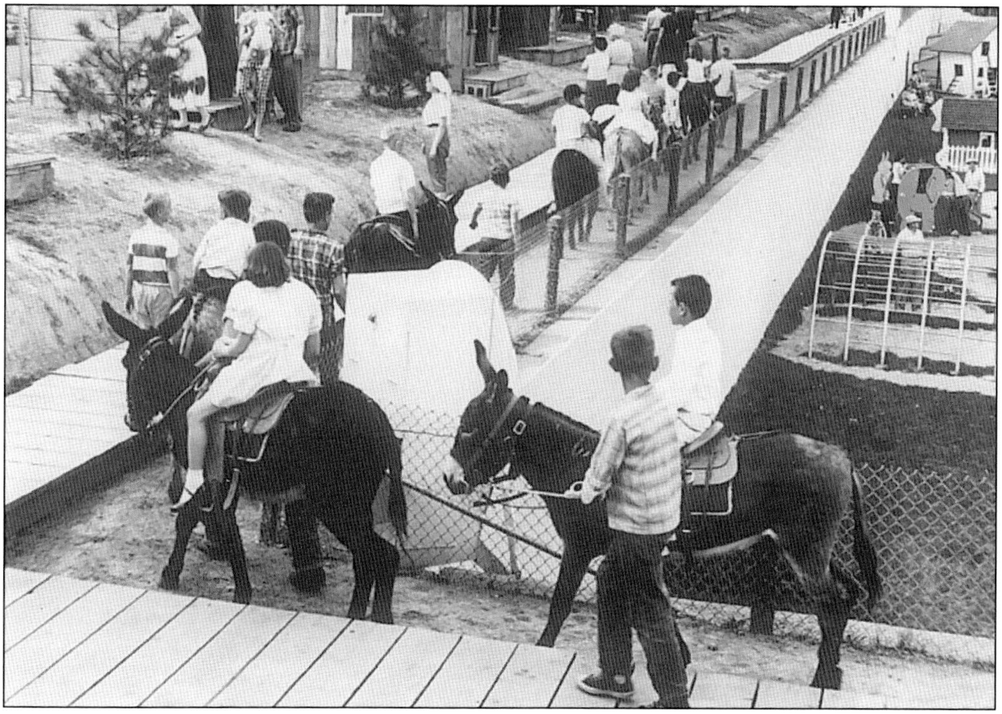

For countless youngsters and used-to-be young-uns, Davenport's Fejervary Park brings back memories of watching monkeys, riding burros, or playing on state-of-the-art gymnastic equipment. Few forget the giant Mother Goose at the entrance that welcomed anyone and everyone for hours of fun. The park came into being thanks to the family and friends of Count Nicholas Fejervary. The Count came to Davenport in 1848, after the Hungarian Revolution. He left his mark on the city in the form of financial and land contributions. He died after returning to Hungary, and his descendants gave the city his land and property.

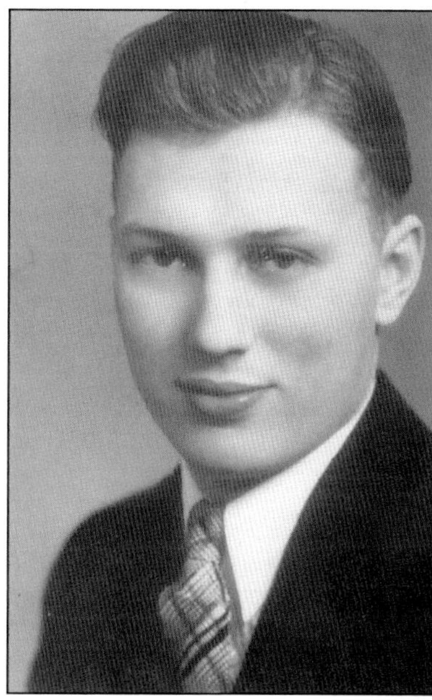

Roland Johnson was like so many from Davenport in the 1930s and '40s. He was a young person just getting established in life, only to join his country's fight for freedom and democracy. He never returned. Roland's interest—more of a calling, actually—was music. Once his formal education was completed, he headed into his role as a musician with a studio in downtown Davenport's Whitaker Building. Then, along came World War II, and sadly, a dream ended. For those like Roland Johnson, who served and died for a grateful country, may they rest in peace.

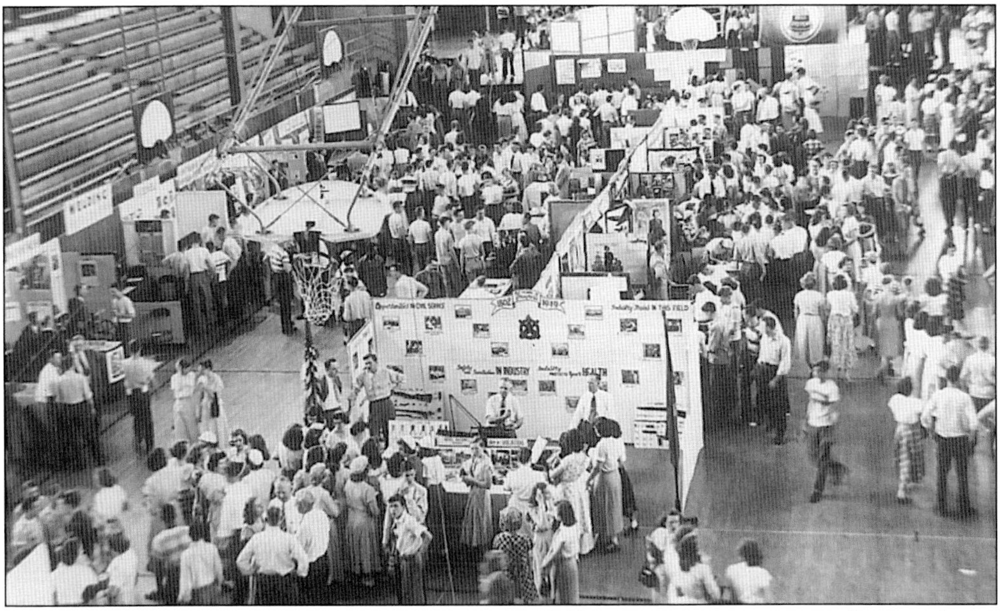

"Are there openings in the teaching profession?" "I'd like to stay in Davenport after I graduate, but I'm not sure I can find a job in the field of writing." "People are talking about a television station that's going to start up here..." The year was 1949, and the students of Davenport Central High School roamed from table to table in the gym during Opportunity Day. Representatives from a variety of professions and occupations eagerly answered questions from, and distributed information to, inquisitive students.

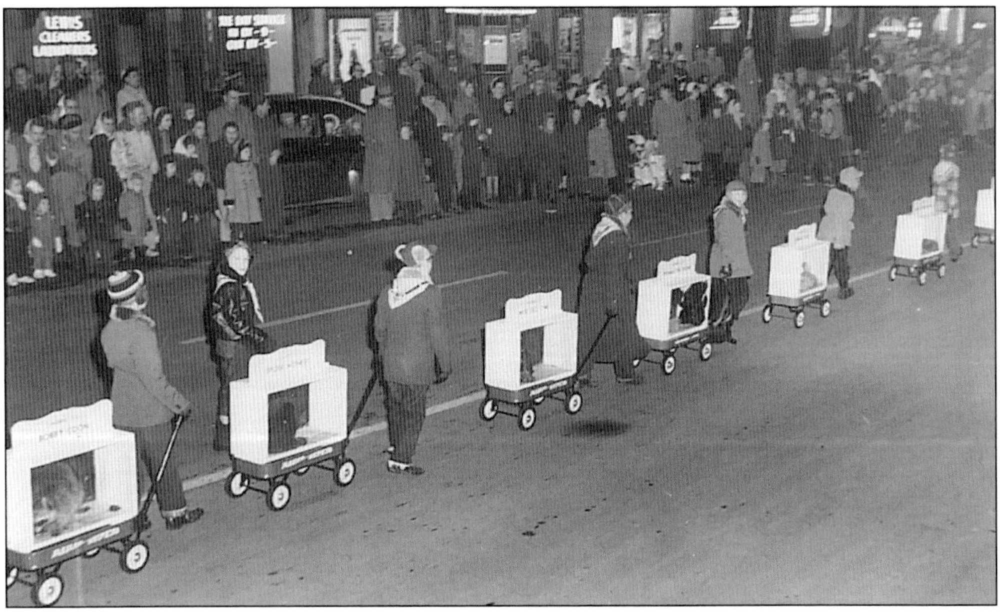

"Lions and tigers and bears, oh, my! Lions and tigers and bears, oh, my!" Well, maybe there aren't any ferocious beasts around—and Dorothy and Toto are not within viewing range, either—but nothing can squelch the spirit and fun of a Davenport parade over the holidays of 1954. Children (of all ages) showed off their "zoo animals" for spectators to admire. Many viewers commented on what "purr-fect" weather shone on Davenport for the parade.

Four

1950 AND ON, WHAT HATH GOD WROUGHT?

Keep your secrets, Cold ballroom walls,
For those who have glided across your gleaming floors
Harbor memories of their own.

Do you remember the past?

The flooded summers of '65 and '93?
Soul-chilling times of 1980s recession and company closings?

Great moments of Bix 7 races and festivals. Businesses closing doors.
The step-by-step determination of German-American society members
As they work to restore the old Standard Hotel.

Davenport's past remembered with sorrow and with joy,
While faces look towards the future.

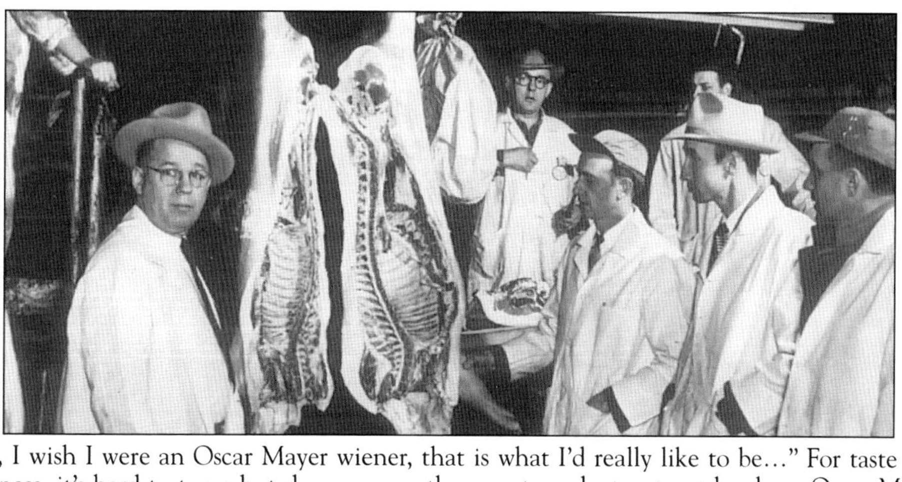

"Oh, I wish I were an Oscar Mayer wiener, that is what I'd really like to be..." For taste and juiciness, it's hard to top a hot dog, or any other meat product put out by those Oscar Mayer folks. Well, maybe with mustard and catsup. Oscar Mayer has been part of Davenport since 1946, when the company started operating out of the old Kohrs Packing Plant. This 1952 photo catches both home workers and visitors at the company's packing plant on West River Drive. The special occasion was the Spring Market Hog Show held in Davenport.

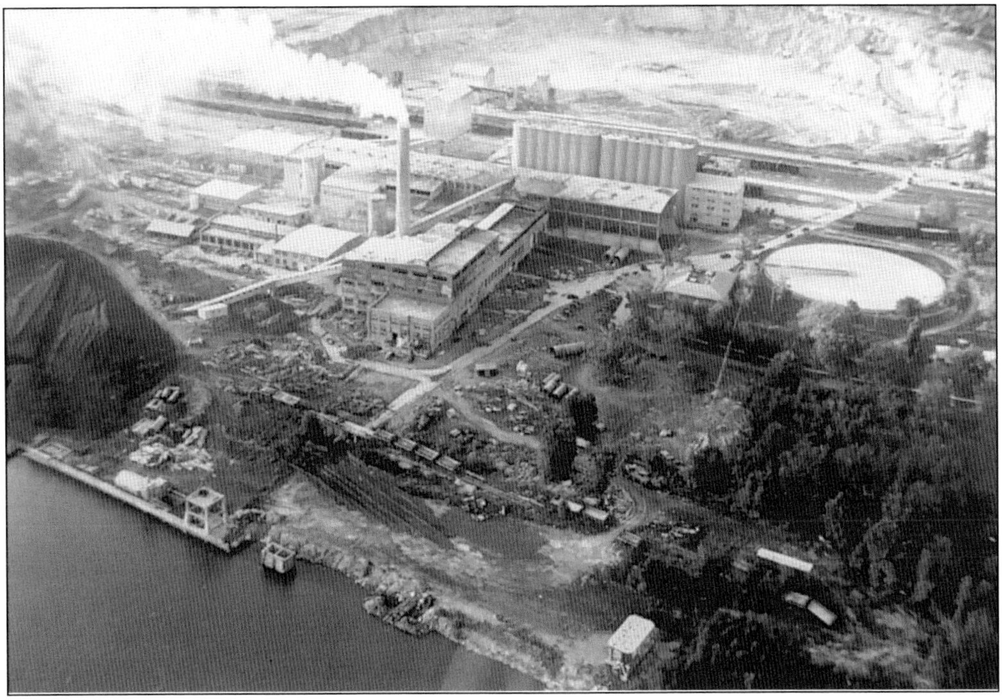

People who view the Mississippi Valley by air often comment on how picturesque the area is, as the Mississippi River snakes through the region like a smooth ribbon. Businesses and residential neighborhoods dot the landscape, and highways look like string, tying everything together. In this visual photograph from 1953, the roadway is Highway 22, and the business is the Dewey Portland Cement Company. Dwight Eisenhower occupied the White House, and, locally, Deere & Company, Harvester, Caterpillar, and Oscar Mayer provided jobs to many.

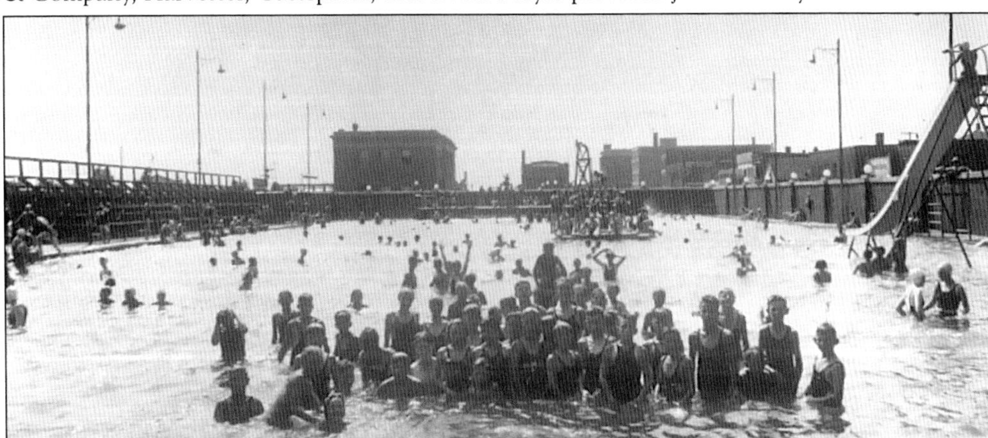

"In the good old summertime, in the good old summertime..." Like lemmings in Norway are drawn to the water, so were swimmers in Davenport during the 1940s and 1950s. Specifically, they were lured to the downtown Municipal Natatorium. The large-scale swimming pool offered refreshing relief from the scorching Iowa summer heat. One "rite of passage" for dare-devilish youngsters involved a quick trip down the slide, screaming all the way. Attendance declined during the 1960s and 1970s, and in 1981 the Natatorium was razed. However, the memories linger, of those water-ful, splash-filled afternoons of long ago.

You can travel to Chicago, Los Angeles, or New York City. You may visit London, Paris, and Rome. But don't be too surprised to find a piece of Davenport on a table or mantel wherever you go. The exquisite Isabel Bloom statuary, large or small, is everywhere. A sculptor almost all her life, the young Isabel first molded fanciful creations from river clay. The family furnace served as a kiln, hardening her work into fixed artistic pieces. Further training at the Immaculate Conception Academy, the Art Institute of Chicago, Vogue School of Fashion, and Grant Wood's Stone City art colony completed Isabel's formal training. But it is the simple and sensitive heart, soul, and hands of the artist that make each Isabel Bloom creation so beautifully unique.

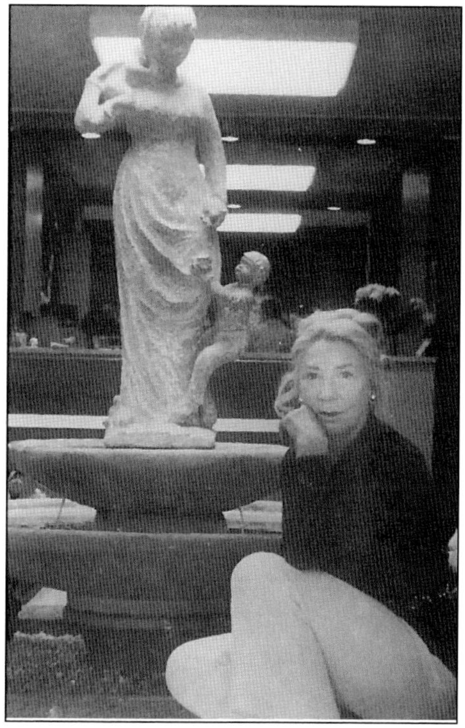

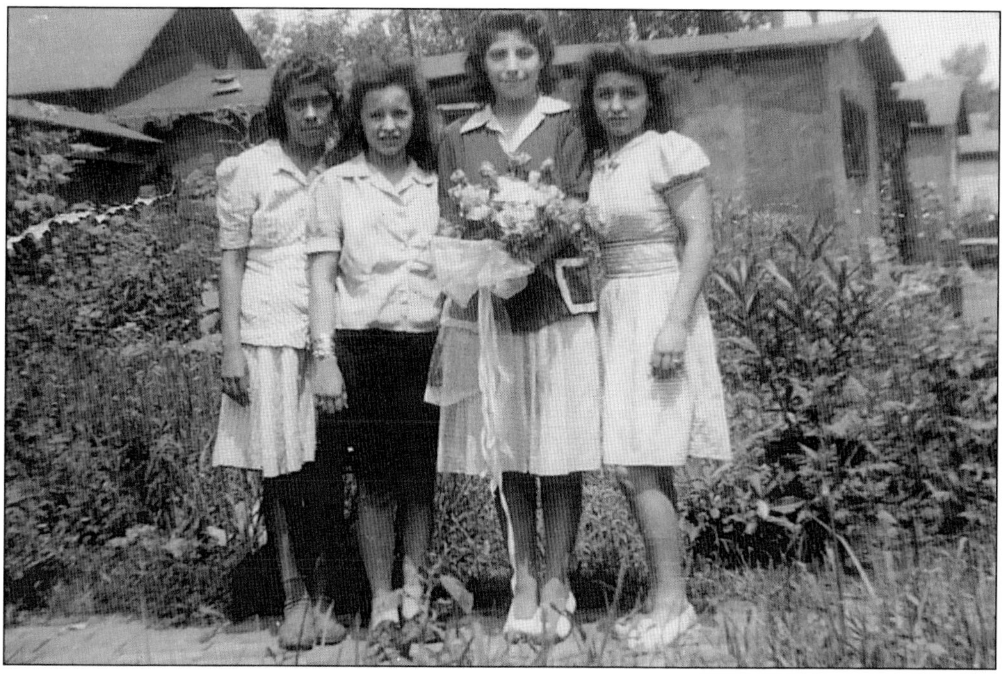

One of Davenport's many positive features is the exciting mixture of cultures that enjoy living in the "Jewel of the Mississippi" area. Many Hispanics immigrated to the living complex known as Cook's Point shortly after World War II. This quartet of señoritas must have been among the most "bonitas." Displaying their wholesome and attractive good looks for the photographer are D. Vargas, N. Garcia., L. Herrera, and M. Garcia.

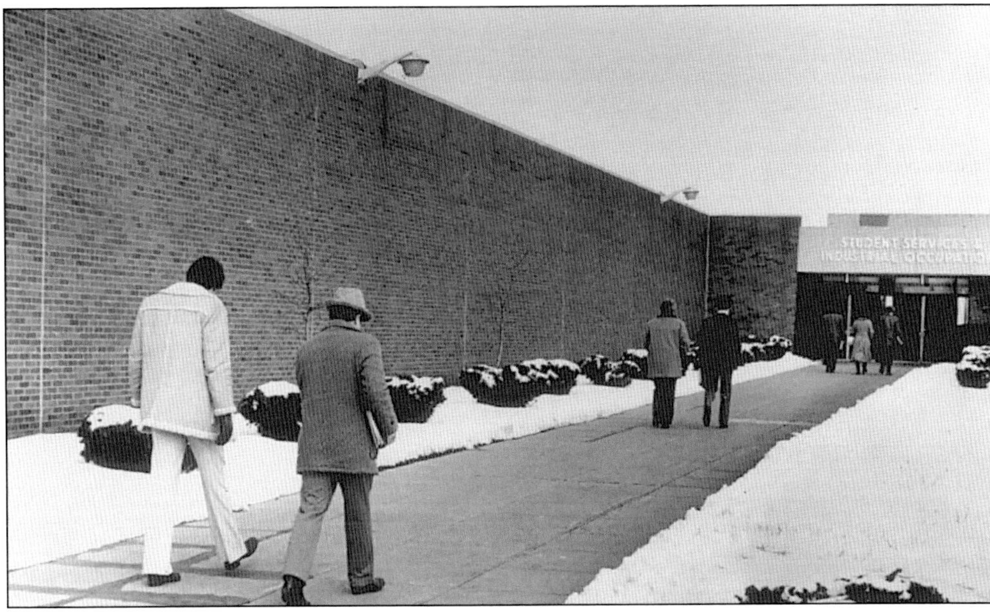

Students learn a variety of vocational skills at Scott Community College. The college evolved from the old Davenport Area Technical Center, which became a part of Iowa's community college system in 1966. This is a view of the college's Belmont Road campus, where the first buildings were completed in 1970.

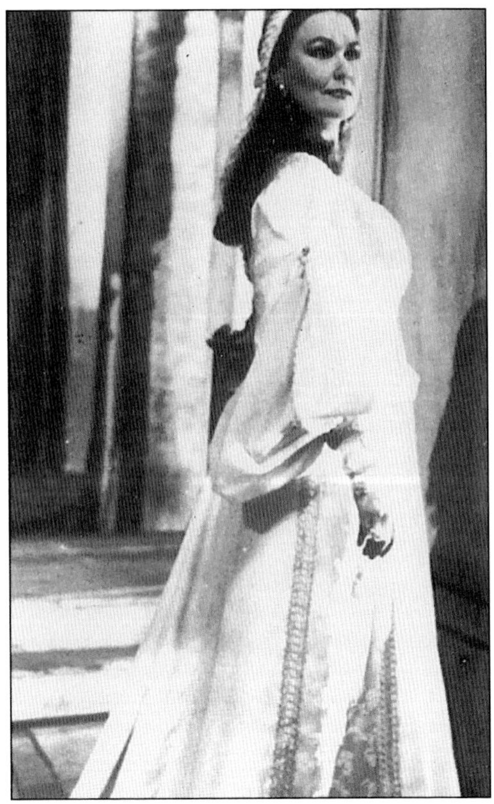

"With poise and precision, Margherita Roberti physically commands the stage, while her voice travels to her audience with power, warmth, and sensitivity." So wrote one critic upon attending a performance, featuring an operatic soprano long associated with Davenport and the Mississippi Valley community. Married to Davenport native Thomas Nobis since 1949, Roberti performed *Aida*, *Tosca*, and many other operas across the country. She was the first American woman to be knighted by the Republic of Italy for her musical contributions there.

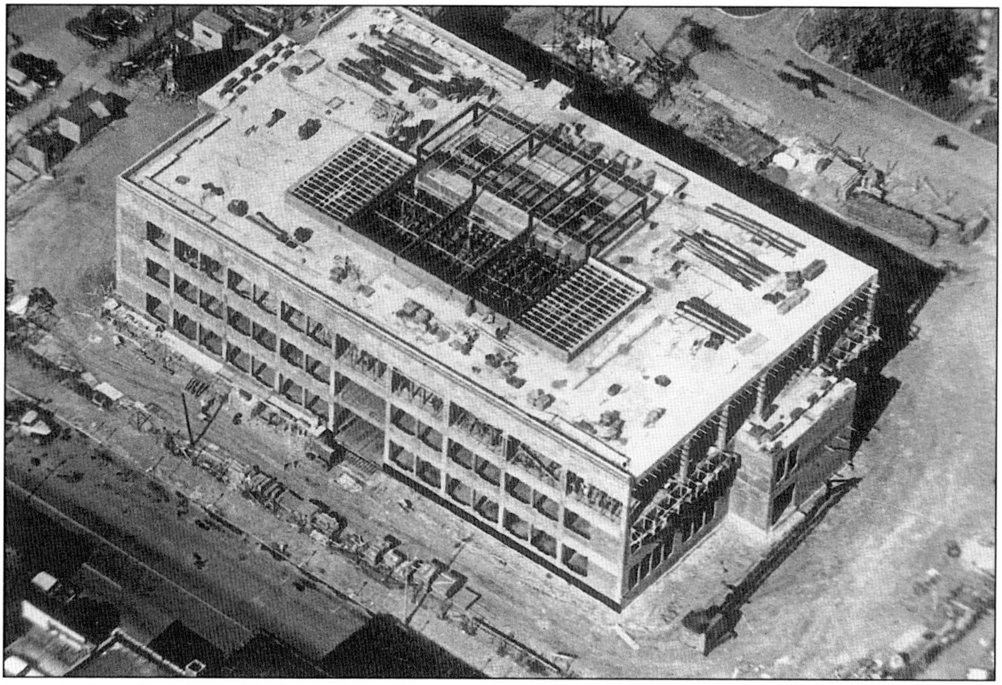

Long before the days of Judge Judy, Judge Jerry, and Judge Joe, efforts were set afoot to construct a courthouse of which Davenport residents could be proud. Certainly, the Scott County Courthouse, built in 1887, had served the area long and well, but buildings do wear out. Leaders talked about putting everything under one roof—that is, government offices and facilities for both Davenport and Scott County. Later, that idea was scrapped, and in 1955, the new Scott County Courthouse went up.

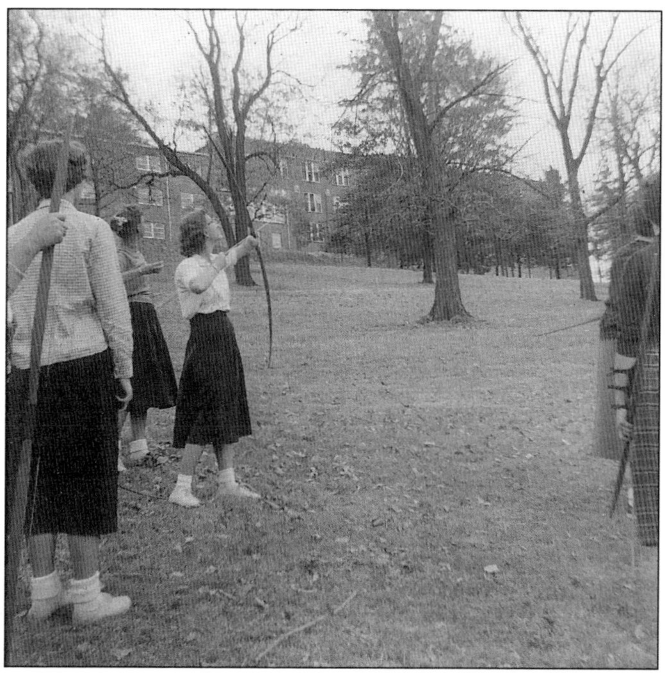

Could they be trying out for Robin Hood's band in Sherwood Forest? Well, the attire is definitely a bit formal. Moreover, upon closer examination, the setting seems to be on the hill located behind Upham Hall, below and behind Rohlman and Lawlor Hall dorms. The time was February of 1957, when Marycrest College was still an all-female institution. Archery is no longer offered at the school. Dwight David Eisenhower was president in 1957, and two film stars—Marilyn Monroe and James Dean—sparked the adoration of countless fans. Both died tragic deaths.

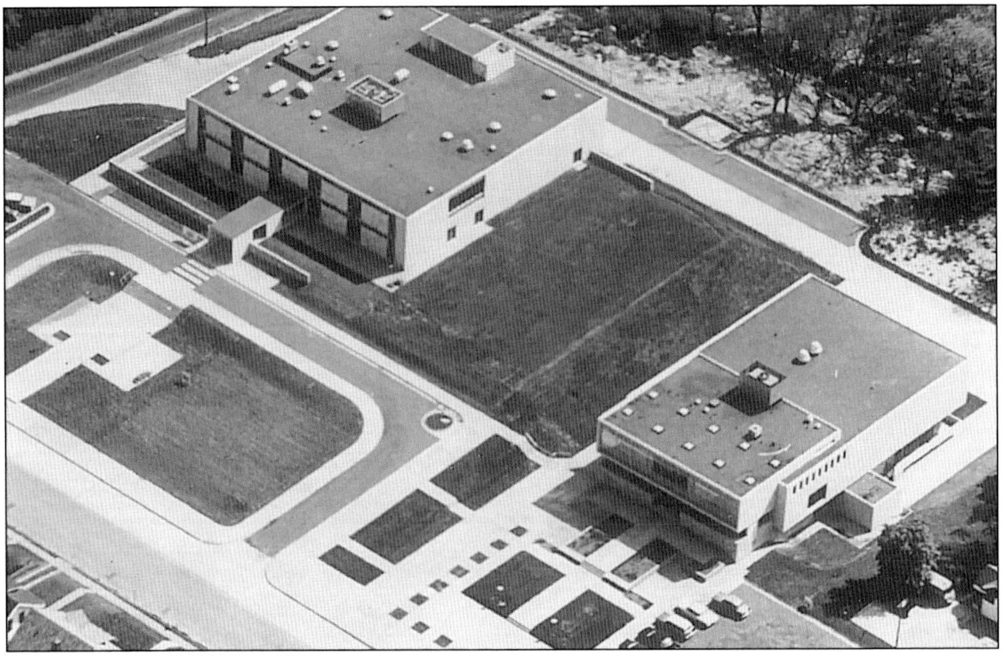

"I want to go to the Davenport Art Gallery." "I want to go to the Putnam Museum." No argument is needed: since the two buildings are close together, visit both! This aerial photo catches both of Davenport's "castles of culture" as they appeared in 1963, the year the museum opened its doors. The art gallery previously resided in the old Armory Building on West Fifth before it was moved into a new building on West Twelfth. Both buildings offer a variety of collections and exhibits each year, while maintaining a wide range of classes and activities.

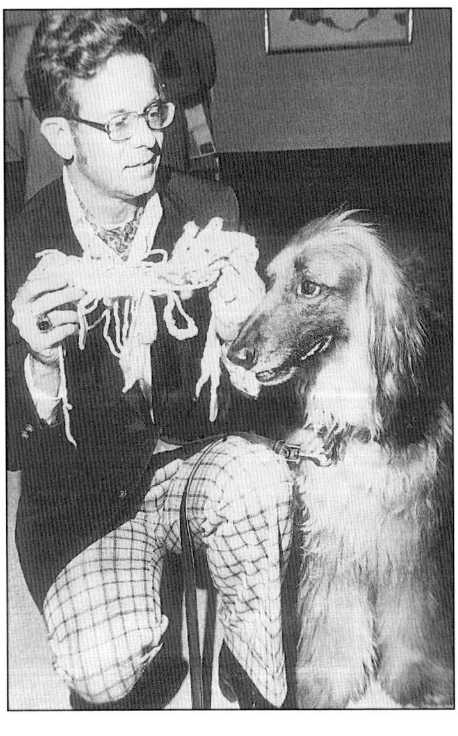

Michelangelo, Leonardo DaVinci, Pablo Picasso, Alexis Boyer, Salvador Dali—hey, wait! Back up a moment! Who is this Alexis Boyer? Certainly, the other names are those of world famous artists, but Alexis Boyer? You say that Boyer was a winner in the 1974 Mid-Mississippi Art Show, with his entry of a chewed mitten, held proudly here by his master Elliot McDonald, the prominent Davenport attorney? Well, it proves the maxim that "beauty is in the eye of the beholder." I'll be doggone...

To be the president of a distinguished college, or the shepherd of a large religious congregation, would demand a special kind of leadership and faith. To hold both demanding positions marks a unique accomplishment. Monsignor Sebastian George Menke was exactly that kind of individual. President of St. Ambrose College during the turbulent 1960s and 1970s, his job required a singular kind of understanding and patience. Following that tenure, he took over Sacred Heart Cathedral, where he became legendary for his energy and compassion. (He also planted countless rosebushes on the grounds!)

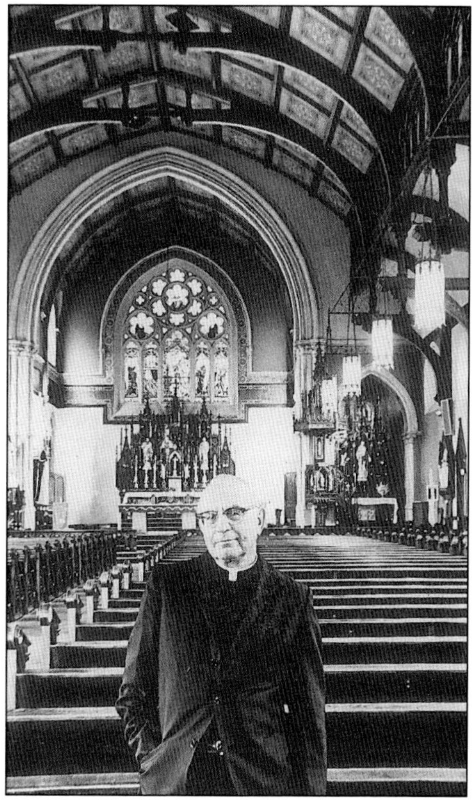

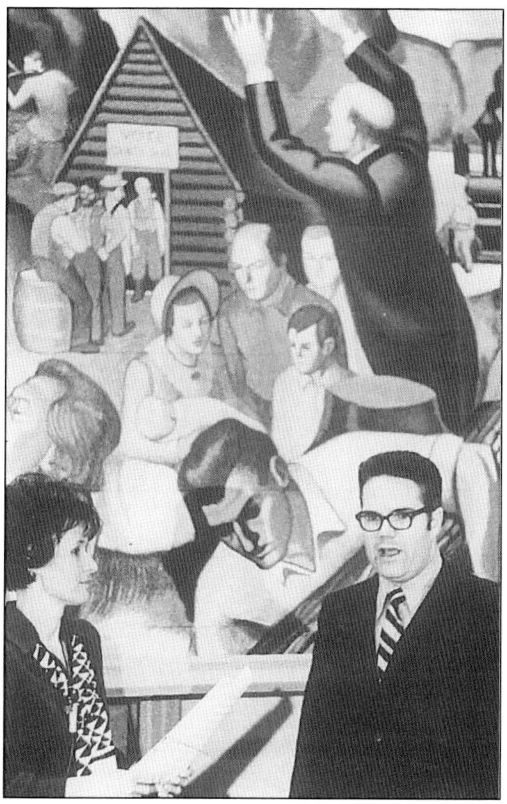

"I can do anything. I am woman..." Across the nation, women were asserting themselves as never before, and Davenport's Kathryn Kirschbaum stepped forth in 1971 to capture the city's mayoral position. First an alderman and mother of two young sons, she later chose to accept a challenge put to her by Davenport Democrats to carry the party's head spot on the ballot. She served two terms as the city's chief executive. This January 3, 1972 photo found her reviewing the score for the "City of Davenport" with the famed Walgreen's mural as a backdrop.

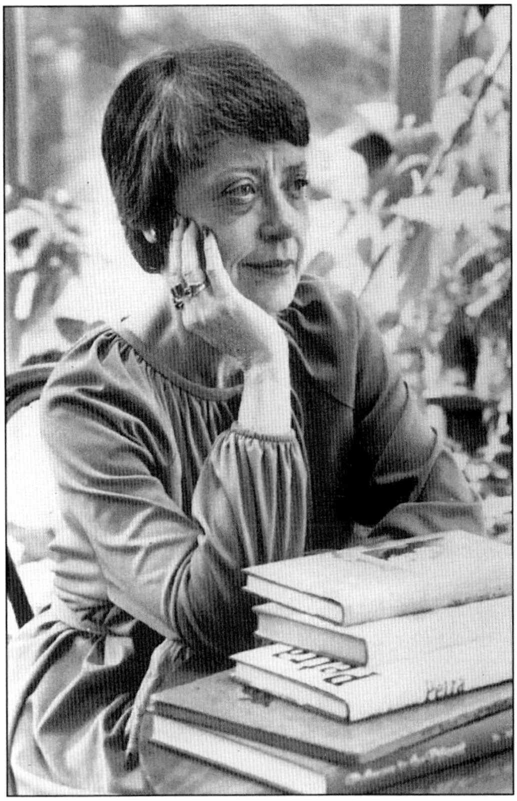

For decades, she has reigned as a reviewer extraordinaire. To receive a positive review from Julie Jensen is to know that your book, your artwork, or your performance has merit and quality. Her byline first appeared above her own play, "The Whispering Mummy," when she was in the sixth grade. So started a career in writing that spread into a love affair with the fine arts. She served many years as chairman of the Iowa Arts Council, squeezing time in to produce such best-selling novels as "Amalie's Story" and "Petra." An art collector and clarinet player, Davenporter Julie Jensen also thrives as Mrs. Elliot McDonald.

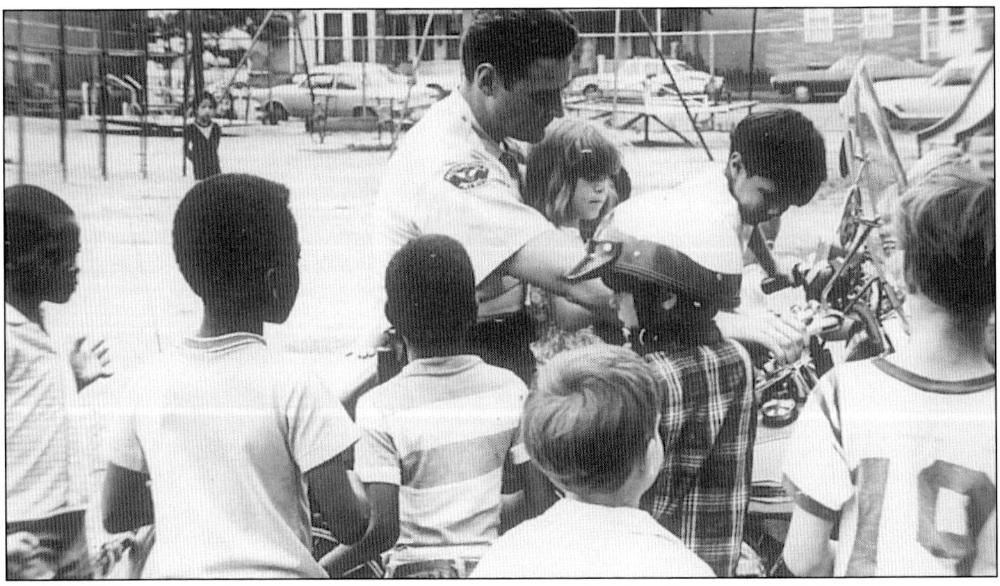

"And you have to be very careful making turns..." The Davenport Police Department maintains an active program designed to keep children safe, secure, and "officer friendly." In this November 1977 photo, motorcycle patrolman Chuck Wright displays his vehicle and explains his duties in law enforcement to inquisitive students. Wright later went on to become a Davenport mayor.

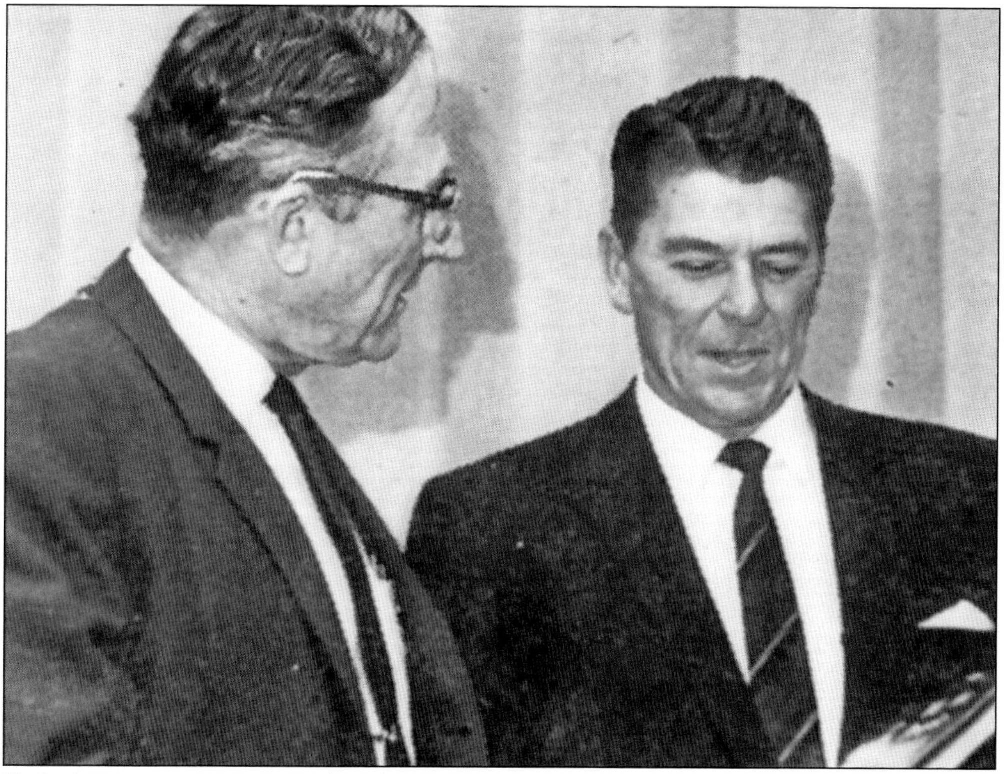

"It looks very impressive, my friend. You've done a lot with your love for history..." In this 1980s photo, Iowa Congressman Fred Schwengel and President Ronald Reagan admire one of Schwengel's latest literary compilations. Schwengel served numerous terms as a representative in the United States House of Representatives before becoming completely involved with historic preservation. Reagan served as a WOC radio announcer while he worked in Davenport during the early 1930s. During his Davenport tenure, he lived in the in the now-razed Vale Apartments.

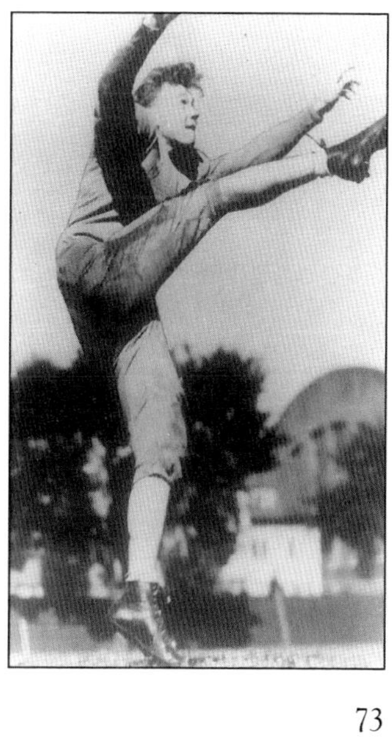

Well, it's sure not Charlie Brown kicking the football! Davenport claims its share of outstanding athletes, and George "Sonny" Franck holds an honored spot with other past Davenport stars of the gridiron. Franck played for legendary coaches Midge Makeever and Jesse Day in Davenport, and then went on to play for Minnesota in an undefeated season. Chosen most valuable player in the 1941 All Star game, Franck was third in the voting for the Heisman Trophy. An elbow injury took him out of professional play, and he returned to Rock Island where he coached for 13 years.

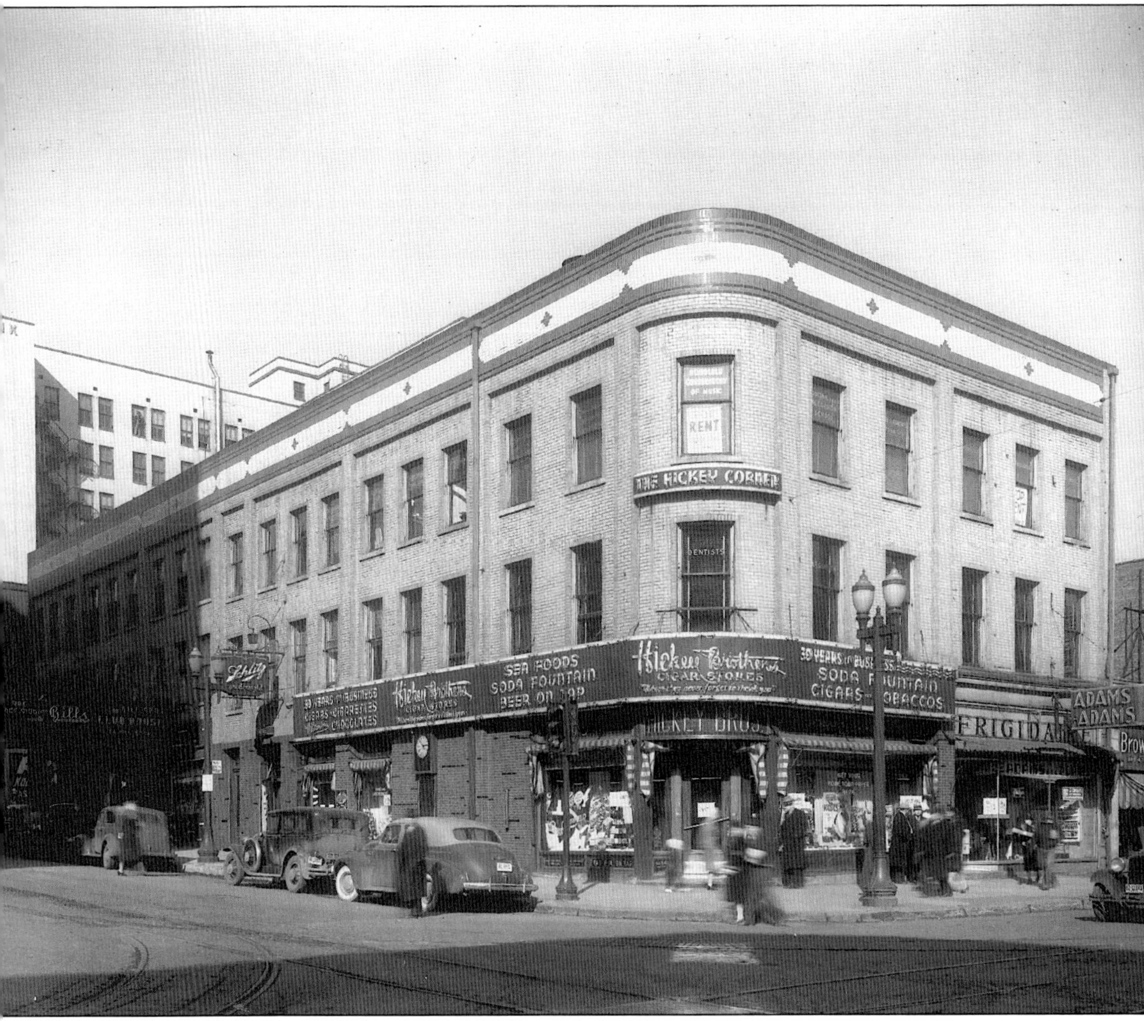

Can you spot a possible business slogan by looking at this picture from the 1930s? How about "Bank on Hickey Brothers"? This national cigar store chain originated in Davenport in 1901, thanks to the leadership of brothers Bill and John Hickey. Offering over one hundred cigar brands, the Hickey Brothers Store also featured pipes, billfolds, specialty candies, and a variety of newspapers. Counter service beverages and foods were offered at the "No. 8" store, shown here, at the northeast corner of Second and Brady Streets. From the beginning, the company motto was "Where they never forget to thank you." The sales were good—over $7,000,000 annually from 130 stores scattered across the nation. Travelers from Davenport found that the best hotels, including the Waldorf-Astoria in New York City and the Drake in Chicago, boasted Hickey Brothers wares. During the early 1950s, the business nose-dived, and in 1957 the final Hickey Brothers store closed its doors.

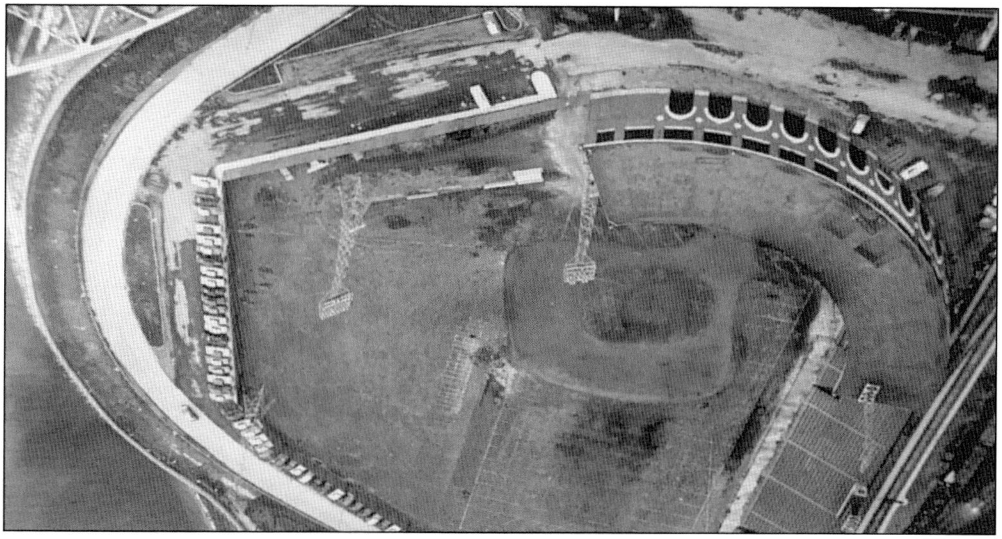

For years, this building was known as Municipal Stadium. It graces the shoreline of the Mississippi, and is the first major city landmark viewed by visitors rolling across the Centennial Bridge. Constructed in 1931, the field hosted all kinds of activities, including patriotic parades, agricultural exhibits, and rousing sports contests. The Quad-City Angels won popular fan support, as did most recently the Quad-City Bandits. In 1970, the Davenport City Council re-named Municipal Stadium the John O'Donnell Stadium, in honor of the popular sportsman and journalist who passed away in that year.

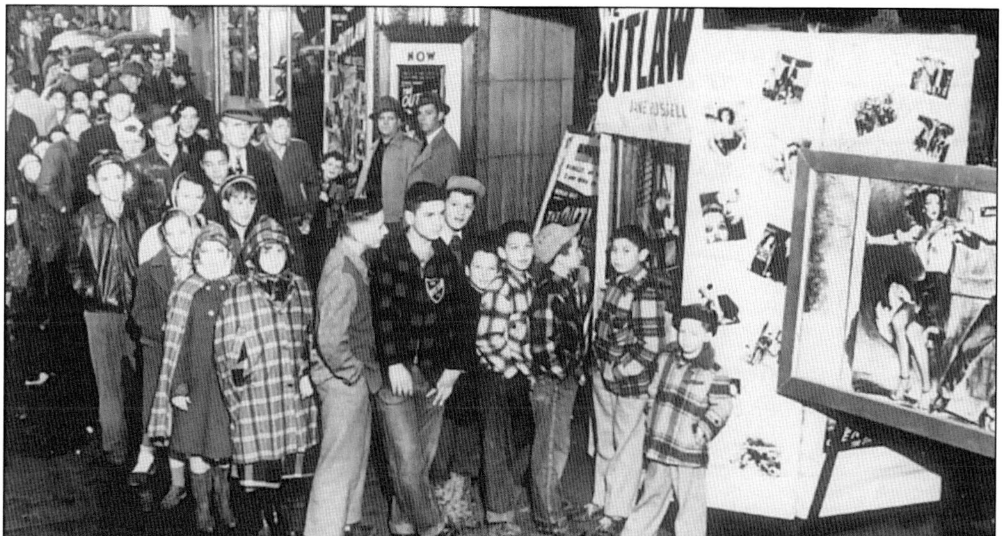

The lines seemed endlessly long at the RKO Orpheum for the 1943 release of "The Outlaw"—a Western that raised eyebrows and provoked controversy among moviegoers. It wasn't the story of Billy the Kid that caused tongues to wag, nor was it the acting by screen veterans Walter Houston and Thomas Mitchell. It was the appearance and decorum of a newcomer to the movies, a certain Miss Jane Russell, that brought discussion to Davenport dinner tables. Admission was 15¢, popcorn was 10¢, and candy bars were 5¢. Saturday afternoons belonged to the kids, but adults enjoyed Wednesday Night Bank Nights, where they could win big cash—up to $350!

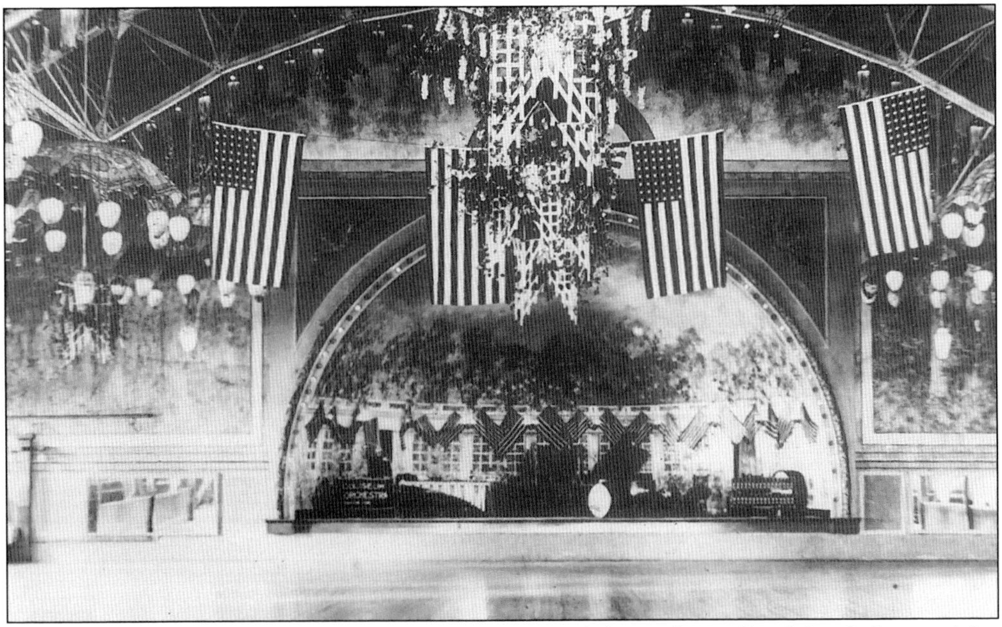

If only walls could talk...How many marriage proposals have the walls of the Coliseum (also known as Col. Ballroom) heard throughout the decades? How many women have grimaced in silent pain from high heels worn too long, or partners treading on their feet? How many songs have these walls heard? Ah, no doubt they would recall that young cornet player from Davenport, who would go on to leave his mark on the history of music. Bix Beiderbecke was his name, and jazz his ticket to fame. Keep your secrets, Coliseum walls, for those who have glided across your gleaming floors have memories of their own.

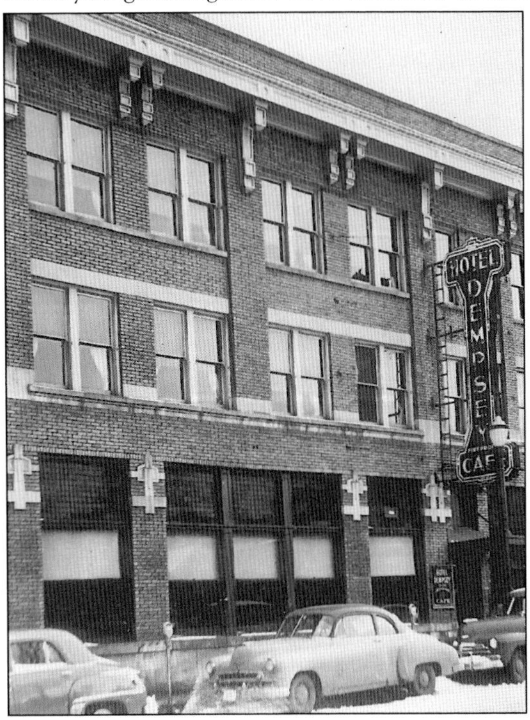

"The Dempsey," people called it, and it was located at 704 Brady. It bore no resemblance to the more majestic Mississippi or Blackhawk Hotels. Rather, the Dempsey was more of a Mickey Spillane setting: nothing fancy, just the basic bed and bathroom accommodations. Yet, there was a charm about the place, and people who ate in the café downstairs testified that the food was good and reasonably priced. "Tom Cruise wouldn't stay there," observed one Davenport old-timer. "Ed Asner would."

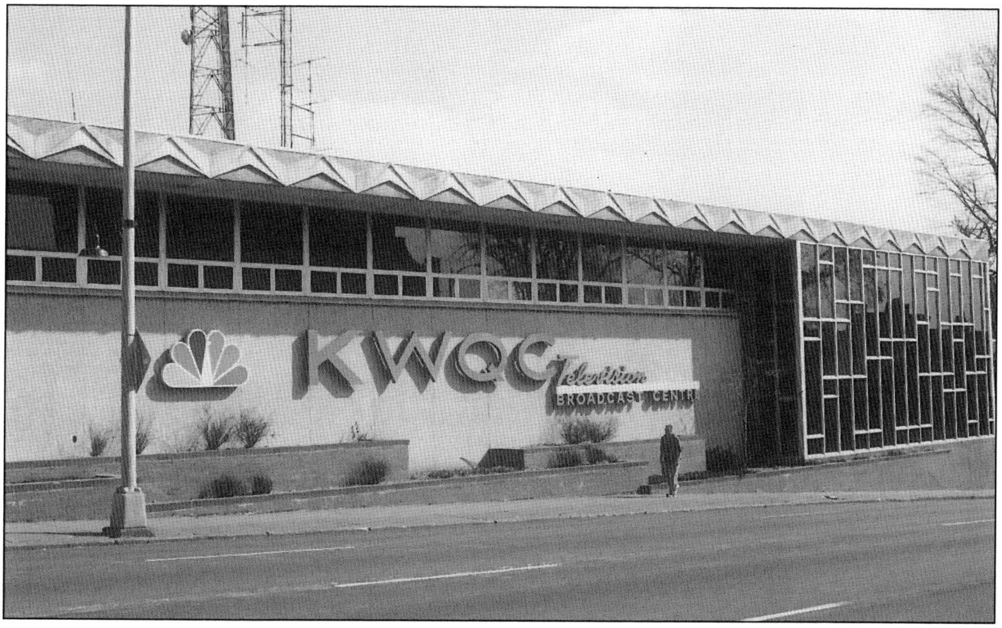

The KWQC building melds into Brady Street Hill. The driveway of the TV station tests unwary drivers, while locals admire the eye-catching design of the building. Since 1989, it has been known as KWQC-TV. However, when it first went on the air in October of 1949 as an NBC affiliate, it was known as WOC-TV. Through the years, viewers came to recognize a variety of familiar faces and names, including Pat Sundine, Ken Wagner, Bill Gress, Paula Sands, and so many more. One of WOC's most popular shows was called "Golden Opportunity," a variety program that allowed local entertainers to highlight their talents.

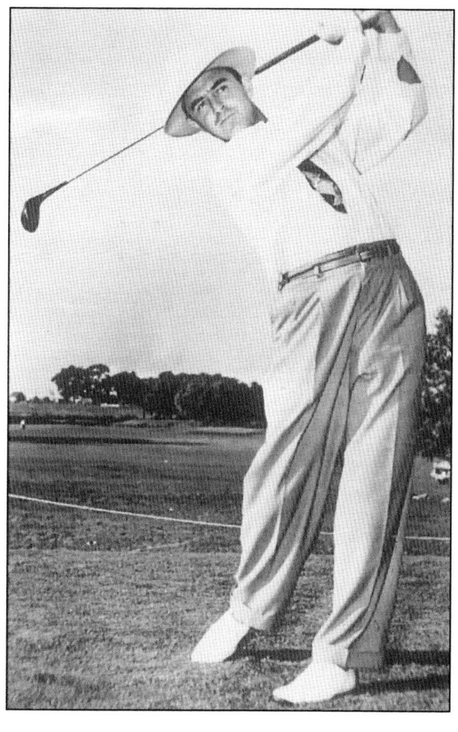

A round of golf is a hobby to some, a recreational sport to others, and a passion to many. Davenport boasts several top-quality golf courses, and whether it's nine holes or eighteen, the links add a lot to the quality of life for many. On this particular afternoon in 1955, the greens at the Davenport Country Club lured one of the nation's super pros—"Slamming" Sammy Snead—to the course. Snead displays his form and poise, but that tense expression suggests he is taking his game seriously.

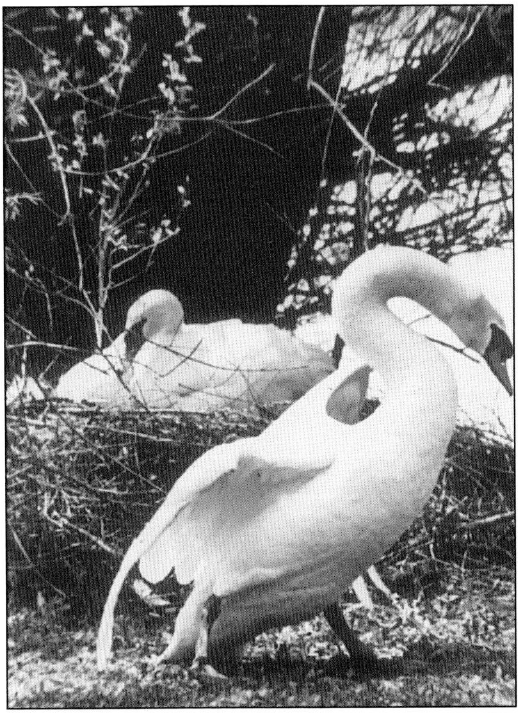

Throughout all of its history, Davenport has boasted spectacular visual images in various parts of the city. Many appear in the form of unusual architecturally-designed homes and public buildings, while colorful murals bedeck walls in residential and downtown neighborhoods. However, few eye-catching scenes could surpass the sight of these graceful and proud swans as they enjoy the quiet setting of Vander Veer Park on a May afternoon in 1955.

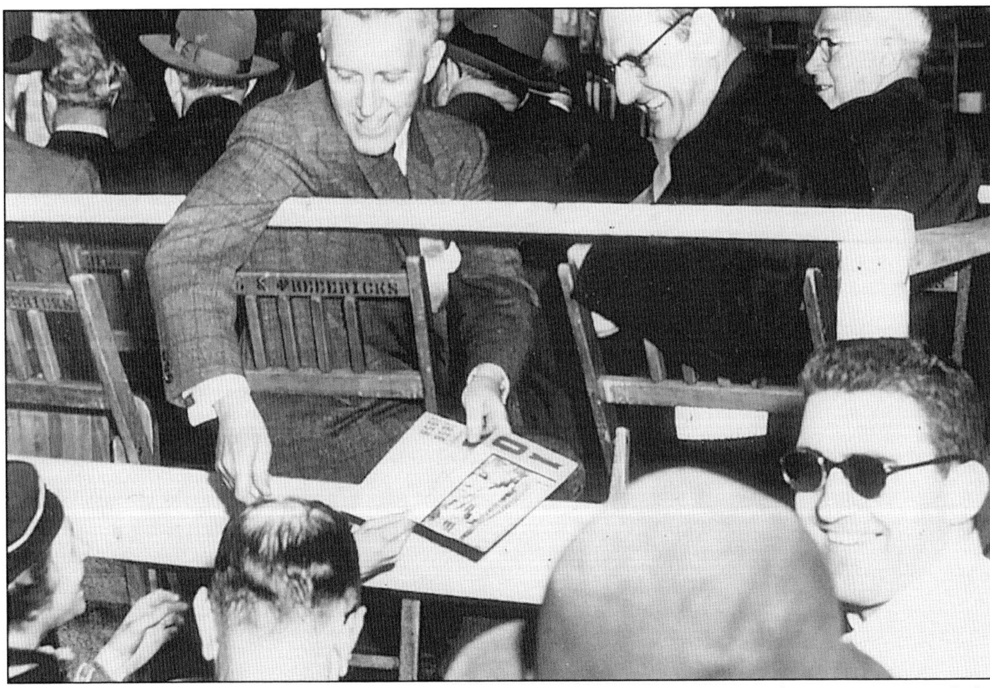

It's time for a celebration! This event in 1956 commemorated the 100th anniversary of the Mississippi railroad bridge construction. What would such an historic observance be without a couple of notable politicians? On hand for the celebration were Iowa Governor Leo Hoegh and Congressman Fred Schwengel. Well-versed in such matters, both men cheerfully oblige a Davenport autograph seeker.

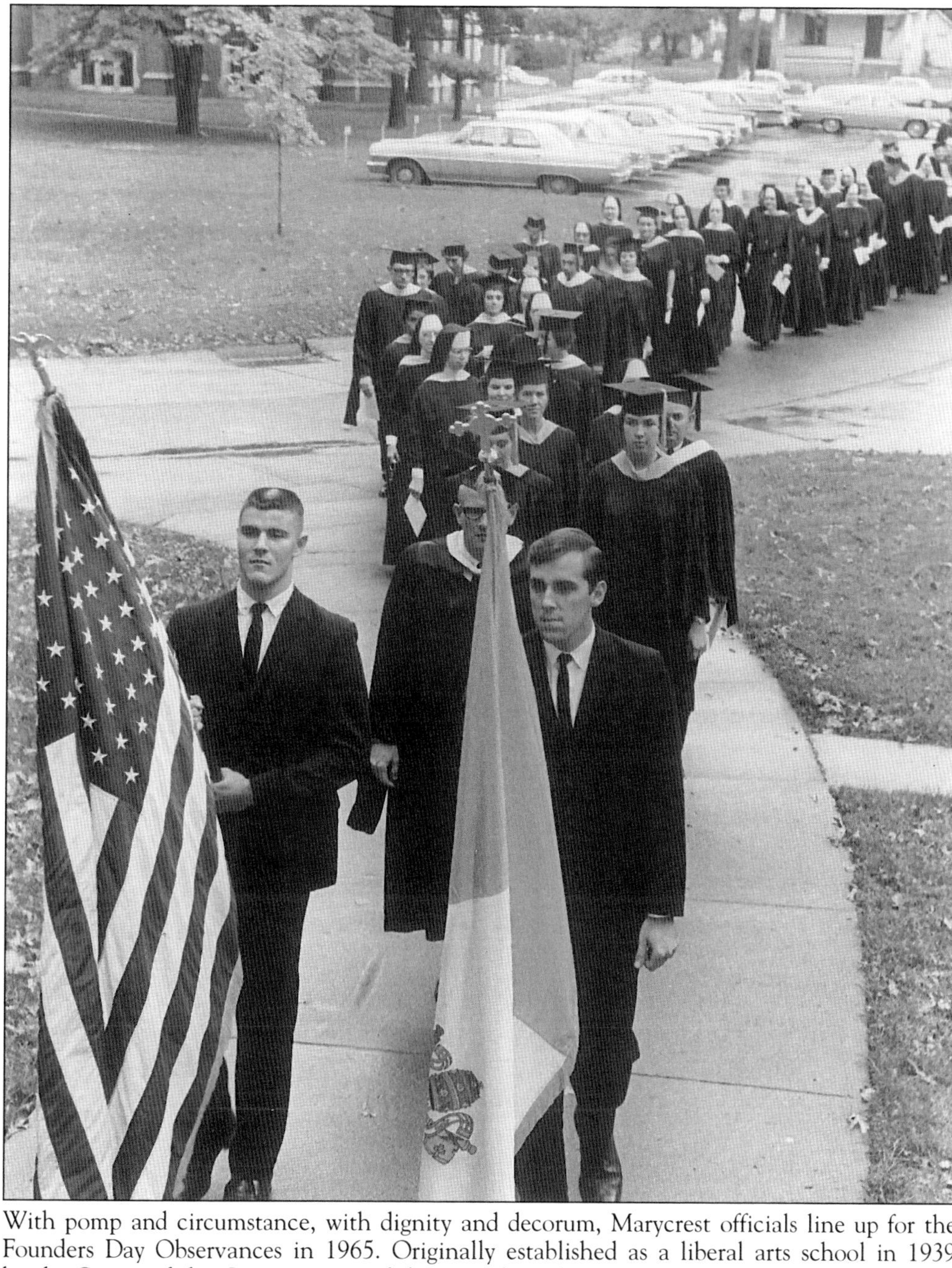

With pomp and circumstance, with dignity and decorum, Marycrest officials line up for the Founders Day Observances in 1965. Originally established as a liberal arts school in 1939 by the Sisters of the Congregation of the Humility of Mary, Marycrest was led by President Mother Mary Geraldine Upham. The all-female institution served as a counterpart to the all-male St. Ambrose College until 1954, when Marycrest became incorporated as a separate institution. Fifteen years later, Marycrest began accepting male students. In 1969, Marycrest also established a Master of Arts program in education. The white building beyond the parking lot in this photo was razed, and a multi-use Activities Center, that housed basketball and tennis courts, was erected in its place. The facility is now used for graduation ceremonies and all of Marycrest's sporting events.

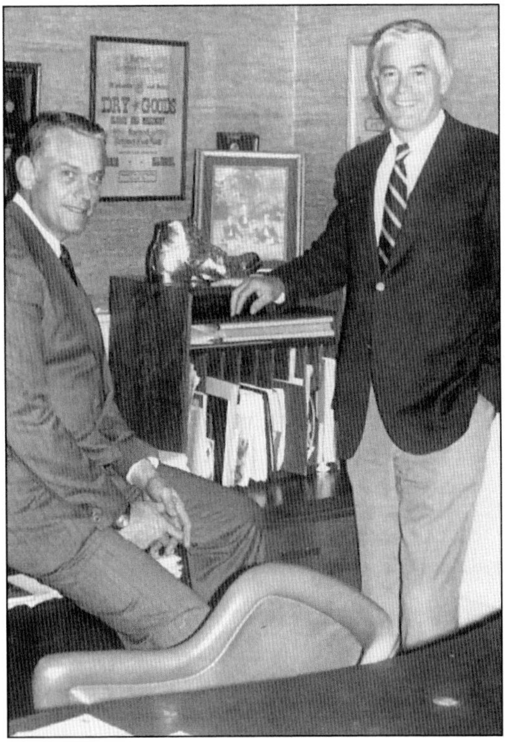

Deciding whom to include in a picture of the Von Maur family is not easy, for few families have contributed more to Davenport in the city's history. Deciding where to place such a picture is simple, because the Von Maur family dates back over one hundred years. Charles and Richard, pictured here, have long been active members in the area business community, and their family stores have popped up far beyond the Mississippi Valley community. How many thousands of Quad-Citians peered into the display windows at Petersen Harned Von Maur at Christmastime? In addition, since we're counting, how many Tri-City Symphony concerts have gone on under mother Elsie Von Maur's expert management?

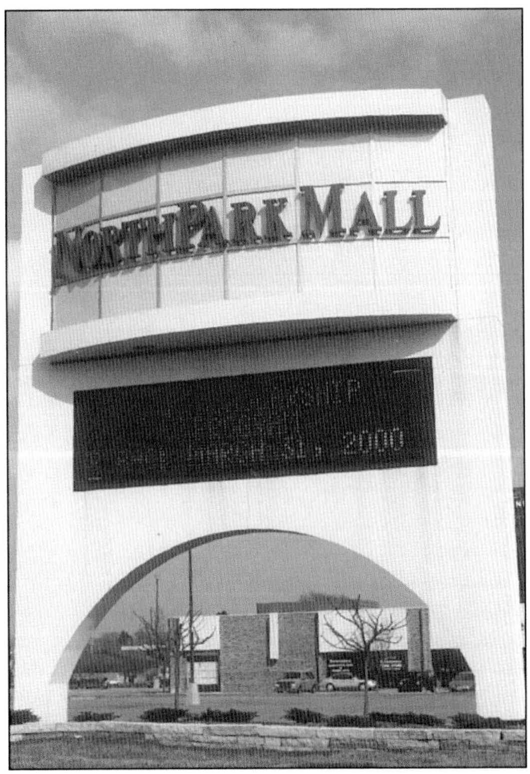

Is there anything that you can't find at Northpark Mall? That is a legitimate question. Furniture, clothing, foods—yup, all the basics are there, as well as more exotic offerings, from high fashion to hair styling salons. Northpark opened July 11, 1973, and the steady flow of traffic has never diminished. A 1982 addition made Northpark the largest shopping center in the entire state of Iowa. "You can spend the whole day roaming around," notes 2000 Iowa grad Joey Schaueneberg, "and you can spend every dollar you own, too." In 1994, mall owners added a food court, carousel, play area, and video arcade.

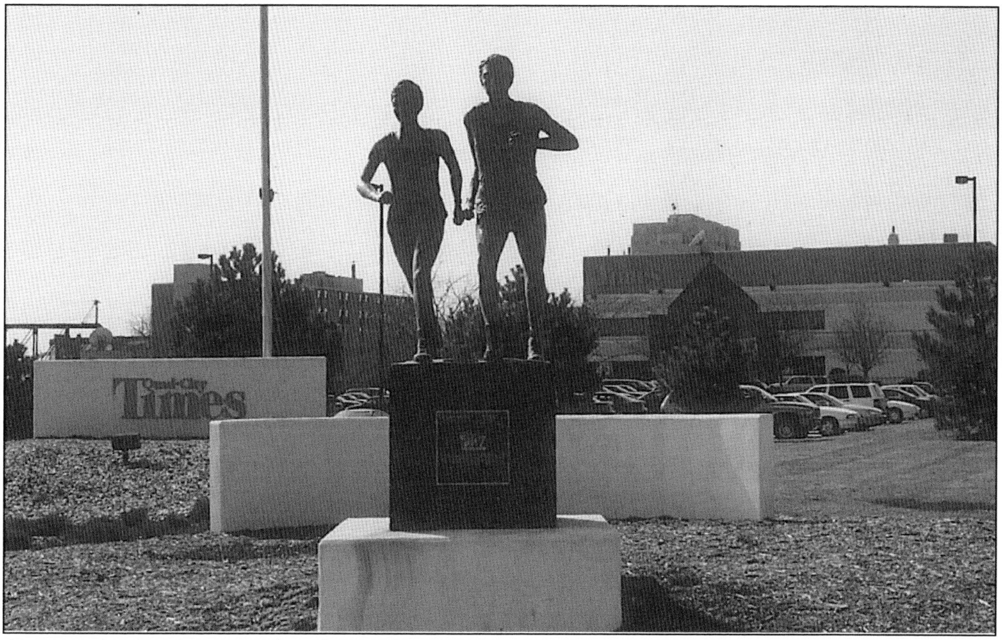

"Run with the Best" is the slogan for the annual *Quad-City Times* road race, a jaunt that attracts the top runners in the world. Walkers are welcome, too, and kids now enjoy their own junior competition. The Bix 7 Run takes participants up and down some of Davenport's most challenging streets and avenues, with spectators who cheer and sprinkle runners with water to cool them down. This impressive statuary, of renowned Olympians and past participants Bill Rodgers and Joan Samuelson, graces the grounds of *the Quad-City Times* complex at 500 East Third.

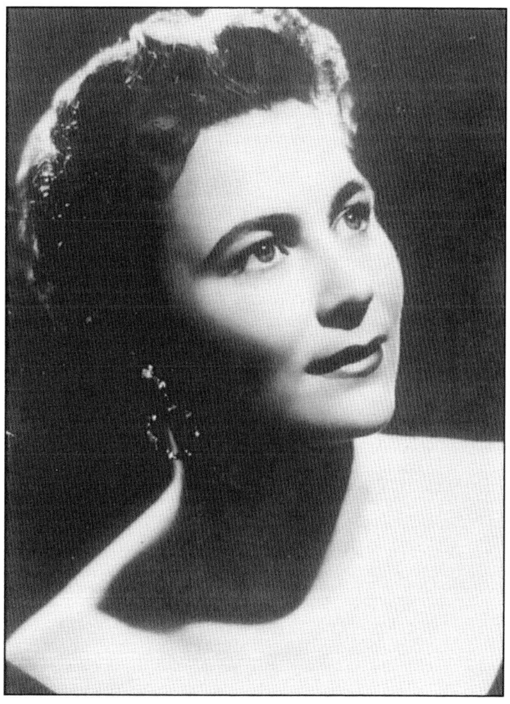

Whether seated at the piano or the organ, Marjorie Meinert's fingers worked magic at the keyboard. A favorite with WOC Radio audiences, she transferred her talents—and good looks—to WOC-TV when the television station became the first to operate in the Quad-Cities in October of 1949. Often, she teamed with the jovial piano man, George Sontag, while Warren Vasen served as MC. "We missed your number by a mile, here's something else to make you smile..." Remember?

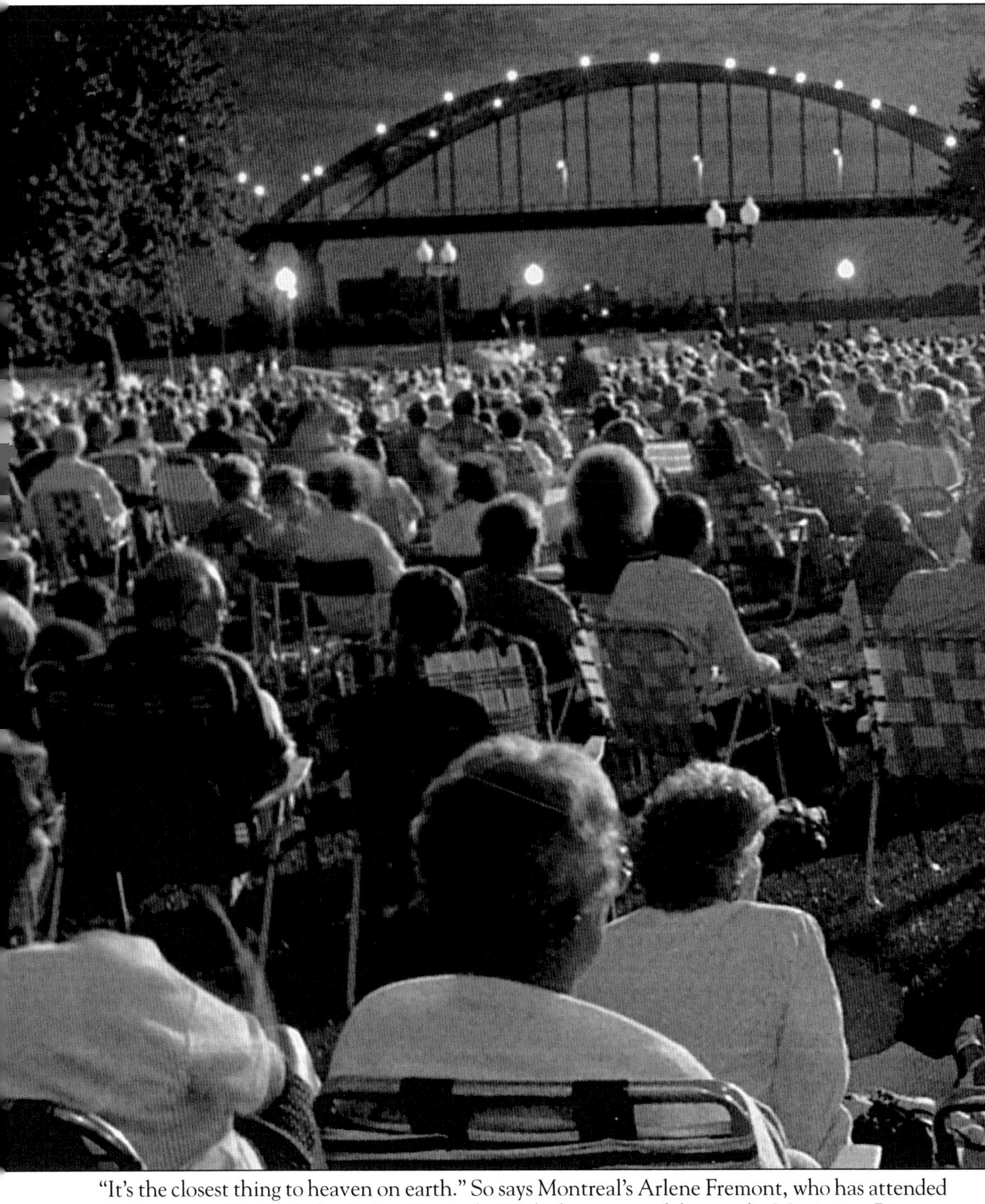

"It's the closest thing to heaven on earth." So says Montreal's Arlene Fremont, who has attended the last seven Bix Beiderbecke Jazz Festivals. With the waters of the nearby Mississippi River to the left and a starry sky above, spectators absorb jazz music at its best, performed by those who play with hands, mouth, heart, and soul. The jazz festival was born in 1972, originating through the efforts of those who had formed the Bix Beiderbecke Memorial Society the year before. The society chose the last weekend in July because that was the closest to the anniversary of

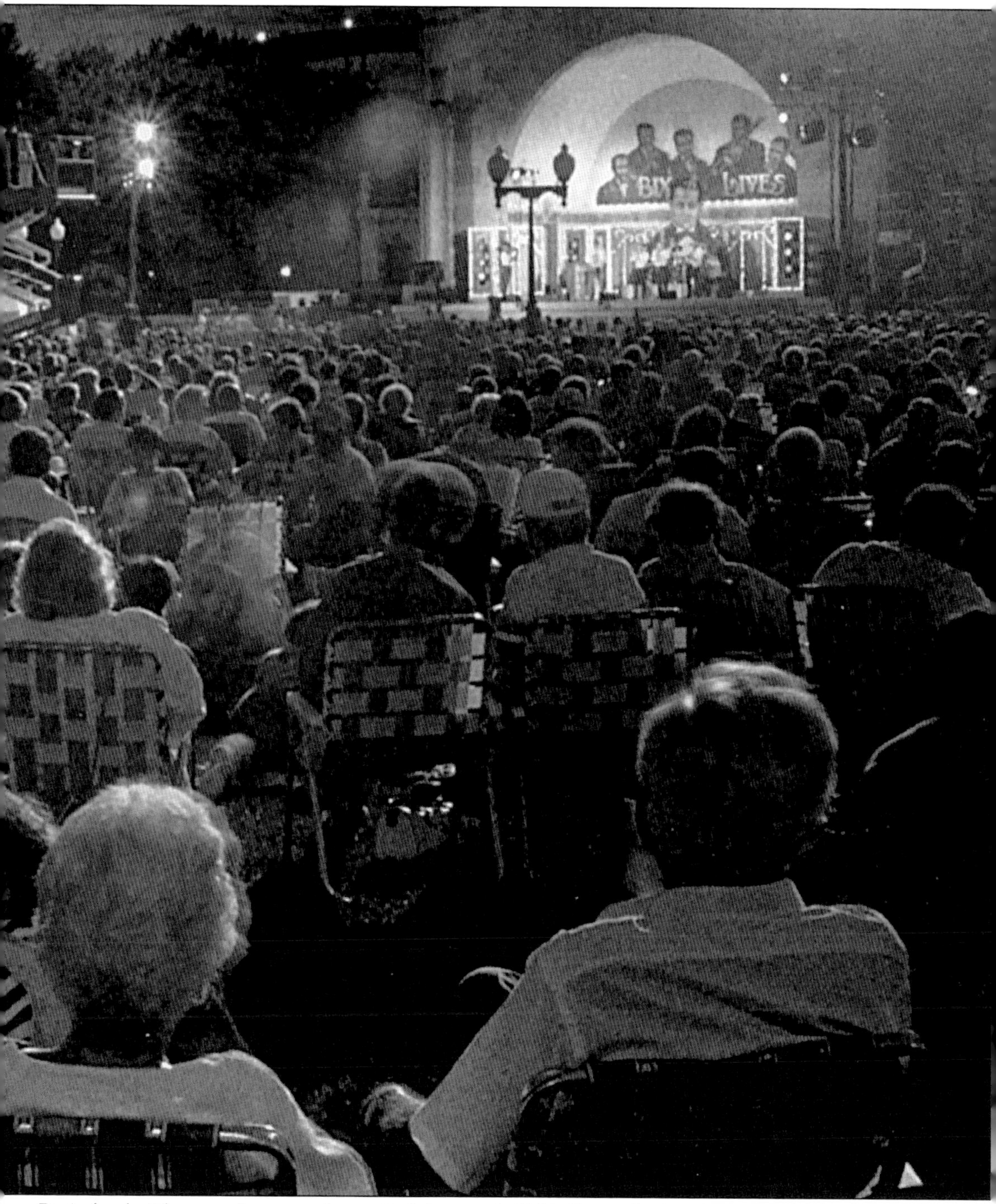

Bix's death. The noted cornet player died August 6, 1931. Soon, food and store vendors joined the celebration, and in 1975, a road race was added. The Bix 7 was so named in reference to the seven challenging miles, up and down Davenport hills, that participants must cover. The *Quad-City Times* took over sponsorship of the race in 1980. But it is the music, the rich unique sound of jazz, that rests at the core of the festival. Whether in a lawnchair or on a blanket, each listener is transported into a special world, a world where jazz reigns supreme.

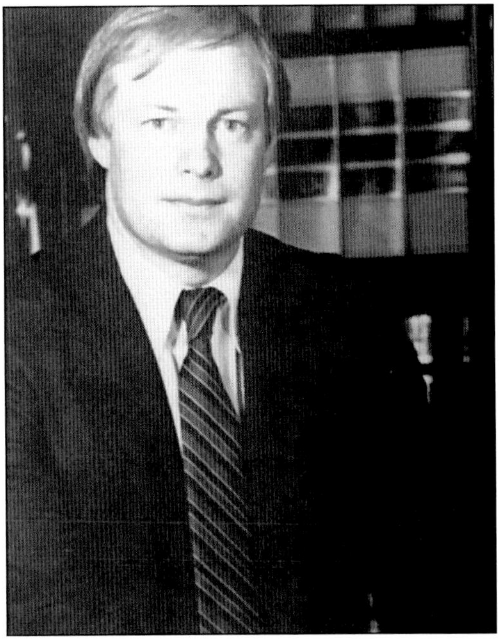

It was the Bicentennial Year, 1976, when James Albert Smith Leach was first elected to the U.S. House of Representatives from Iowa's First Congressional District. Since that time, Scott County voters have kept him there. Leach is the top Scott County vote-getter on the ballot for any local, state, or national office. Born in Davenport in 1942, Leach bears a noteworthy educational background including Princeton, Johns Hopkins University, and the London School of Economics. He is a major hitter in federal finance, and always willing to promote the farmer's cause. His wife, Deba, is an architectural historian and genealogy expert.

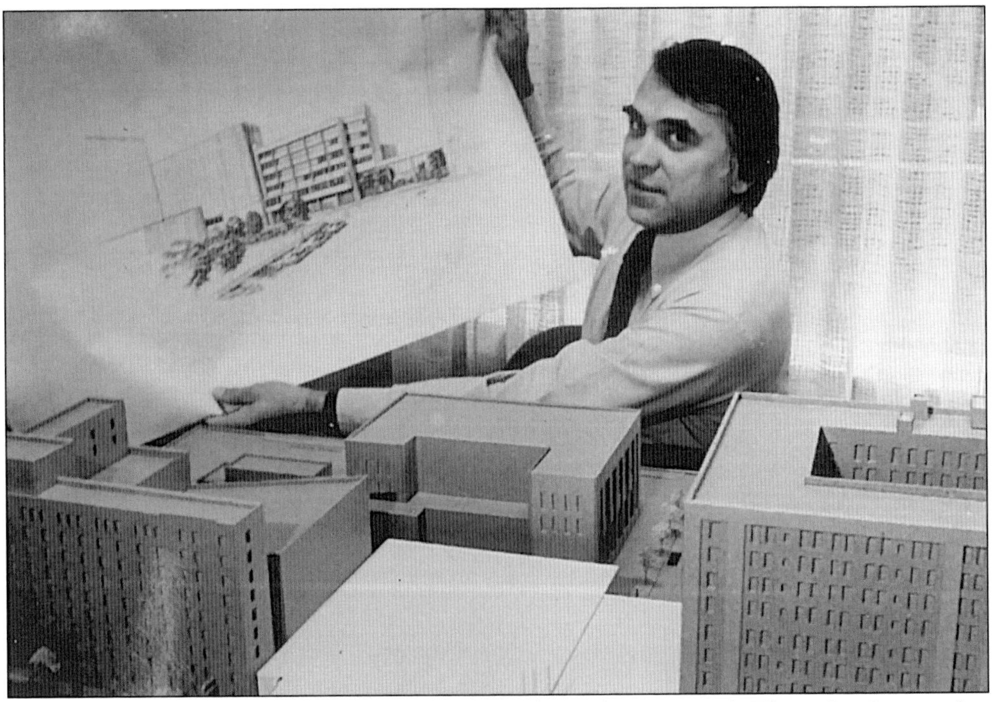

At first, buildings are merely images hovering in the architect's mind. Then, the dream takes shape and form through pen, paper, and computer screen. The anticipated building in this case was the Davenport River Center, a civic structure that city planners hoped would give the city much-needed space for multiple uses in the downtown area. The dream sparked into reality in 1980, as architect Roman Scholtz showed off his drawings and a miniature replica of the proposed center. Today, the building vibrates with activity, offering plenty of proof that dreams do come true.

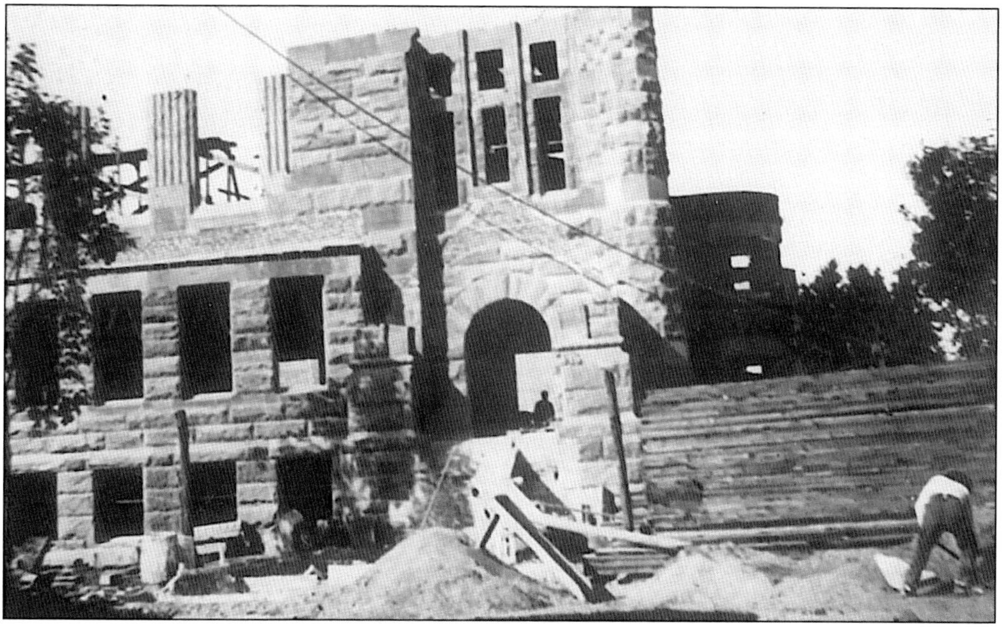

The year was 1953. President Dwight David Eisenhower was in the White House. In Davenport, tongues wagged over the evils of rock and roll music, and kids wore coonskin caps popularized by the Disney movie "Davy Crockett." Passersby investigating the Davenport downtown area paused to inspect the razing process of the old 1887 Scott County Courthouse. Designed by Arthur Ebeling, the new county courthouse cost $1.4 million, and was erected on the original Bolivar Square.

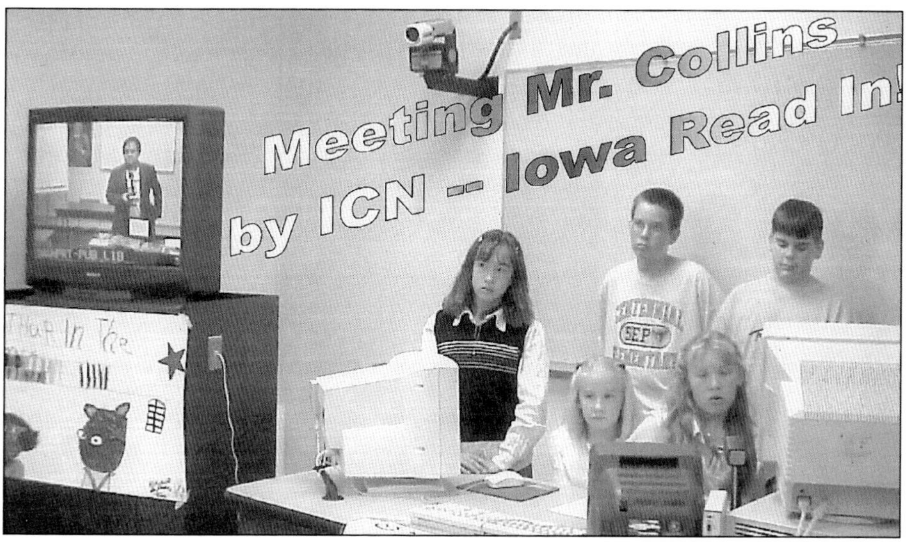

"School days, school days..." Davenport prides itself on quality public and parochial schools, aiming to offer the best education for its young people. While relying on well-tested programs and a curriculum designed to challenge and expand student minds, administrators and teachers constantly seek new and better methods to enrich the learning process. Technology plays an essential role. Here, the ICN Room at the Davenport Public Library provides a statewide hookup, as students across Iowa question local author David R. Collins about how a writer gets ideas.

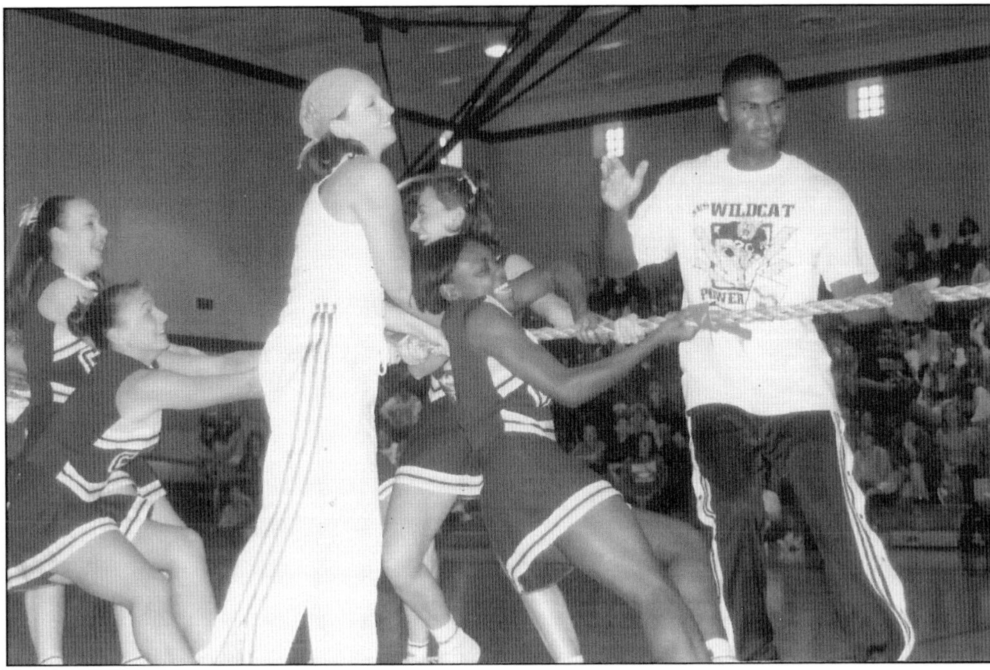

"Pull! Tug! Pull!" Homecoming at area high schools offers a blend of traditions, and the featured attractions are usually a football game and dance. However, there are also splinter activities that represent a particular high school. In this case, North Scott seniors Stacie Logsdon, Kelly Nodarse, Mimi Hoogerwerf, Erica Rauch, and Shayla Johnson flex their muscles in the annual tug-of-war contest inside the North Scott Gym. Until 1985–1986, North Scott had been a junior high, and the big gym was the first step in updating the facility to a high school. In 2000, the second step will be taken in a new Center for the Performing Arts.

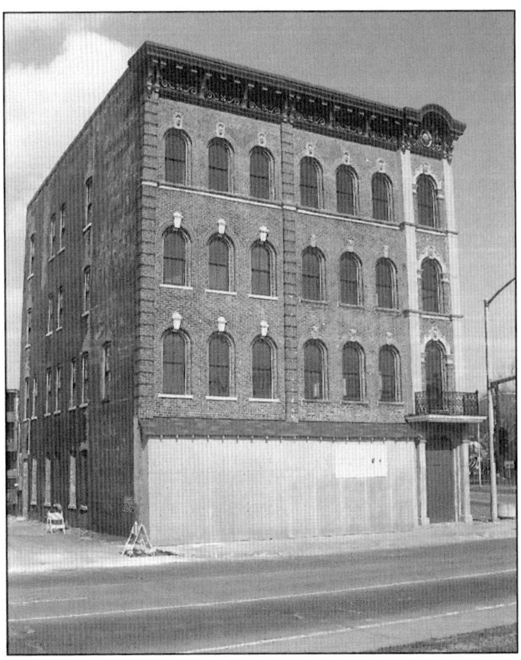

Surely there would be an abundance of tales to come from this structure, the first to greet people as they roll off the Centennial Bridge from Illinois. The Standard Hotel is but a memory now, as is Miller's Saloon that occupied the lower level, but for decades they welcomed travelers to Iowa. Now, the sturdy, four-story structure is undergoing remodeling and development, so that it can one day house offices and facilities for German-American culture. "We have big plans to preserve a major part of Davenport's past," observes Sharlotte Blevins. "Heritage and history are important partners."

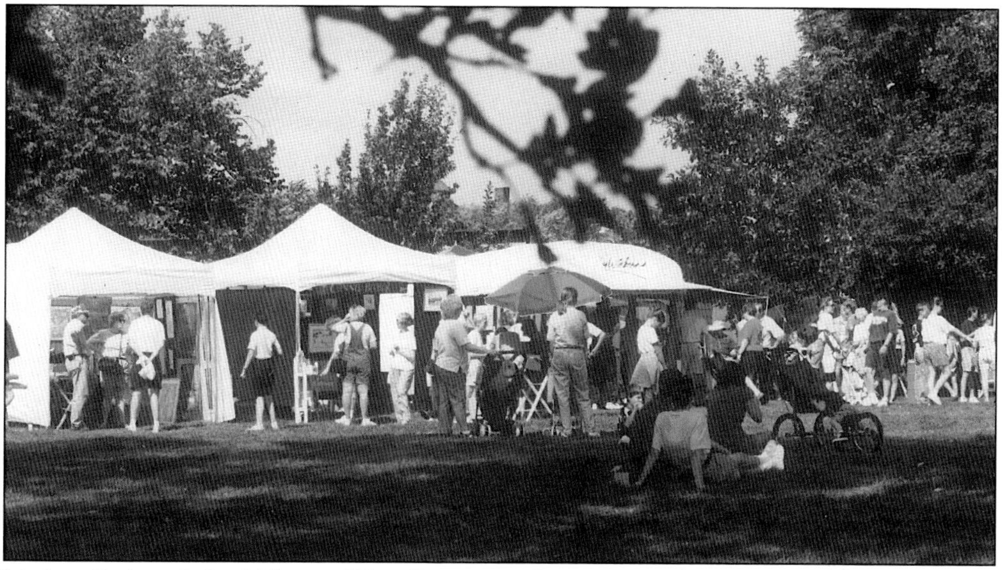

Lindsay Park and the Village of East Davenport lure area residents with a variety of events and activities. They once included the Civil War Muster and Mercantile Exposition which began around the time of the Bicentennial. It gave local history buffs a chance to turn back the calendar by reenacting battles and staging exciting, costumed conflicts. The following decade brought "Riverssance" to Lindsay Park, another celebration featuring art, crafts, music, and food. This late September happening spotlights culture at its best in the Mississippi Valley.

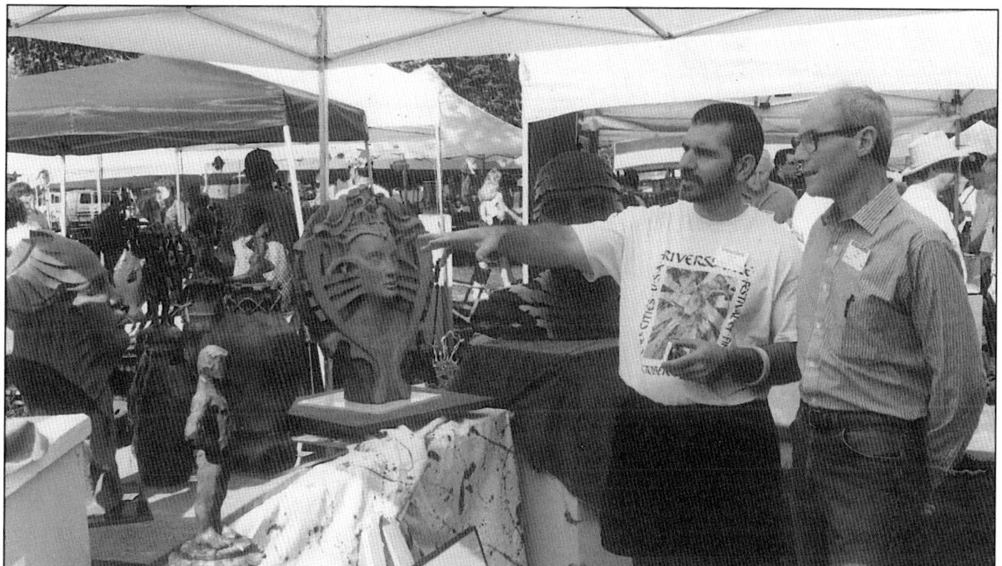

The annual "Riverssance" held in Lindsay Park brings together both artists and art appreciators, who share their work and comments under brightly-colored tents. With a background of pleasing music and delicious smelling foodstuffs, visitors, like these two gentlemen, discuss the variety and quality of artwork brought together. "The 'Riverssance' Festival provides a showcase for area musicians and visual artists," notes retired Black Hawk College professor and "Riverssance" organizer Bill Hannan. "It's amazing just how much talent we have in this immediate area."

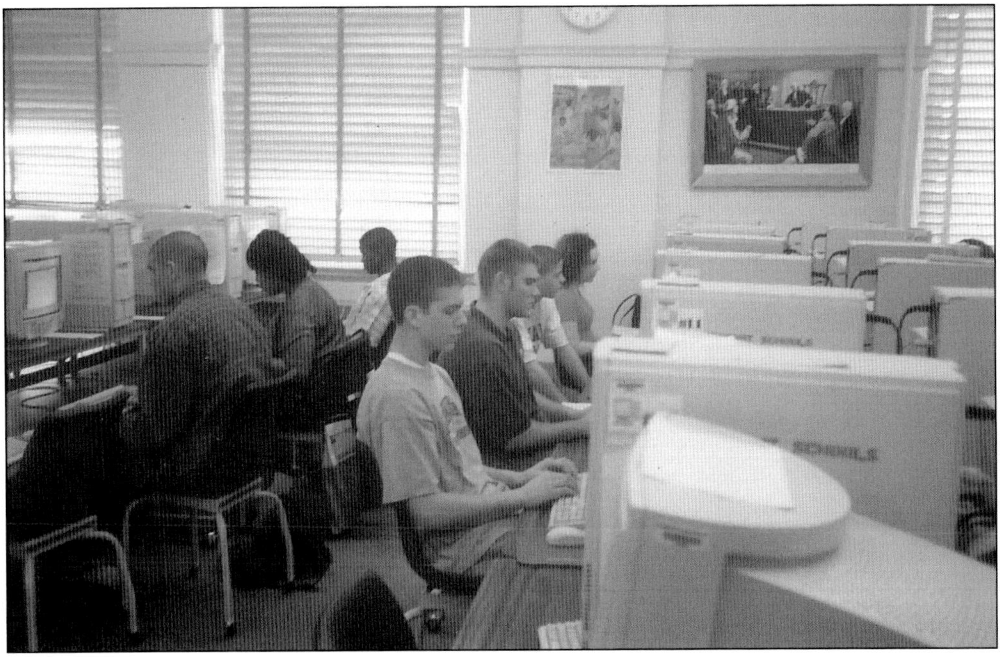

"Don't forget to save regularly" is sage advice, especially for students working diligently at their computers. This group of "super writers" hails from Davenport's Central High, specifically from the class of Mrs. Kit Redeker. Schools in Davenport pride themselves on offering students the latest technology from the 21st century. Central's Instructional Media Center is often filled with students who hardly have time to look up from their screens. Who would have ever thought, 50 years ago, that pupils would hold "mice" in their hands—and enjoy it?

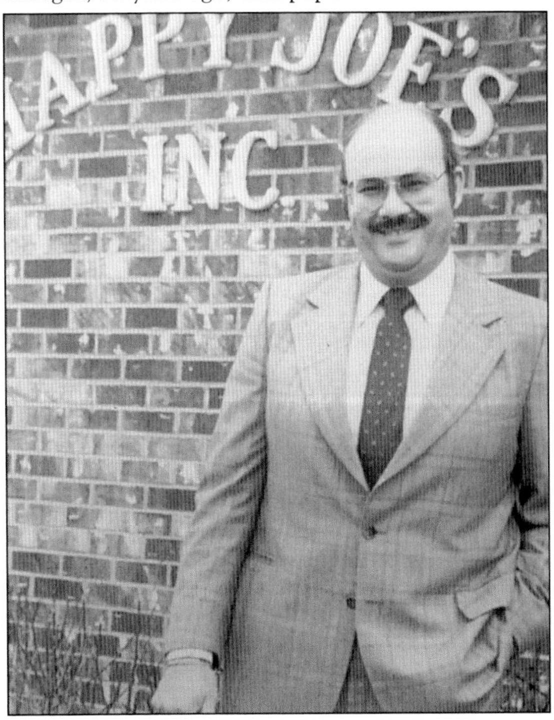

His eyes sparkle, his smile is contagious, and his business sense is astute. He's met presidents and ambassadors, yet he'd much rather be surrounded by a group of youngsters—chomping down pizza, of course! Few Davenporters are more easily recognized than "Happy Joe" Whitty, a fellow who has built a business empire out of dough, toppings, and a genuine sense of community concern. His secret for success? "Everyone should be poor once," he says. One might add, "And everyone who is rich should share with others as you do." Few folks have shared as much happiness as "Happy Joe."

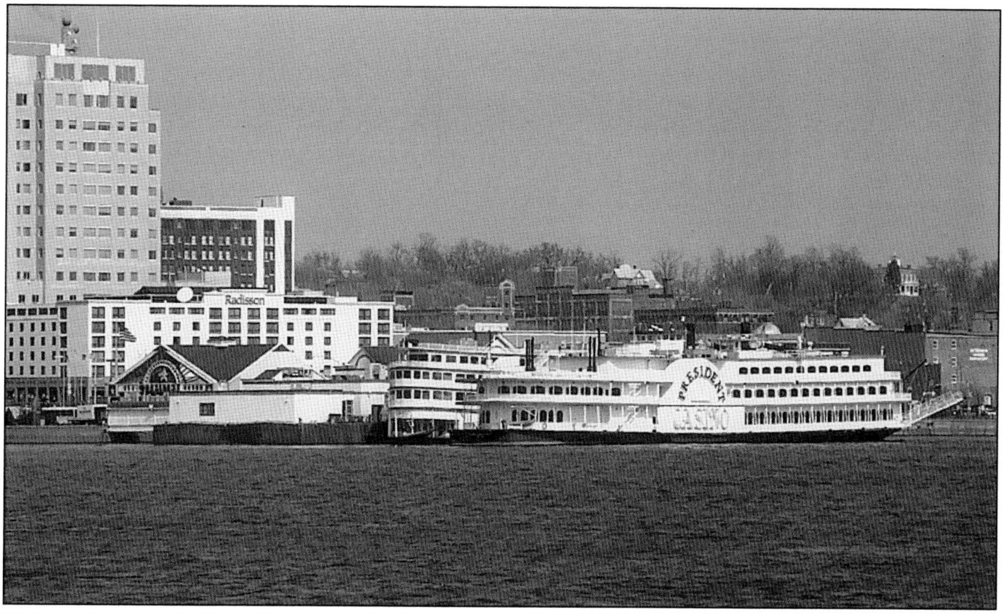

Before the cars, before the trains, before the trucks, before the planes, there were the boats. Farmers and traders of the 19th century sent their corn and manufactured goods down the Mississippi, selling products at various stopping points, and finally selling the carrier boats themselves. Travel on the river blossomed with the invention of the steam engine, allowing for the advent of steam-propelled paddle wheelers. The *Eclipse*, the *J.S.*, the *Quinlan*—so many names, so many memories. Today, riverboats like the *President* and the *Vice President* draw people in to roll the dice, play the slots, and seek mini-fortunes. By March of 2000, it was the riverboat industry itself that sought "lady luck" to fight off rising debts.

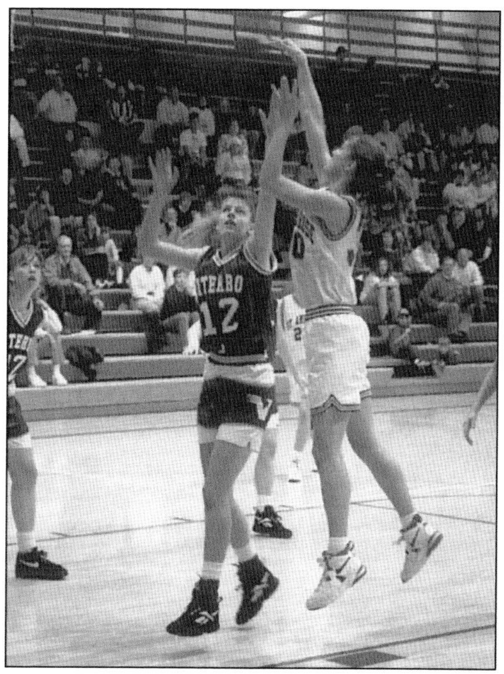

"She's dribbling down the court, glances for an open teammate, spotting none, she turns, fakes, and leaps into the air, shooting toward the basket…it's a swisher, and the Lady Bees take the lead!" St. Ambrose not only boasts a fine academic curriculum, but an outstanding sports program as well. Men and women alike share the spotlight, and Davenport fans remain faithful to their college teams. St. Ambrose's football, basketball, baseball, softball, and volleyball teams are part of the NIA Division II. Lee Lohman Arena in the PE Center, pictured here, sees plenty of fast action.

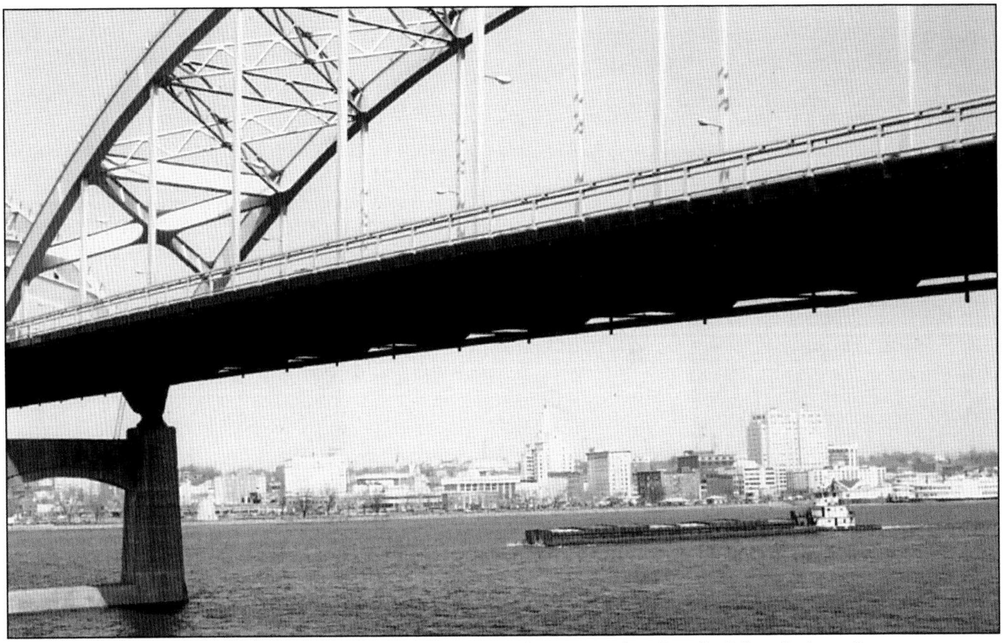

"Old Man River, that Old Man River..." Standing on the Rock Island shoreline, one can capture a familiar picture as a barge glides along the waves headed west. Across the watery expanse, the Davenport skyline appears proud and imposing. The *President* riverboat is visible to the right. The strong steel girders of the Centennial Bridge complete the picture. The Centennial, which spans the mile-long width of river between Davenport and Rock Island, carries over 16,000 vehicles daily.

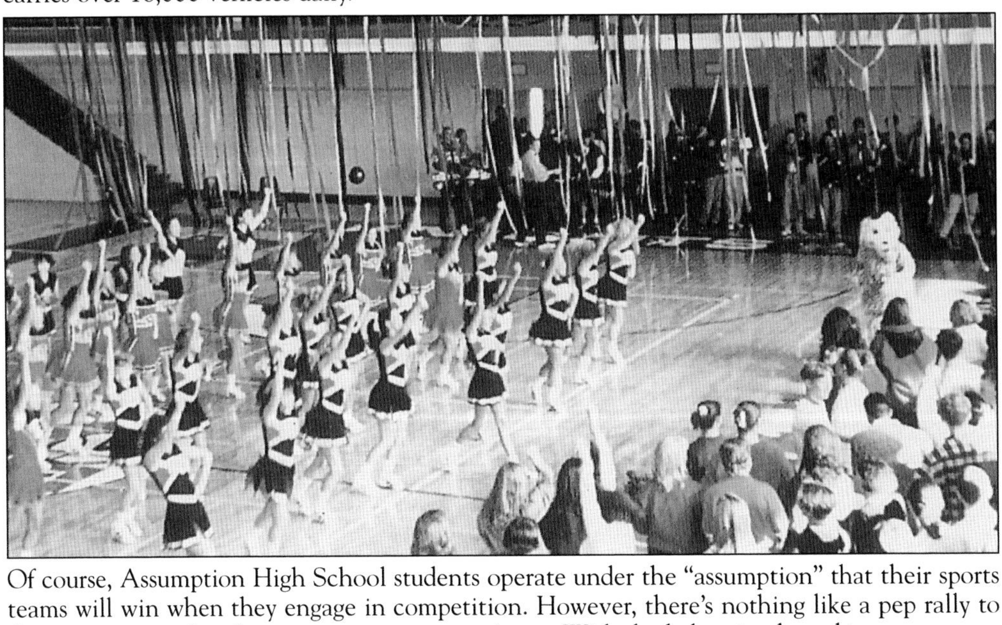

Of course, Assumption High School students operate under the "assumption" that their sports teams will win when they engage in competition. However, there's nothing like a pep rally to drum up spirit and enthusiasm to guarantee a victory. With the balconies draped in crepe paper, Assumption cheerleaders yell their lungs out to get the assembled crowd to do the same. Did it work? Well, it's a cinch: the boys' basketball team got the message, and brought home a state championship. Rah, yea, Assumption!

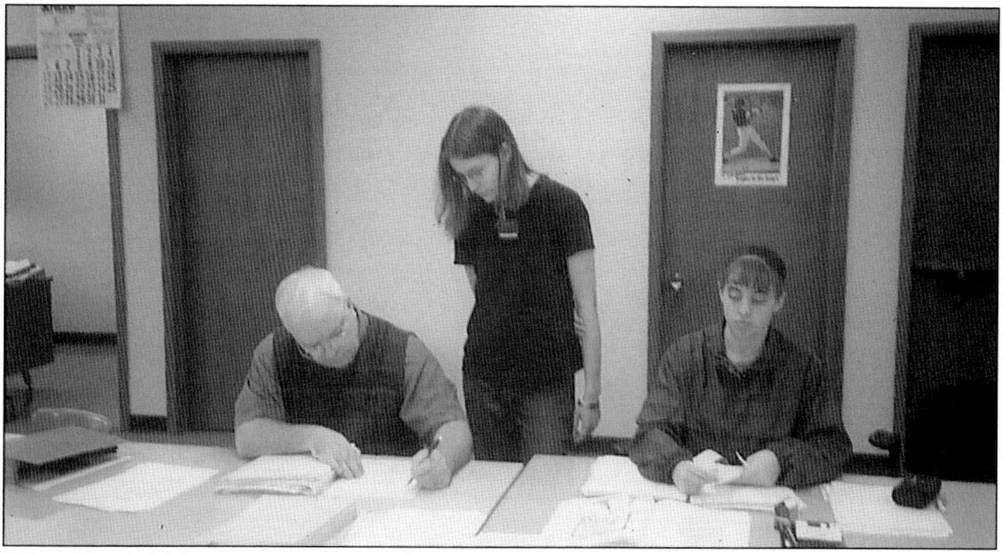

What "devilish" business is going on here? It takes three pairs of eyes to check every comma and period in the "Devil's Diary," Central High School's literary magazine, before it goes to press. Mr. John Miller, faculty advisor, gratefully receives help from Leslie Spring (standing) and Deborah Rogal, one of the student editors. Davenport schools provide a variety of extracurricular activities to embellish a stellar curriculum. In this case, future Stephen Kings or Danielle Steeles get an opportunity to share prose and poetry efforts before the Central High reading community.

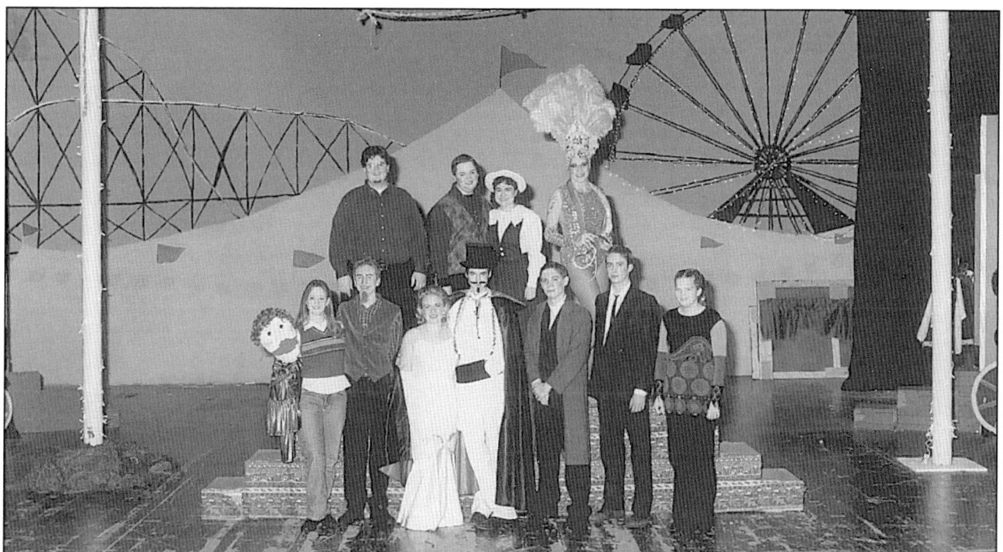

Ah, what heightens the spirit of stage thespians more than the smell of greasepaint and the sound of applause? One would only have to ask this theatrical ensemble from Davenport West High School, as they prepare to delight an audience with the immortal classic, "State Fair." The transformation into another character, totally removed from one's own, lures many to the stage every year. Of course, there are jitters before opening night. "Will I remember my lines?" "Will I pick up my cues?" "Will the audience like the play?" Yup, "there's no business like show business…"

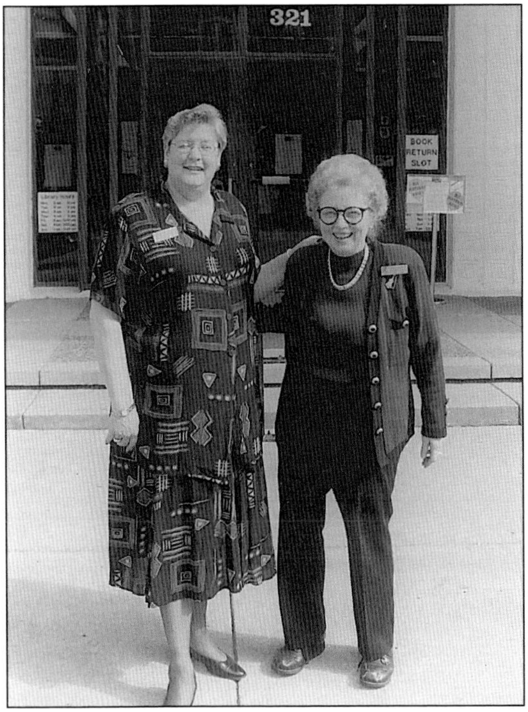

Yes, the smiles are sincere and the desire to serve never ceases. Two of Davenport's friendliest gals can be found within the city's favorite "hangout"—the Davenport Public Library. The library's director, Kay Runge, has guided the building's evolution from a typical book exchange to a multi-faceted service center, enriching the cultural lives of area residents through countless activities and materials. For over 40 years, Children's Department Director Rochelle Murray has touched the minds and hearts of young people, offering constant help and attention mixed with a giant spoonful of love.

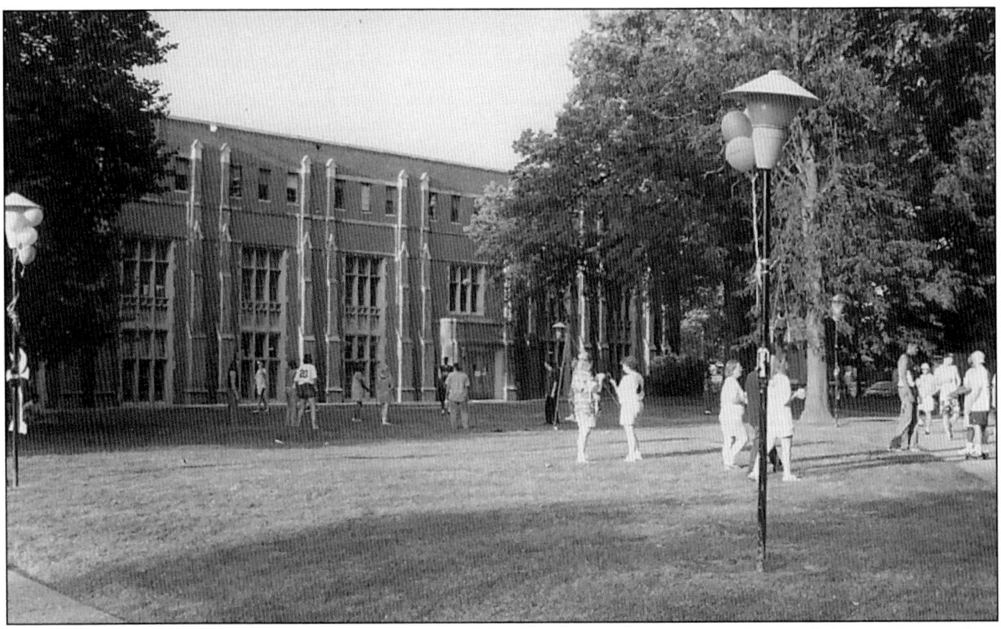

"Where is Upham Hall?" "Someone told me the Admissions Office is in Clifton Manor, but I'm not sure where that is." "I want to see Dr. Discovery. Is he around?" It's Orientation Week at Marycrest University in the fall of 1999, and questions abound! Eager newcomers roam the "Quad" in front of Petersen Hall as they embark on a major journey in their lives. Thankfully, the weather cooperated, allowing students to enjoy a leisurely beginning to their college days—or daze! By the way, Dr. Discovery is really Dino Hayz, performing arts director and a frequent guest on "Paula Sands Live."

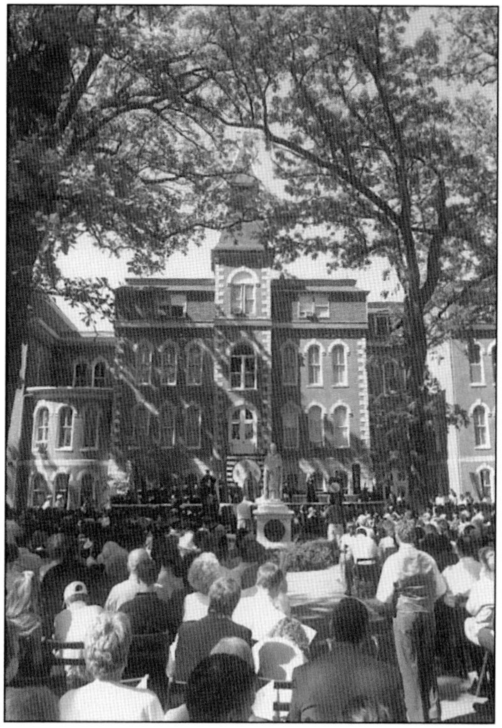

It's an afternoon in May, and spectators bask in the sunlight before the regal and imposing St. Ambrose Hall, a fixture at the university since 1882. It is commencement, a time for bidding college days farewell, and sentinels offer a special protective covering to the people at this graduation. There is little doubt that feelings of pride, love, accomplishment, and yes, a touch of fear and uncertainly, mingle among those present. It is a time of celebration, and of opening another door in life, as time takes another step.

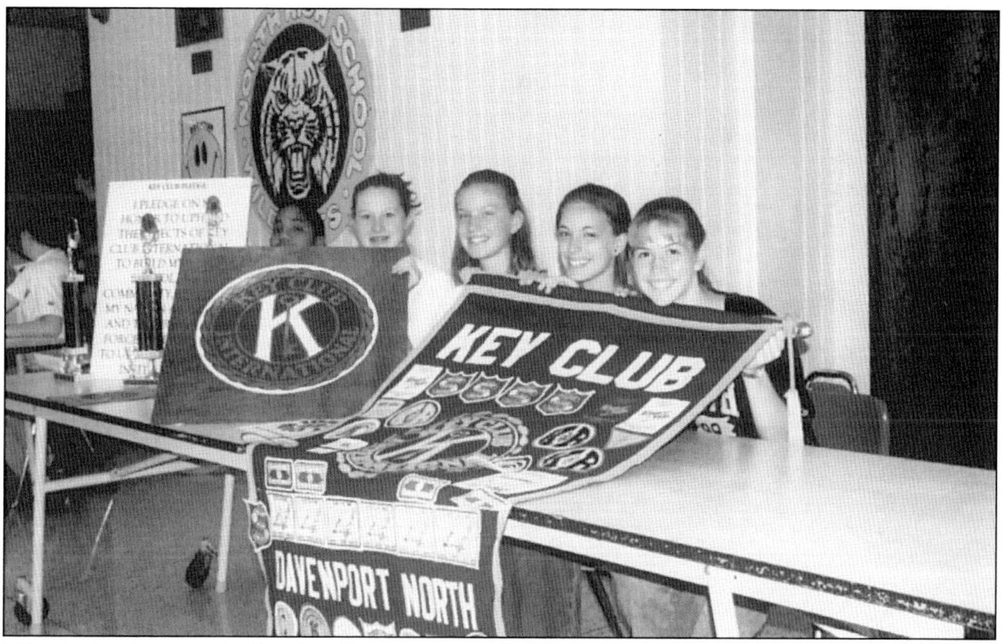

What's the key to a high school's success? Well, this smiling quintet from North Scott High School might well answer, "an active Key Club." Freshman orientation activities offer incoming ninth graders a chance to investigate extra-curricular life at the high school. Key Club is one of the largest organizations on campus, reaching out to enrich the community. Apparently, North Scott is doing something right, because the institution has won the F.I.N.E. (First in National Excellence) Award.

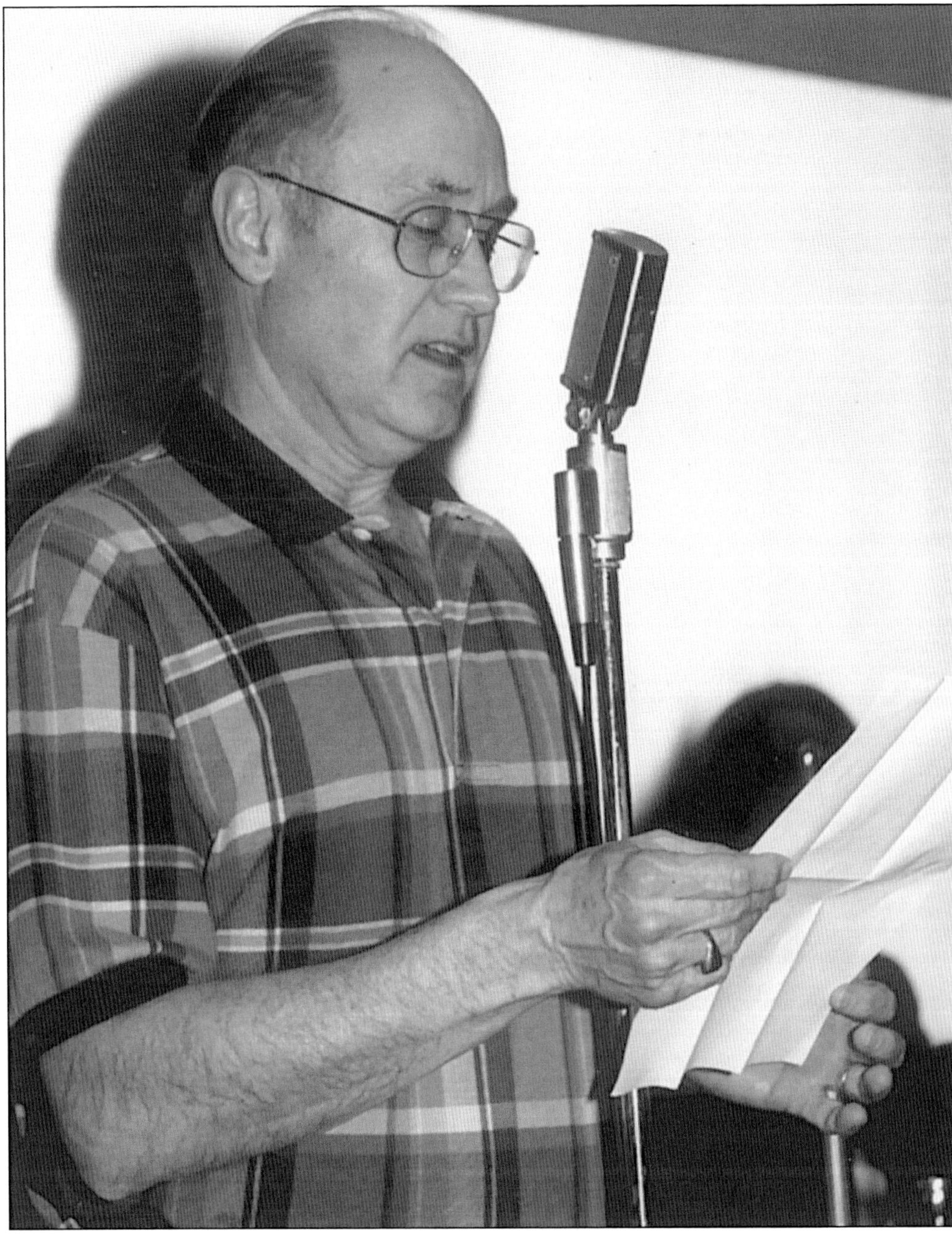

If the United States has its poet laureate in the form of Robert Pinsky (a "Super Author" visitor sponsored by the Quad-City Arts in March of 2000), Davenport counts local poet and teacher Dick Stahl as its own royal man of letters. For decades, Stahl has shared his memorable musings, winning poetry contests near and far and publishing a fine collection of his own words. Among his titles are *After the Milk Route* and *Under the Green Tree Hotel*. A permanent staff member of the annual Mississippi Valley Writers Conference, here Stahl presents his first place winning "Ode to Bix" at the March 6, 2000, Beiderbecke Birthday Bash. Fortunately for Davenport youth, Stahl teaches at Davenport Central High, thus passing along valuable guidance to future Sandburgs, Frosts, and Stahls.

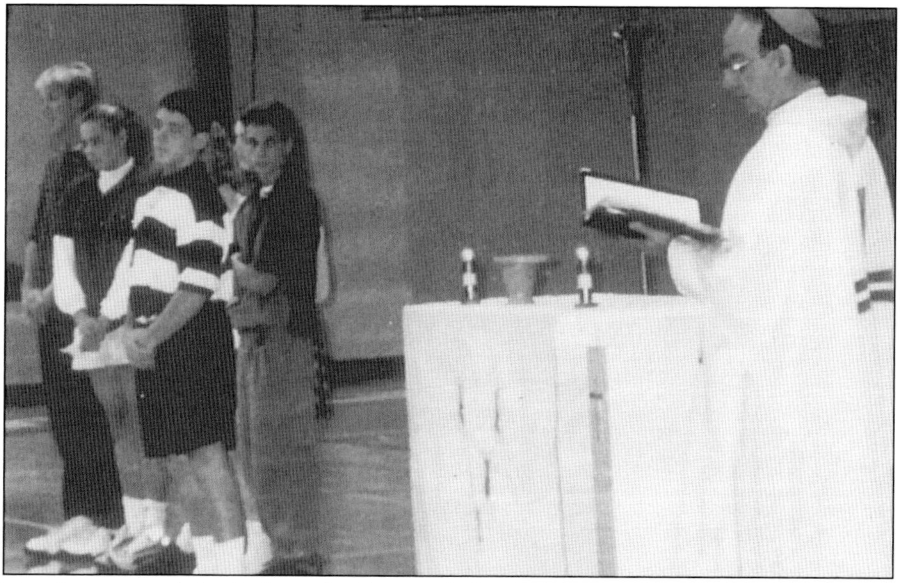

"And in the name of the Father, the Son, and the Holy Spirit..." Bishop William Franklin, of the Diocese of Davenport, joins Assumption High School students in a Mass held in the school gymnasium. As a Catholic high school, Assumption offers a spiritual backdrop within the framework of its curriculum, clubs, and athletics. Operating under "A Path to Excellence," Assumption aims "to inspire and help young men and women develop their opportunities through a quality, Catholic, educational program." In April of 2000, the Assumption community mourned the death of former Bishop Gerald O'Keefe.

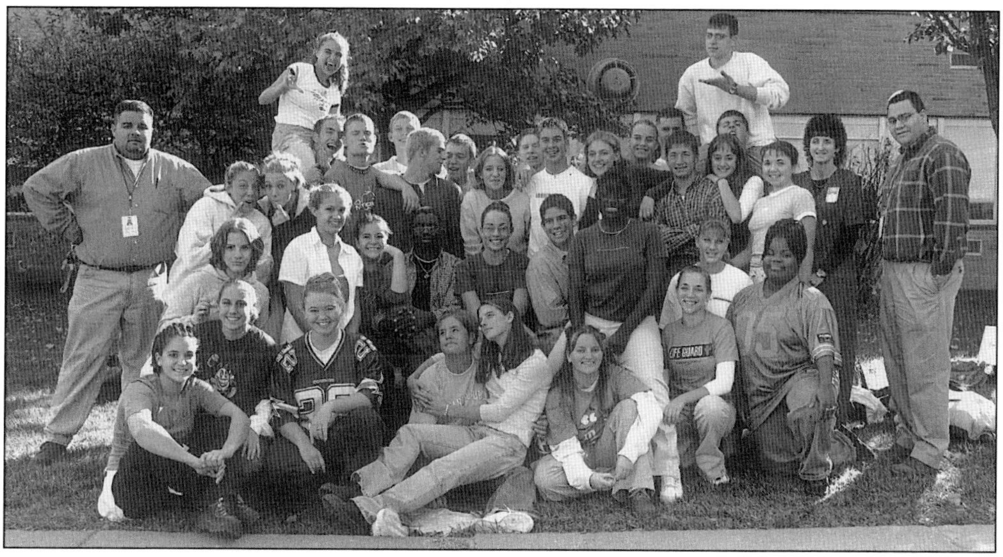

Remember cramming to get a good grade on that high school math final? Or how about staying up until all hours to get that research paper finished? The pressures from the classroom are many and intense, but lessons are absorbed in other ways as well. The smiles on the faces of these Davenport West Senate members stem from the fact that their school won the annual food drive competition held among area high schools. Although generosity coupled with school spirit may not be a graded class on an official transcript, it is reason for special attention and congratulations. Way to go, West!

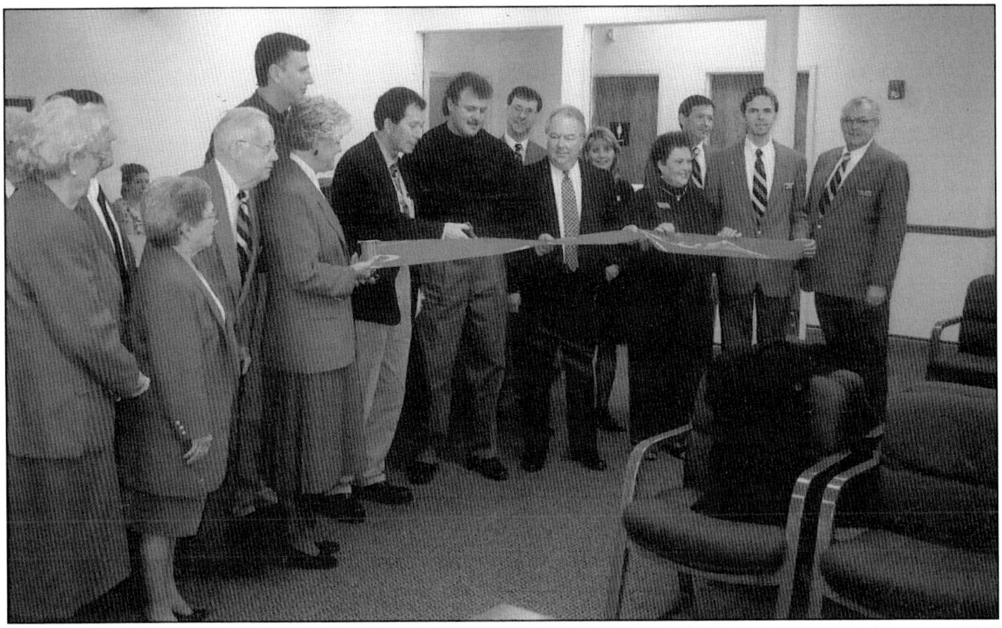

Ah, here is one of the glamorous rewards of being the Mayor of Davenport! His Honor, Phil Yerrington, shares smiles and frivolity with Davenport constituents, a welcome relief from the more stressful rigors of the city's chief executive duties. From delicate personnel matters to zoning questions, from decisions about taxes to arguments about new businesses entering the city, the day-to-day duties of mayor demand constant study and attention. Whether it is presenting awards, cutting ribbons for openings, or running city council meetings, Yerrington seems to thrive on activity and a bit of controversy. In his job, there are plenty of both!

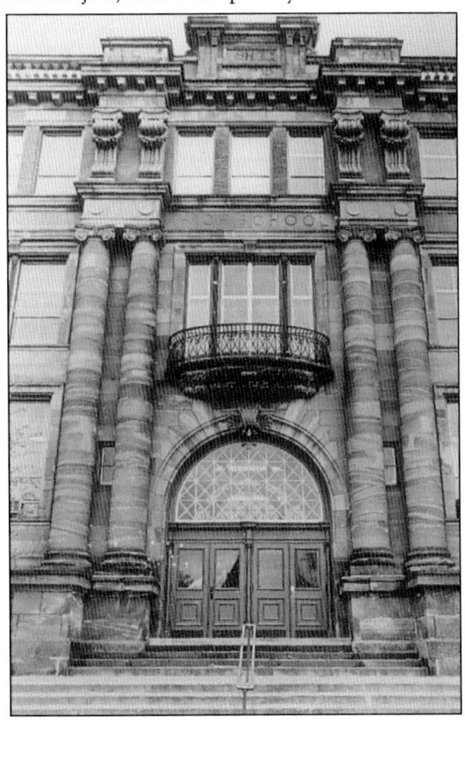

"Hail to the chief..." In May of 2000, President Bill Clinton visited Davenport Central High School, constructed in 1994. Central joined eight elementary schools that were built during the tenure of schools superintendent John B. Young who served nearly 30 years in his position.

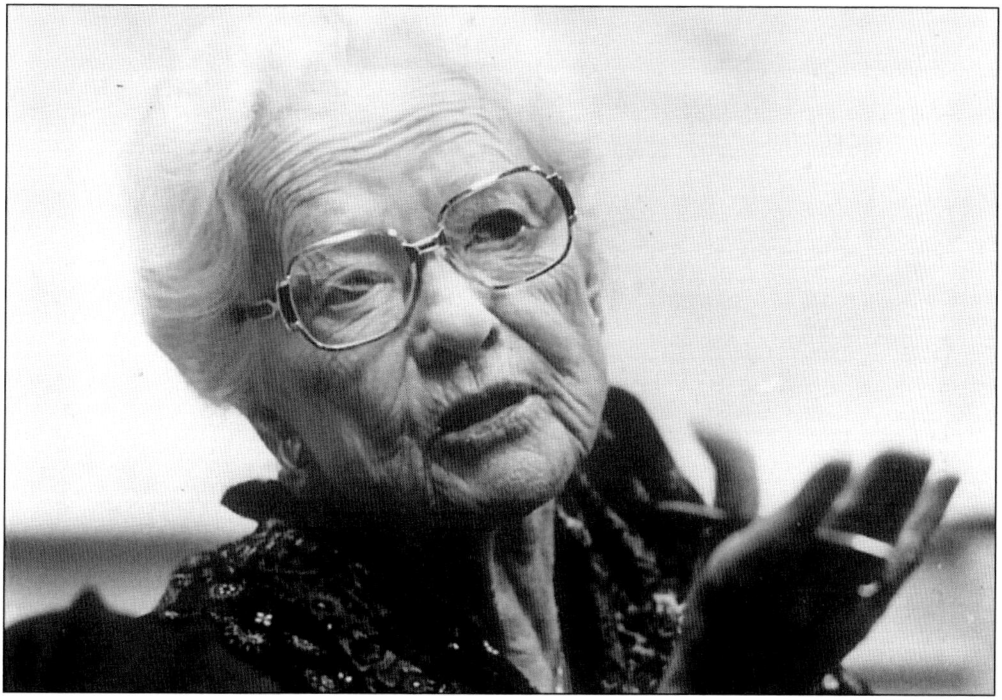

Helen Hayes was dubbed "The Queen of the American Stage." Well, the show always went on when Mary F. Nighswander, the "Queen of Davenport Theater," was around. Nighswander, who died in 1991, battled for more than 30 years to make her dream of a permanent home for young actors and actresses come true. She also proved that the Quad-Cities would support Broadway shows. "There's no business like show business!" And there was no one quite like Mary Nighswander!

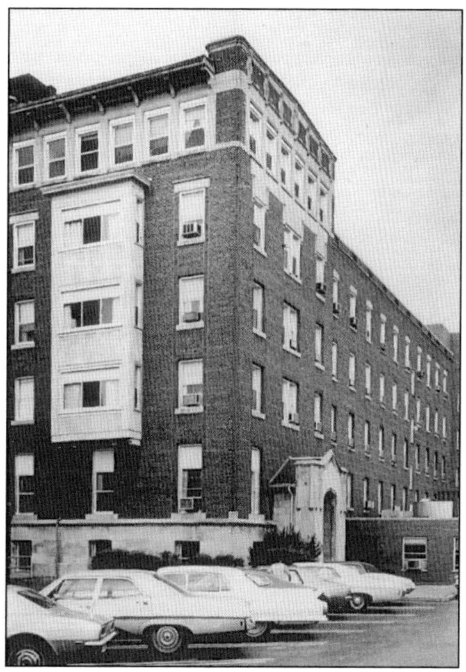

St. Luke's Hospital—today the east campus of Genesis Medical Center—dates back to 1895. This photograph shows the old hospital building that was completed at High Street and Bridge Avenue in 1919.

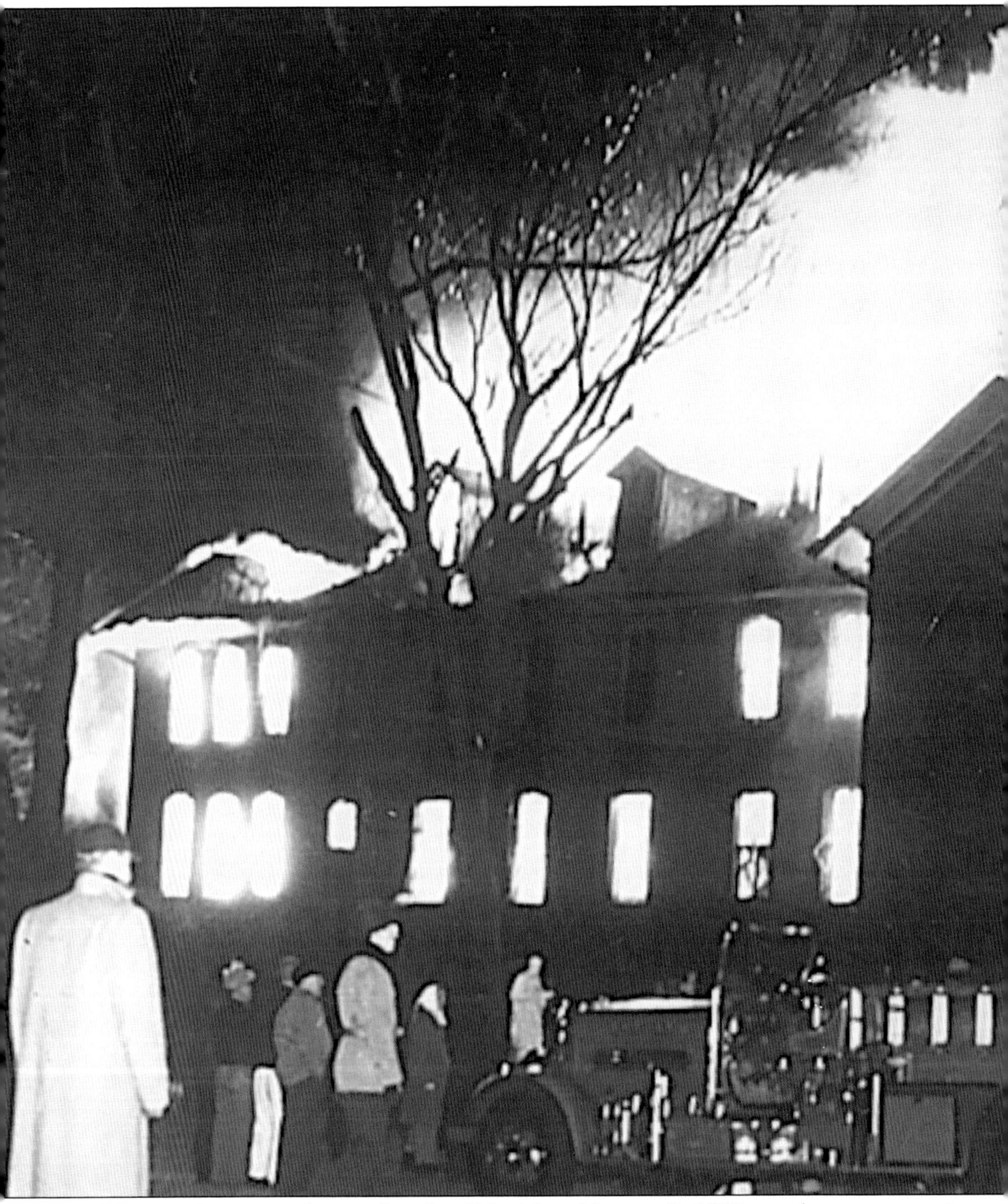

Fifty years have passed since that dreadful night of January 7, 1950, yet there are many in Davenport who still remember that deadly winter's night of so long ago. Here, spectators watch as fire consumes the St. Elizabeth's mental ward in the old Mercy Hospital. The blaze, started by a patient, killed 40 female patients and one nurse. It remains the deadliest fire in the history of the Quad-Cities. Firefighters encountered barred windows, making it difficult to rescue the screaming, confused patients. Winds and cold temperatures compounded the problems of

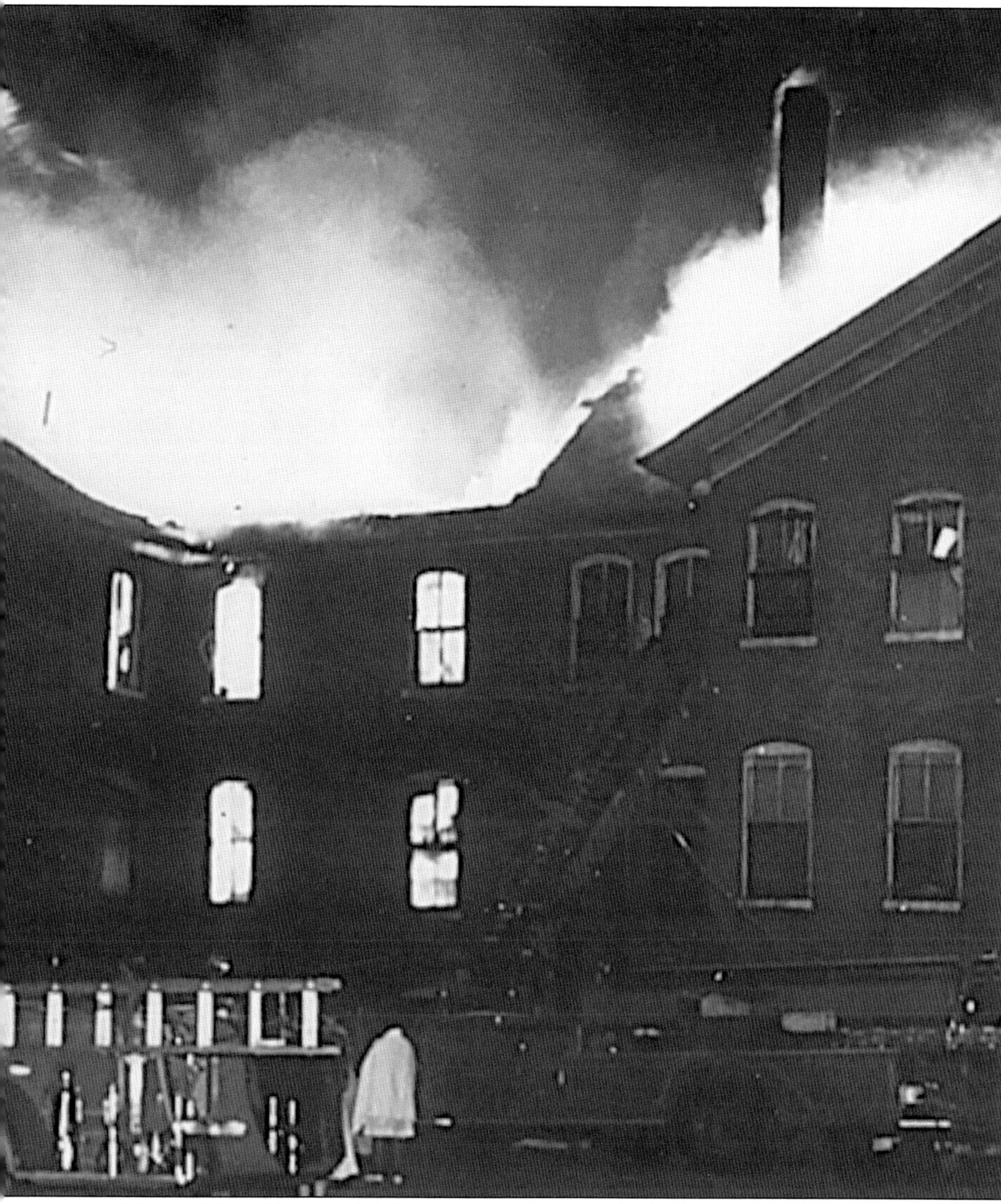

extinguishing the blaze. The tragedy led to a variety of improved safety measures. "I lost an aunt in the fire," recalls longtime Davenport resident Alice Kearns, "and it was just awful to think how she died—she and her friends. The firemen tried so hard and were so brave. It doesn't seem like fifty years ago, but I guess it was. I have planted a special flower every year for her in the backyard, from 1950 until 2000. It just doesn't seem possible."

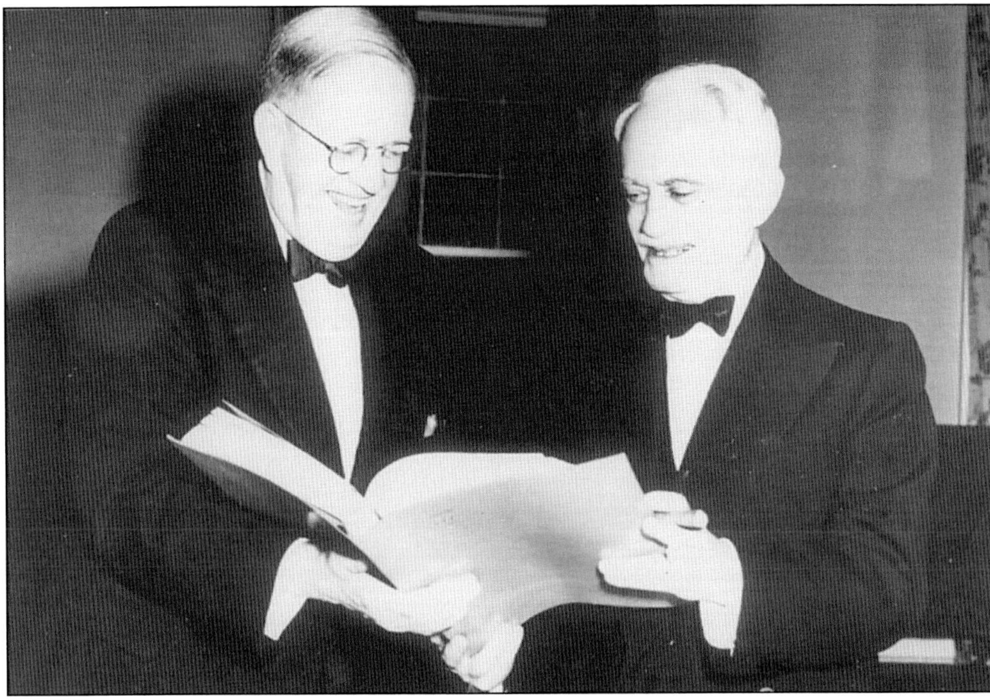

Newspaper publisher E.P. Adler (right) was a powerful force in Davenport for most of the first half of the 20th century. He served as president of Lee Enterprises Inc. from 1907 until his death in 1949. As publisher of *the Davenport Daily Times*, a predecessor of the *Quad-City Times*, he rallied the community to save Davenport Bank and Trust Co., its largest bank, during the Great Depression. He is shown with Lee Loomis, who succeeded him as president of Lee Enterprises.

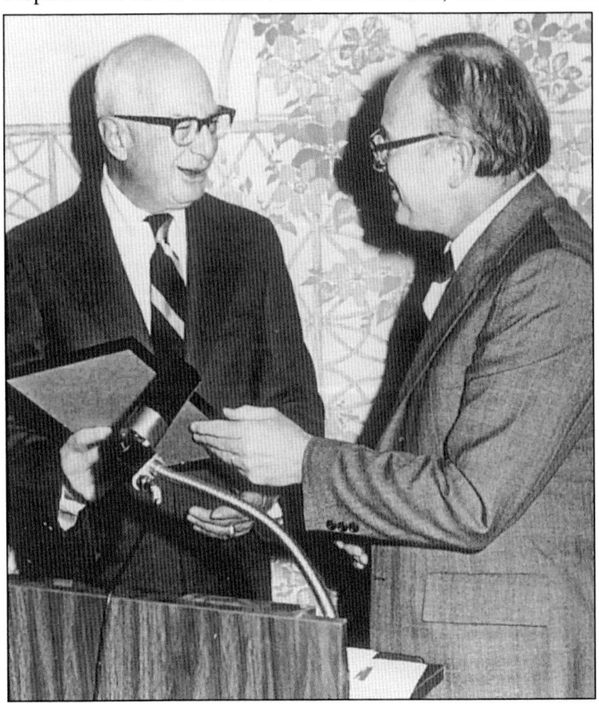

Philip D. Adler (left), son of E.P. Adler, continued his father's legacy of public service as publisher of the *Davenport Daily Times*, and its predecessor, the *Times-Democrat*. He also was president of Lee Enterprises Inc. He worked summers as a printer's devil, and graduated from the University of Iowa. He is shown during his induction into the Hall of Fame of the University of Iowa Journalism School. Making the presentation is William Zima, past Iowa chapter president of Kappa Tau Alpha.

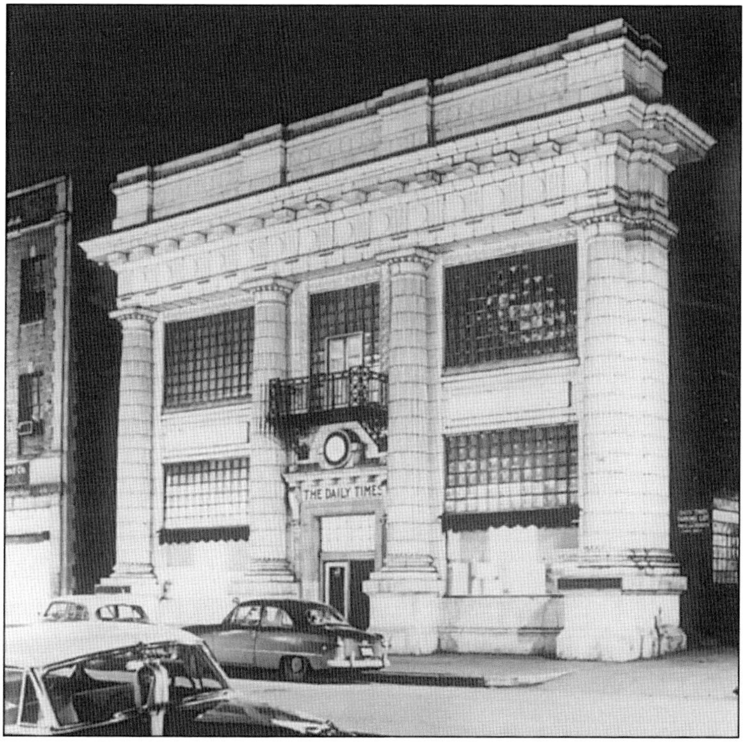

The *Davenport Daily Times* commanded Second Street from this Greek Revival style headquarters for much of the 20th century. In later years, the *Davenport Democrat* shared the building. The two papers merged in the 1960s and the building expanded into the neighboring structures. A new facade unified the complex. The site was cleared in the 1990s to make way for the MidAmerican Energy Building, and the city parking garage.

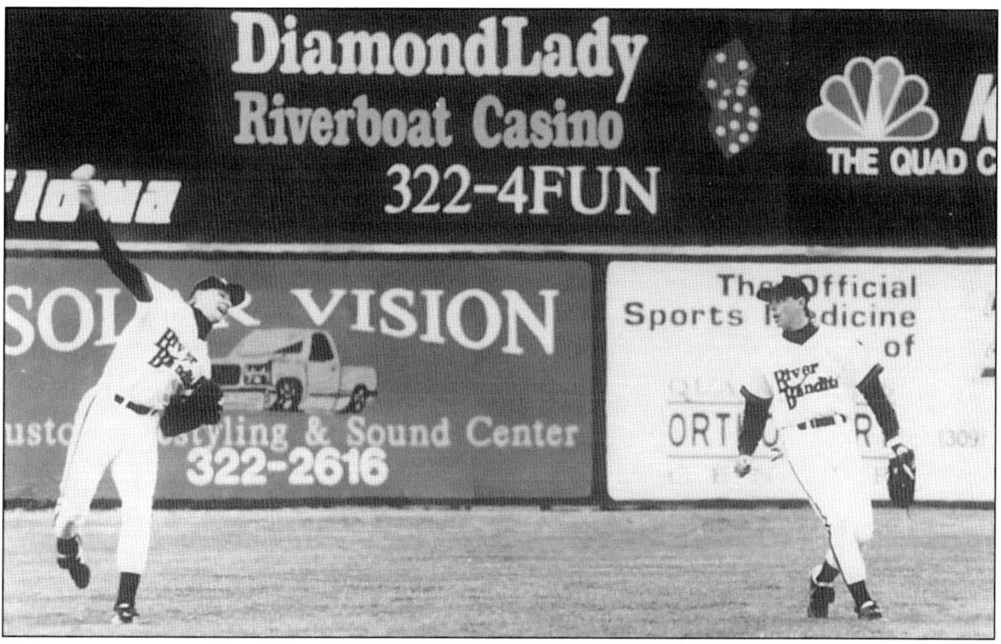

"It's root, root, root for the home team," as in this case, the Quad-City River Bandits, who play at Davenport's historic John O'Donnell Stadium. The ballpark, overlooking the Mississippi River at the foot of Gaines Street, opened May 26, 1931, with a contest between the Davenport Blue Sox and the Dubuque Tigers, both of the old Mississippi Valley League. It is the nation's fourth oldest professional baseball park still in use.

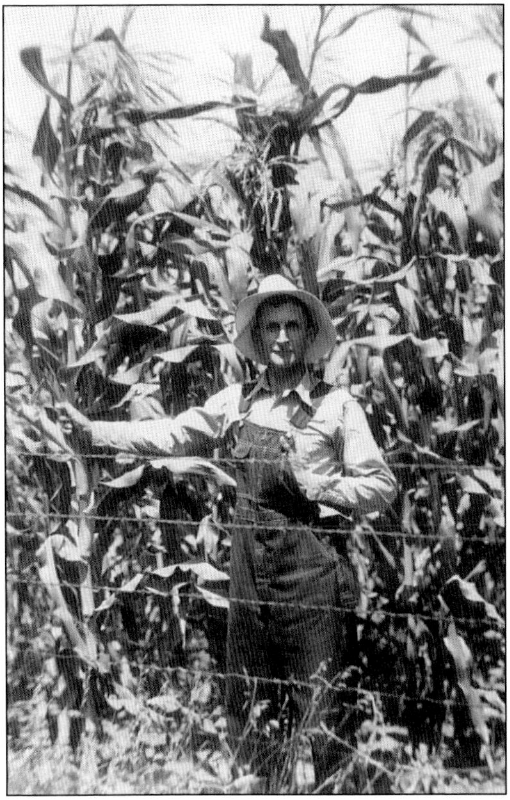

Well, if you're thinking this is kind of a corny picture, you're right. Nevertheless, this fellow represents all the farmers in and around Davenport who take pride in growing top-quality corn. That entitles him to assume a Napoleonic stance, hand in his overalls. Why, if he were in the military, he would immediately be promoted to "kernel" for such a fine harvest. Boy, wouldn't it be fun to play hide and seek in his cornfield? You wouldn't have anyone stalking you…

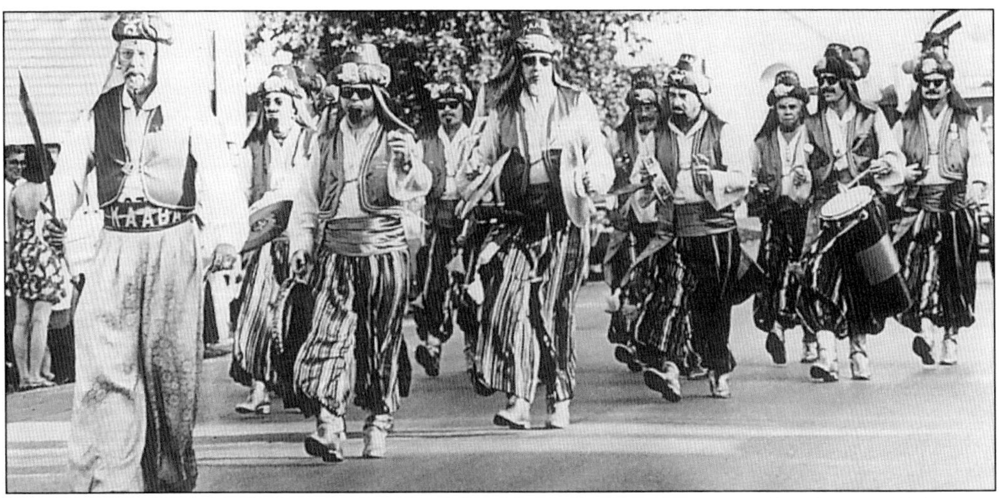

Well, you cannot beat this group for colorful costuming! Can you guess who they are? Maybe a few hints will help. They are devoted to helping children with physical and mental difficulties. Each year they campaign on behalf of unfortunate youngsters, helping to raise money for their treatment, and providing entertainment at children's hospitals. When there's a parade, they will be marching, attracting attention to their cause while they delight spectators. If you guessed the Kaaba Shrine, you're right on the money. Oh, and while you're counting your cash, throw a little their way—it's for a good cause.

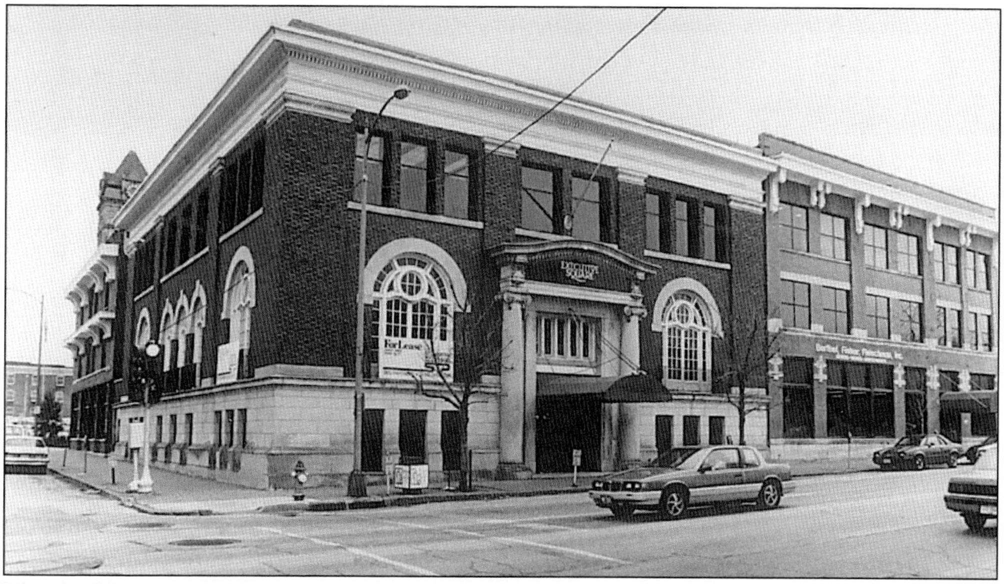

This building at 400 Main Street was built in 1905 for the Davenport Commercial Club, which later became the Davenport Chamber of Commerce. Here, cigar-smoking businessmen could enjoy elegant dining and a game of billiards in the billiard room. A Ladies' parlor and a basement rathskeller were also among the amenities. Later, the club's ornate oak fireplaces, chandeliers, and oak woodwork took on a new usage when the structure was renovated into the Executive Square office building during the mid-1980s.

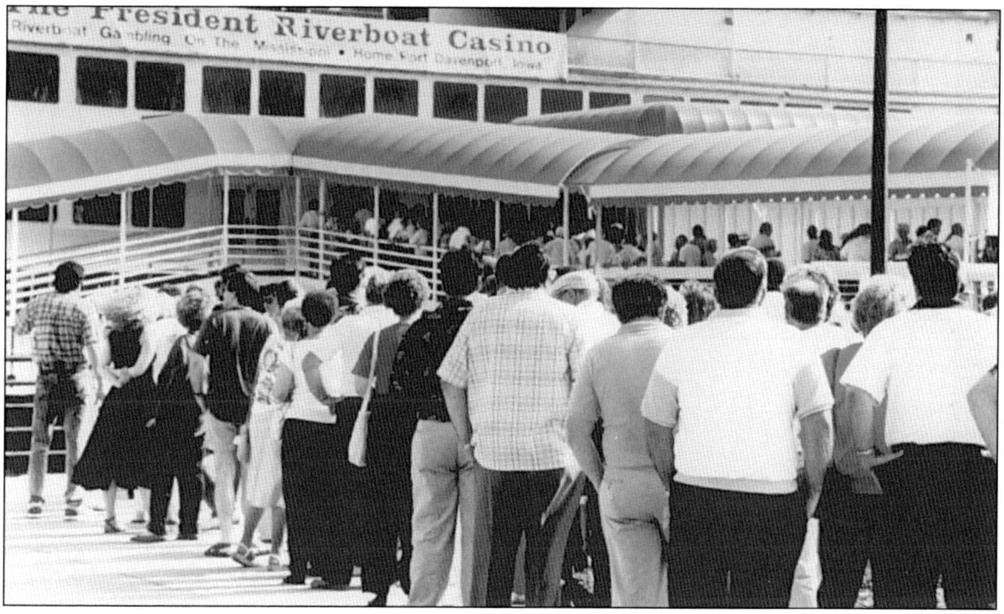

Tourists traveled to Davenport's riverfront to try their luck at slot machines, roulette, blackjack, and other games of chance after the Quad-City area became the first in the nation to offer legalized riverboat gambling. The President Casino opened on April 1, 1991, with the promise of jobs, a lively riverfront, and additional revenue to support a variety of civic and social projects. Assistance from the Riverboat Development Authority has provided many local schools and organizations with much-needed project dollars.

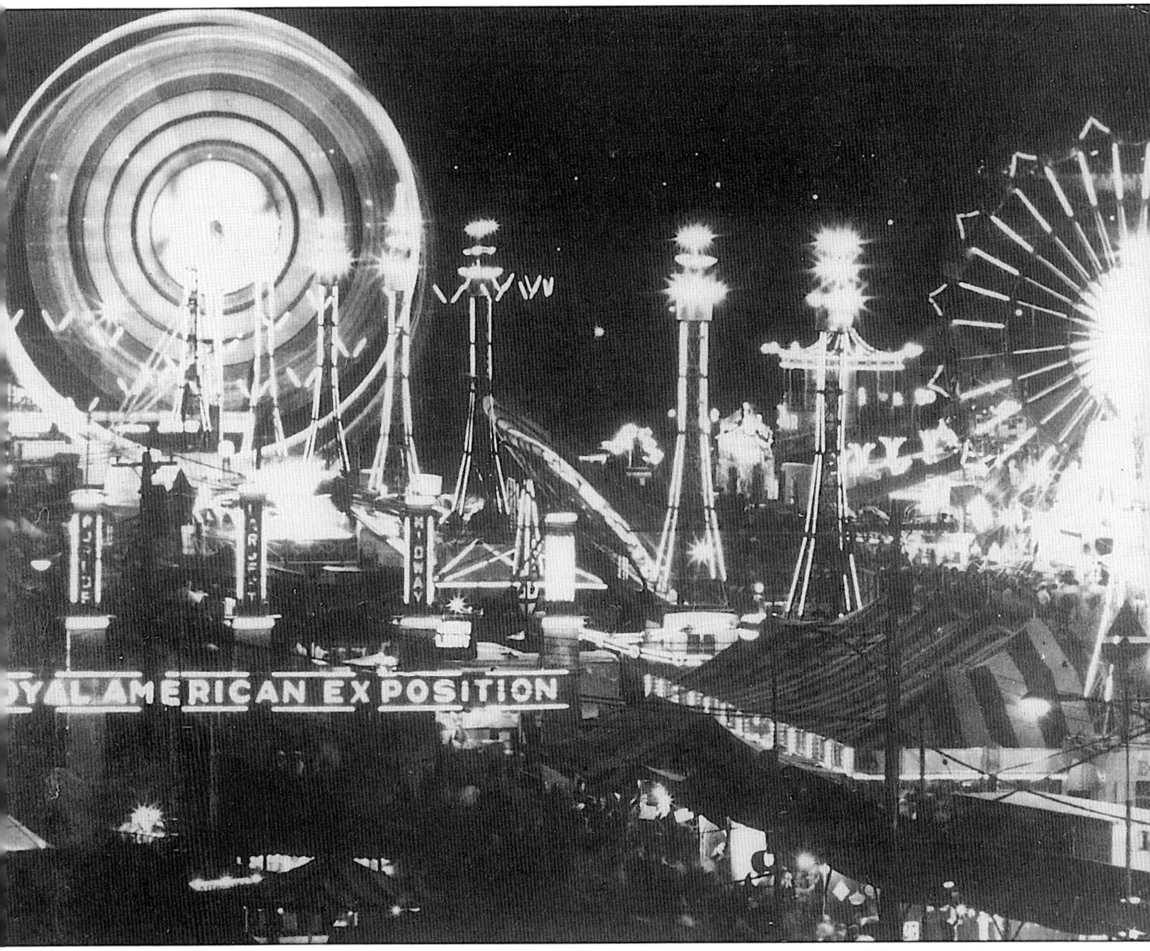

The Davenport Levee exploded in light when the Royal American Shows came to town. An early summer tradition, the show set up on the grounds west of the Centennial Bridge. In addition to thrill rides, the show's attractions included hucksters who pitched games, and vendors of cotton candy and hot dogs.

Kimberly Road, one of Davenport's busiest commercial thoroughfares, was little more than a country road when this photo was taken in 1941. Today, thousands of vehicles use the busy four-lane road to get to the Northpark Mall or "Sell-More" Avenue for hours of shopping, eating, and other leisure activities.

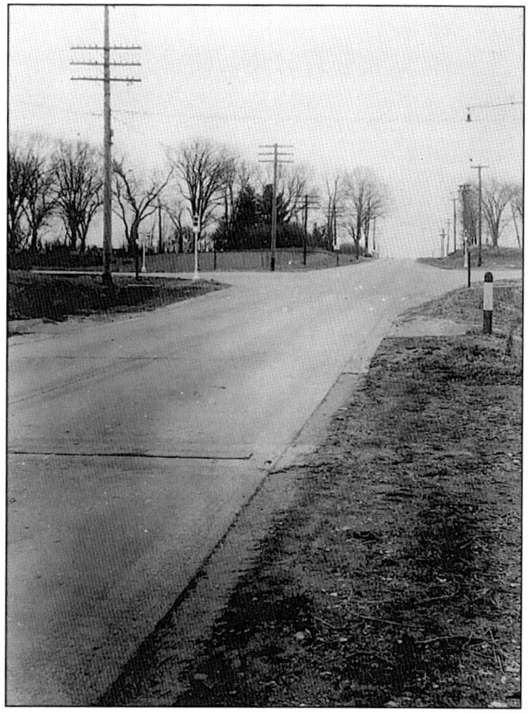

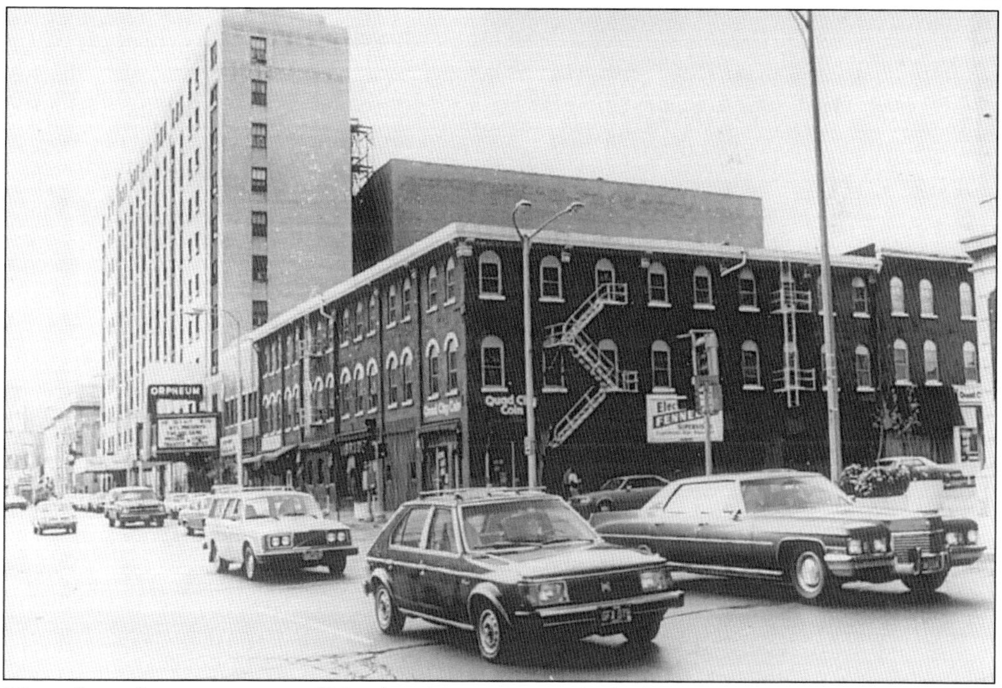

This is how the intersection of Third and Perry Streets looked in 1980, before the River Center was built. The corner building, originally a hotel, housed several retailers on the lower level, including Brud's Tavern, Ziffren's Pawn Shop, and the Louisiana Bar B-Q. A corner of the Blackhawk Hotel, visible at far right, has a sign advertising its old restaurant, the Sundance Social Club. Ah, remember the days...

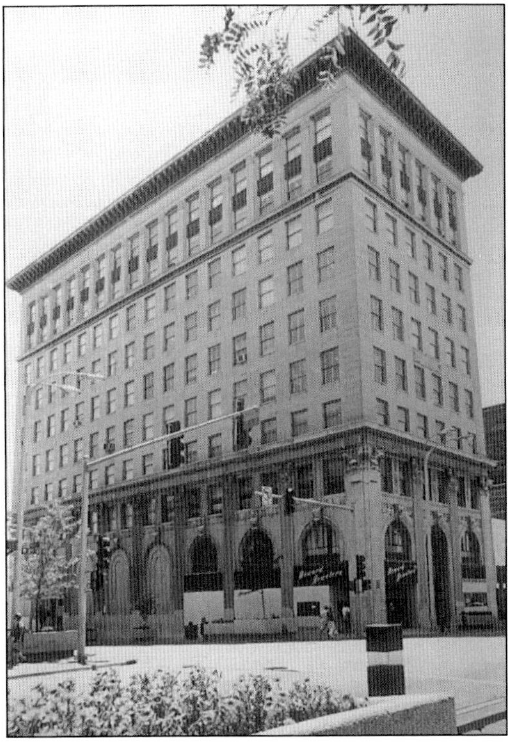

The First National Bank Building, today Firstar Centre, was built immediately after a 1923 fire destroyed an earlier First National Bank on the same site. For many years, the building housed shops on the first floor and offices on the upper floors. From 1985 to 1986, the building was restored to its original use and appearance as a bank.

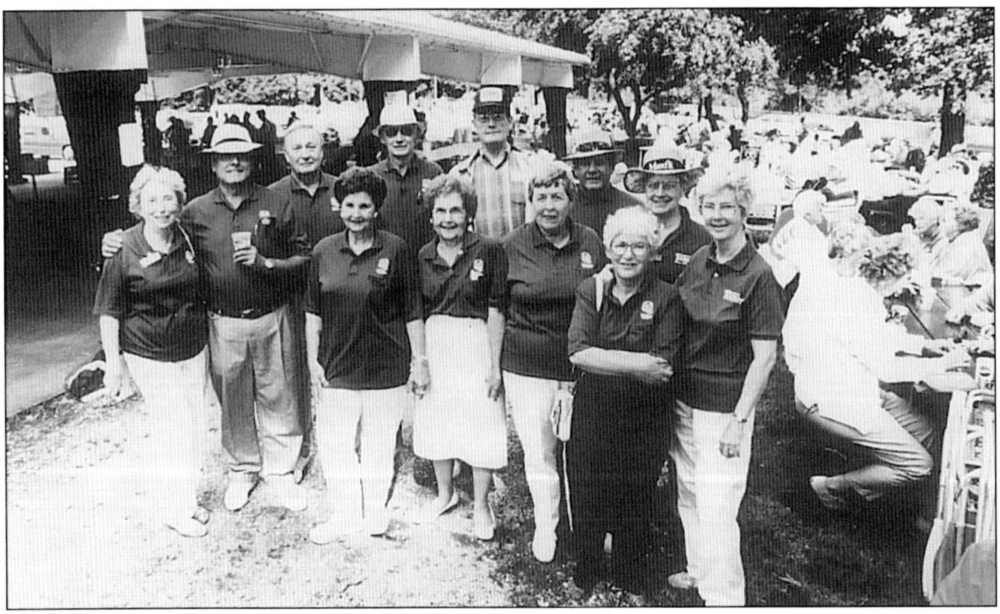

Later years can indeed be the golden years, as evidenced by the indefatigable Shirley Davis (far left), who has worked more than 40 years at the *Quad-City Times*. As coordinator of the newspaper's Plus 60 Club, she leads active seniors on tours with destinations that range from Chicago, to Paris, to the Great Wall of China. Here, she gets together with the Plus 60 board at a recent club picnic. When not packing her suitcase for Plus 60 trips, she writes travel features. "She always sparkles," observes one Davis fan. You'll find no argument here.

John Holladay earned a national reputation for his whimsical college athletics posters, and others depicting various professions and sports. In 1990, he was licensed by the National Football League to create a complete line of posters and shirts. He teaches art at Assumption High School in Davenport. He is also a presenter at the annual Children's Literature Festival held every April.

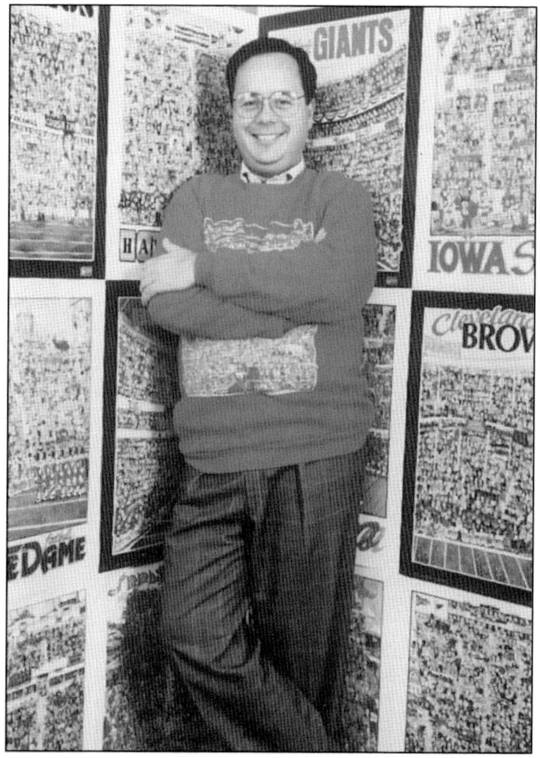

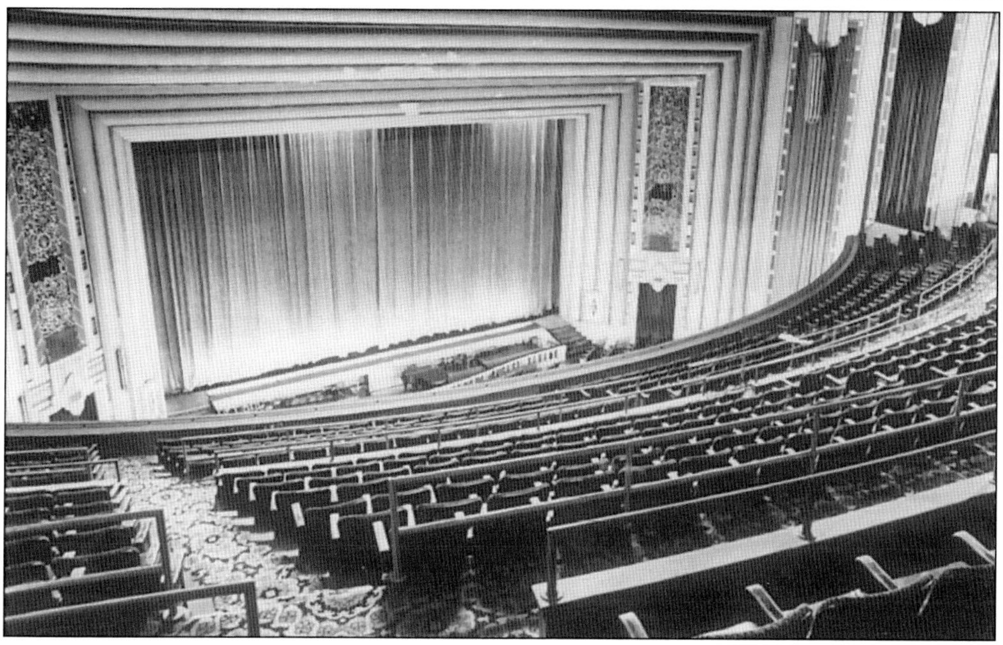

The last, great movie palace built in the Quad-Cities was Davenport's Orpheum, today known as the Adler Theatre. This photo, taken before the theater was restored into a performing arts center in 1986, shows the original proscenium of the Art Deco masterpiece. After it closed as a first-run movie house, the Orpheum became a popular venue for rock concerts. Sister Sledge, the Pointer Sisters, Cheech & Chong, and other acts appeared there in the 1970s.

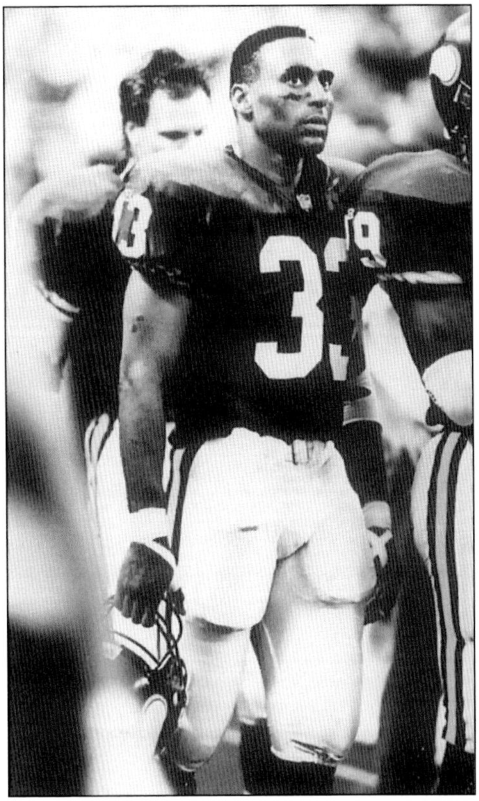

Davenport native Roger Craig played 11 seasons in the National Football League, as one of the most versatile running backs of his era. He starred on three Super Bowl championship teams with the San Francisco 49ers, and later played with the Minnesota Vikings. After graduating from Davenport Central High School, he went on to become the number 10 all-time rusher at the University of Nebraska. It is the classic story of a hometown boy making good and returning home to share his good fortune by opening a delightful sports nightclub.

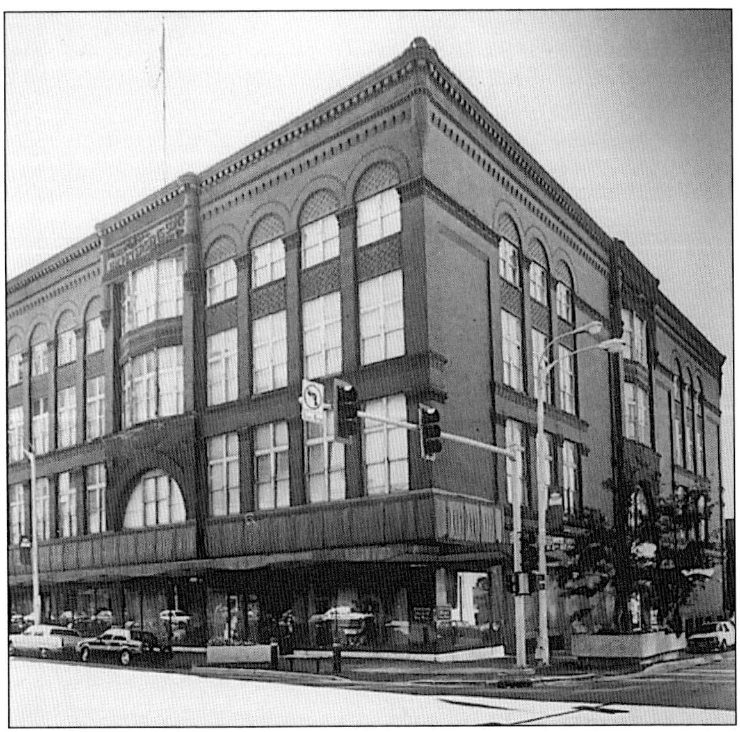

The ornate Romanesque structure at the southeast corner of Second and Main Streets was the flagship store of the Petersen Harned Von Maur department store chain, until the company closed its downtown operations in 1986. John H.C. Petersen, who bought his merchandise at auction in Chicago and resold it locally, founded the company, today known as Von Maur, in 1872. Shoppers still enjoy upscale shopping at Von Maur, located in Davenport's Northpark Mall.

The late Father Edward M. Catich was a respected authority on calligraphy during his 40 years as a teacher at St. Ambrose University. He was also a talented artist whose images of Christ once angered the Vatican. Today, Vatican officials embrace his work, because they say it has withstood the test of time. His work is preserved in St. Ambrose's Edward M. Catich Memorial Gallery.

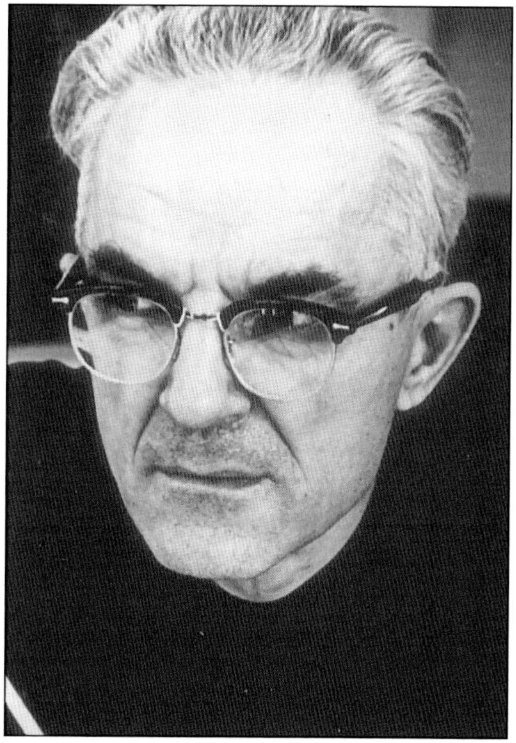

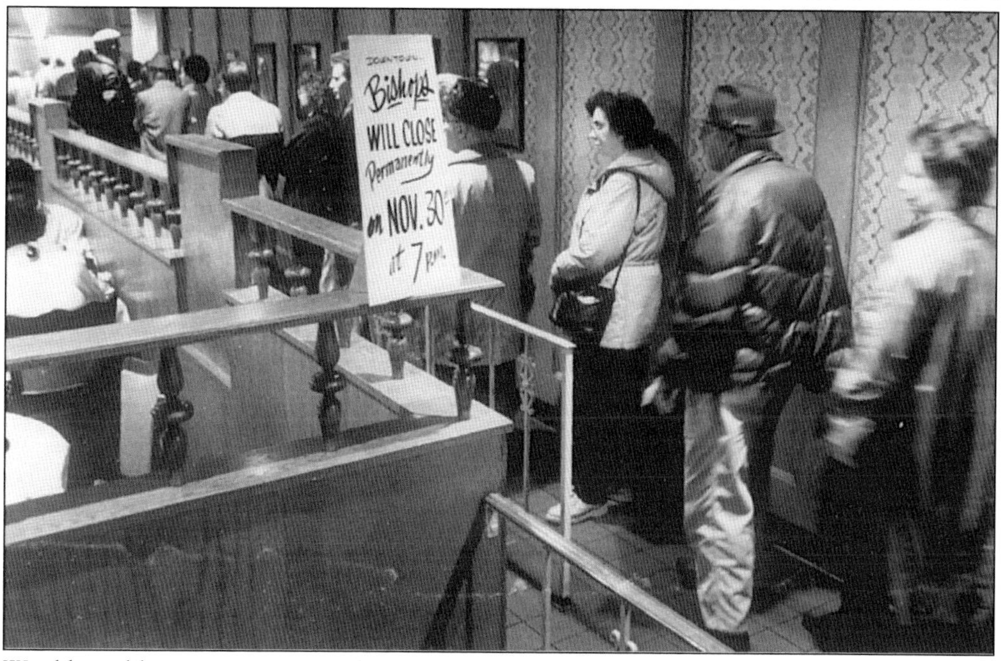

Would you like more peas? Roast beef? On November 30, 1989, customers lined up for the last time at the Bishop's Buffet that once stood at the northeast corner of Second and Brady Streets in downtown Davenport. The popular downtown eatery, which opened in 1965, was razed to make way for the MidAmerican Energy Building and a city parking ramp. Ah, and let's not forget that delicious "Ambrosia" chocolate pie!

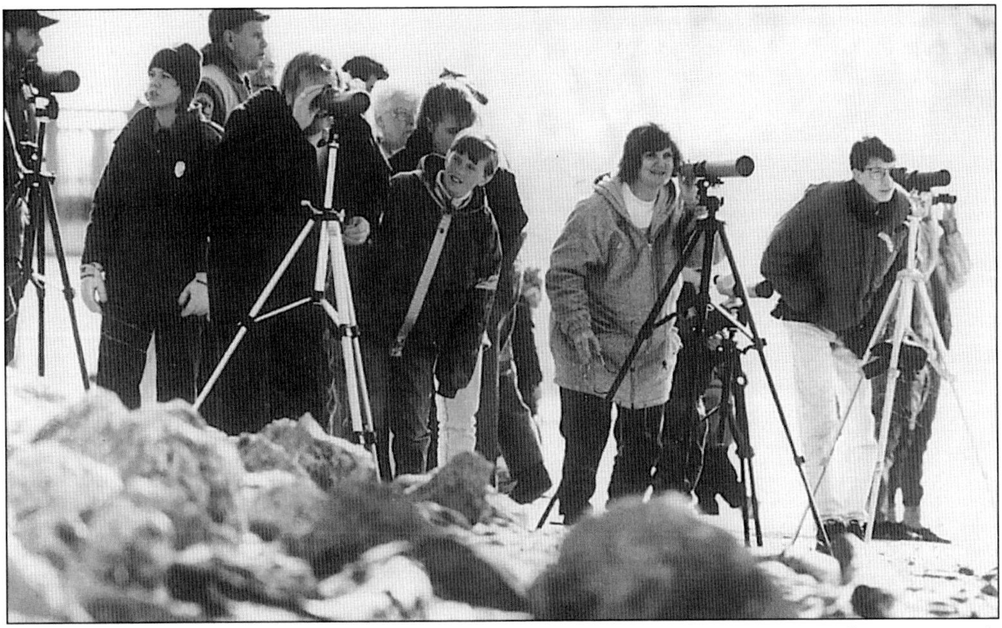

Come winter, people from throughout the Midwest flock to Davenport's riverfront to watch bald eagles. Some watch from the shelter of their cars, but others, bundled well against Iowa's chilly blasts, stand outside and search for eagles through binocular-aided eyes. The magnificent birds winter in the Quad-Cities, and fish in the open waters of the Mississippi River next to Lock and Dam 15. The annual Bald Eagle Days, held in January, is a good time to get up close and personal to our national symbol.

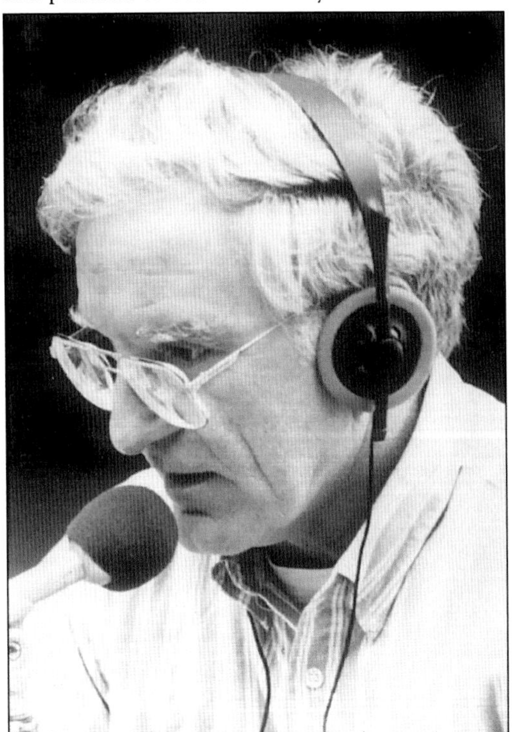

Some love him, some detest him, but when Jim Fisher comes on the air, the phone lines fill up. Fisher, a talk show host on WOC-AM, is known as a local radio legend for his no-holds-barred style. Fisher is a native of Mason City, Iowa, and worked in Cedar Rapids, Iowa, before coming to Davenport. In addition to being a gifted announcer, he is an avid outdoorsman with a passion for fishing.

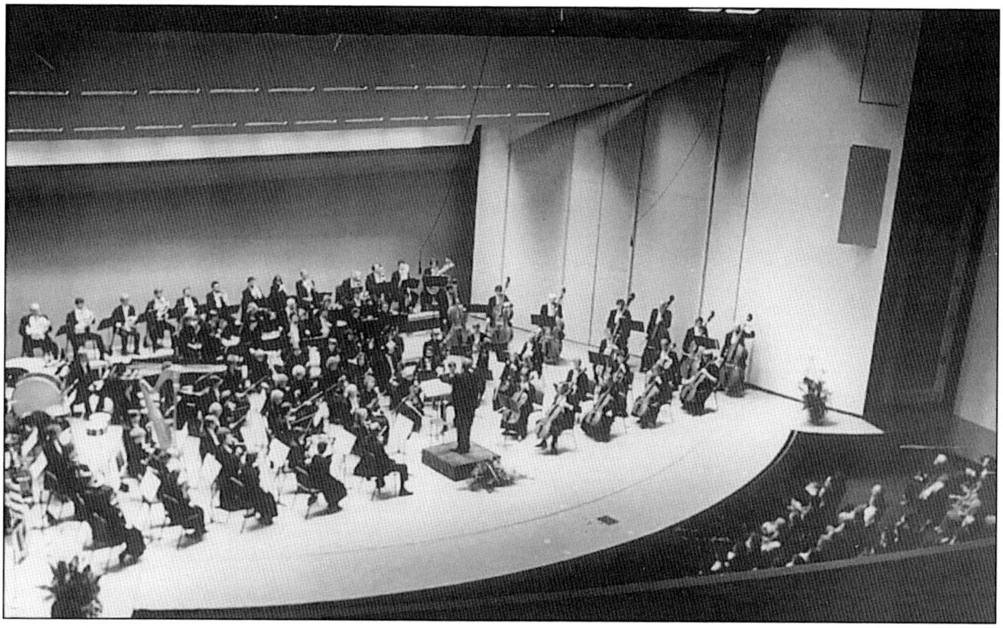

A raised hand, a swish of the baton, and *voila*, another evening of soul-stirring music has begun. The Quad-City Symphony Orchestra performed for a near sell-out crowd of 2,300 during its first performance at the renovated Adler Theatre in February of 1986. Since its founding in Davenport in 1916, the symphony has been one of the community's most revered and enduring cultural institutions. It is among the oldest symphonies in the United States.

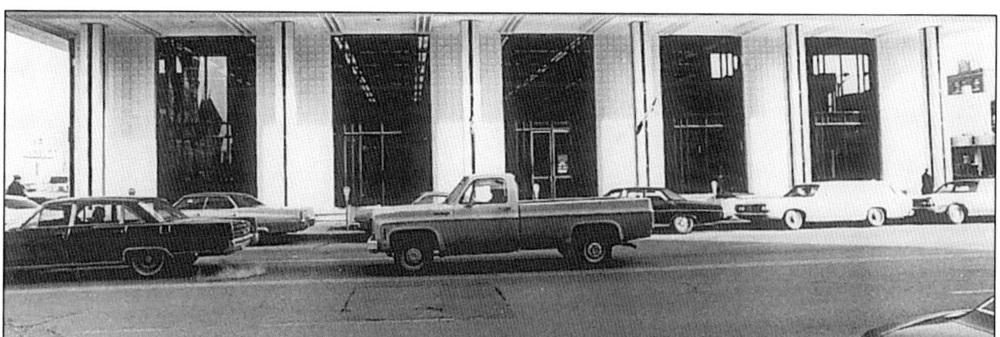

Davenport brought in the talents of an excellent architect when it planned its new library at 321 Main Street in the 1960s. Edward Durell Stone designed the structure. Opened in the fall of 1968, it reflects the style of his other works, including the John F. Kennedy Center for the Performing Arts in Washington D.C., and the Museum of Modern Art in New York City.

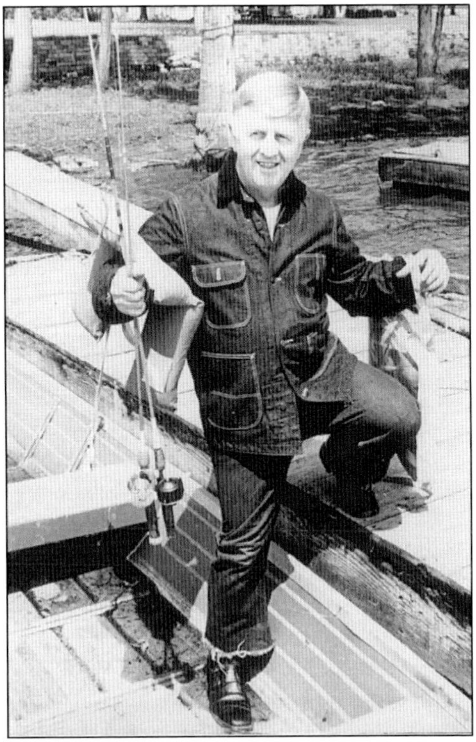

Father James Conroy, the former pastor at St. Anthony's Church, is known for his charity, goodwill, and boundless energy. For years, Conroy pastored the flock of St. Anthony's church—an edifice that has cared for the spiritual needs of Catholics since the mid-1830s. With the help of Sister Ludmilla Benda, he launched the free "McAnthony's meals," and other programs to help homeless people and others down on their luck. Now retired, Father Conroy finds a bit more time for fishing and enjoying his weekend home located near Buffalo.

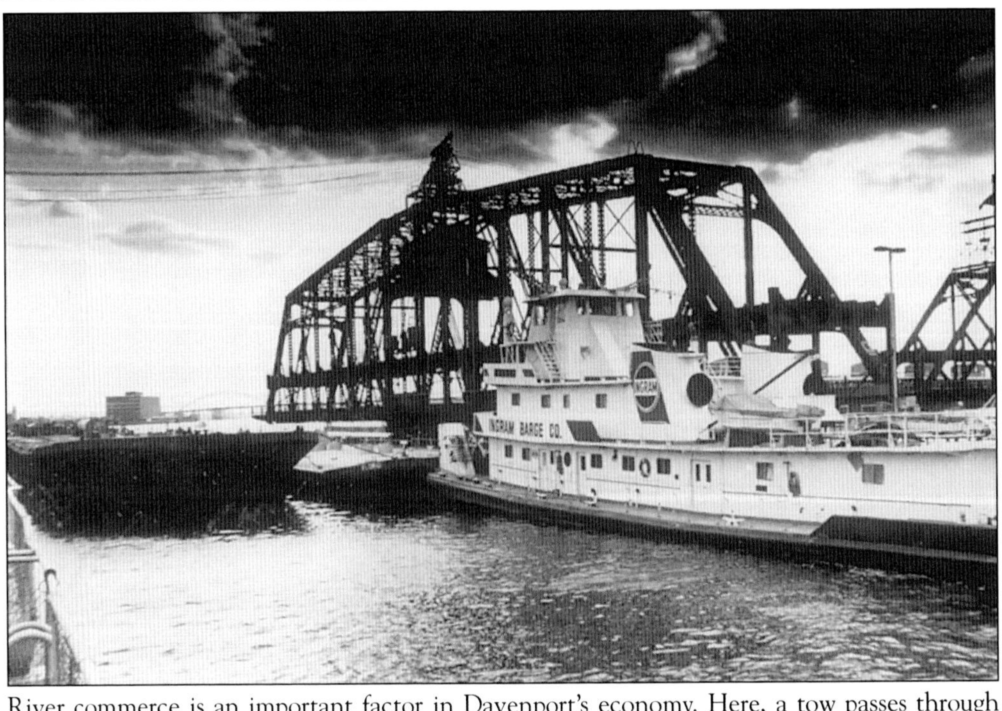

River commerce is an important factor in Davenport's economy. Here, a tow passes through Lock 15 on its way down the Mississippi River. Constructed during the 1930s, the locks system provides a 9-foot channel for navigation. The swing bridge that allows boats to pass through has operated since the turn of the century.

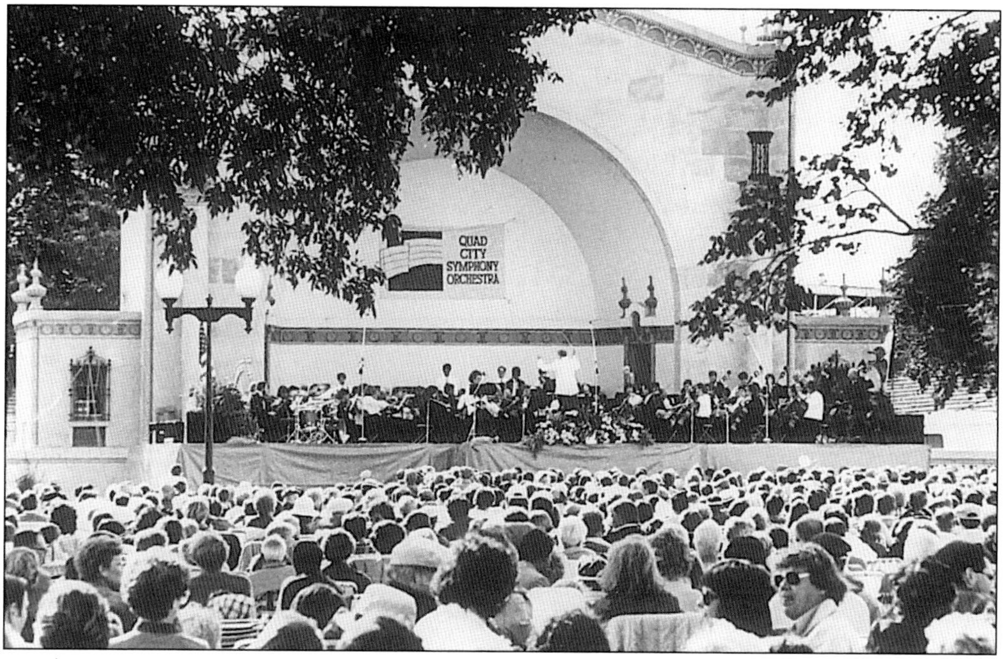

Sunshine, river breezes, and lush classical music entice thousands to Davenport's LeClaire Park every September for the Quad-City Symphony Orchestra's Riverfront Pops concerts. The concerts always end with a rousing version of the "Stars and Stripes Forever," complete with cannon fire supplied by National Guardsmen.

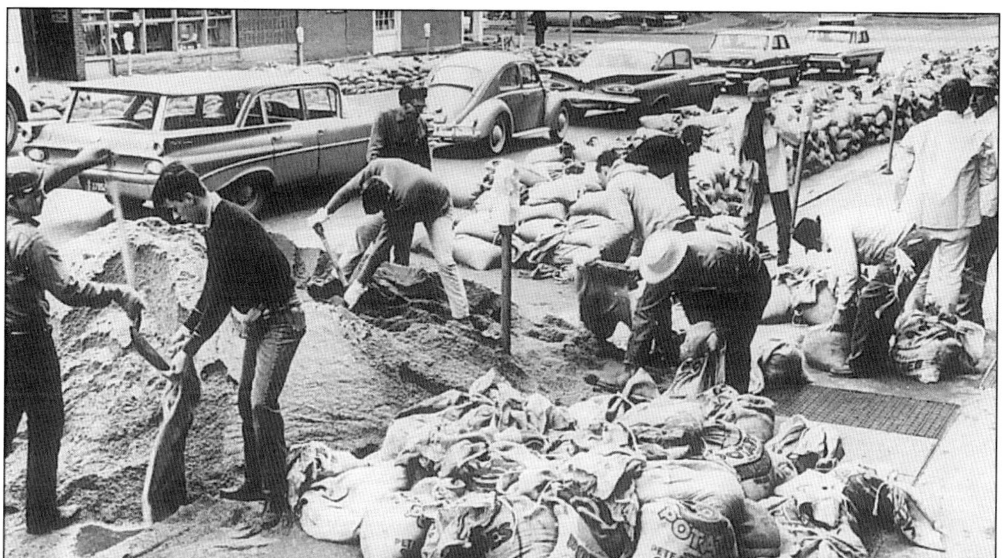

"Hey, how high do you think the water will go?" Aching muscles aside, a platoon of sandbaggers scrambled in 1965 to protect businesses along Main Street from the waters of the rising Mississippi River. The '65 flood crested at 22.48 feet in the Quad-Cities—a figure that river watchers thought would stand forever (the figure, not the river). However, in 1993, the Mississippi unleashed its full fury, first cracking the '65 mark, then swamping it with a crest of 22.63 feet on July ninth.

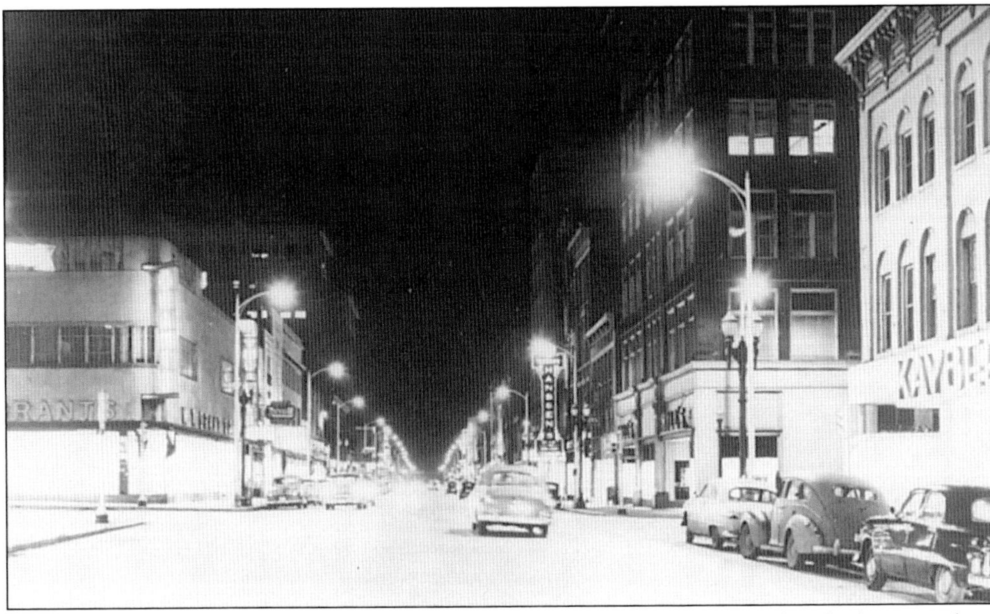

A mingling of old and new street lights can be seen in this 1954 view that looks west along downtown's Second Street. That year, the older picturesque lights were replaced with modern fixtures that lent the street a daytime glow. Ironically, replicas of the old-style streetlights are coming back to downtown Davenport to lend a nostalgic ambiance.

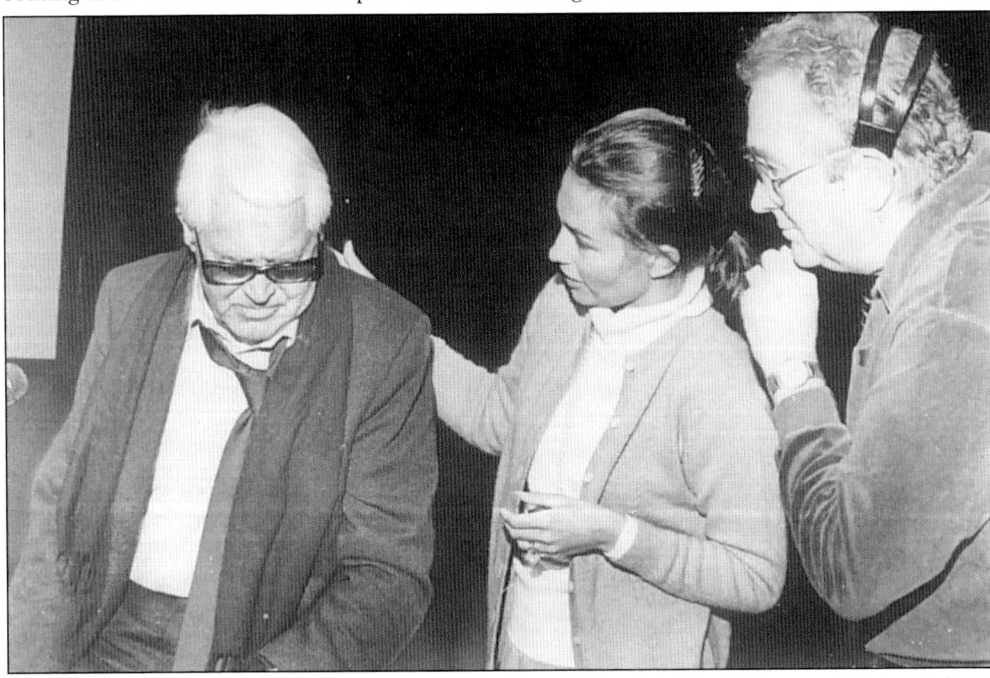

Cary Grant conferred with his wife, actress Barbara Harris, and Jack Dexter, chief stagehand at Davenport's Adler Theatre, during rehearsal for the performance he never gave. He died on November 30, 1986, just before going on stage at the city's first Festival of Trees gala. The death of the Hollywood legend put Davenport in the international spotlight, as journalists rushed to get the story and photos.

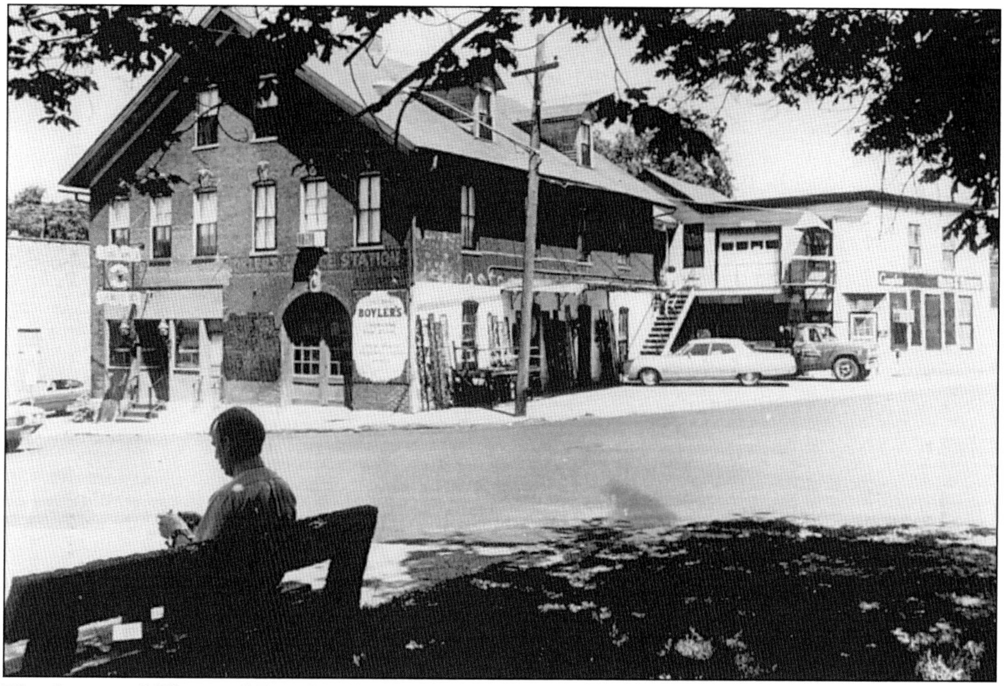

The historic Village of East Davenport, established in the 1850s as a logging center, grew to be one of the Quad-Cities' most popular shopping districts. Davenport officially annexed the city in the early 1900s. This view shows a Victorian building that housed Boyler's Ornamental Iron Works. Many of the Civil War era buildings have been restored, and Village merchants celebrate their heritage with a variety of special events.

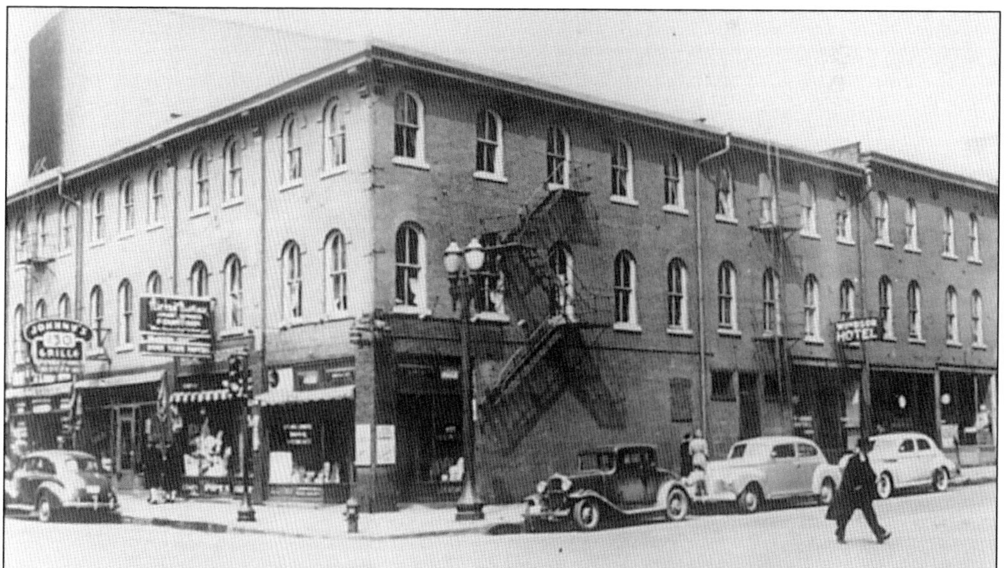

By April of 1941, fewer Davenport men and women thronged the downtown streets to visit the Hickey Brothers cigar store, Johnny's Grill, and the Louisiana Bar B-Q located on the northwest corner of Third and Perry Streets. Many had donned uniforms, and were fighting in the European or Japanese war theaters. The River Center occupies the site today.

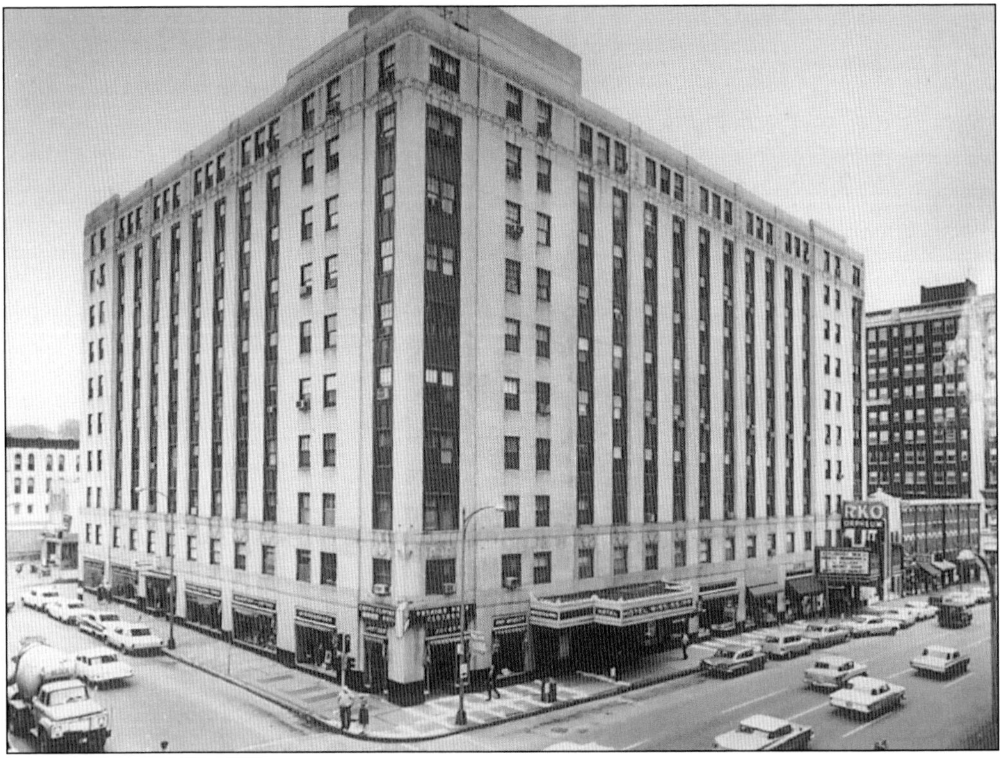

The opening of the Mississippi Hotel at the northeast corner of Third and Brady Streets was nothing short of an economic miracle. The hotel and its centerpiece, the Orpheum Theater, opened in November of 1931, during the depths of the Great Depression. Banker and real estate developer George Bechtel hired a Chicago architect to create a piece of "modernistic American architecture." Willing workers were not hard to find in those days.

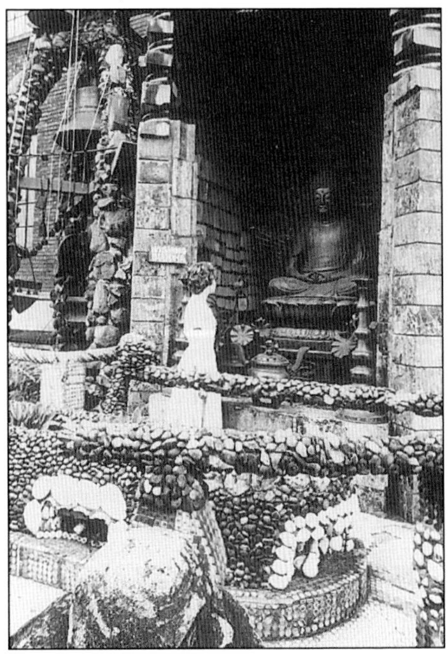

Chiropractic guru B.J. Palmer collected sculpture, porcelain, and artwork from around the world. He incorporated his treasures into his Brady Street home and the gardens of "Little Bit o' Heaven." Using his sense of humor, B.J. dubbed the entrance to "Bit o' Heaven," "Purgatory." The Palmer College of Chiropractic opened "Little Bit o' Heaven" to the public in 1924, and closed it, following B.J.'s death, in the 1970s.

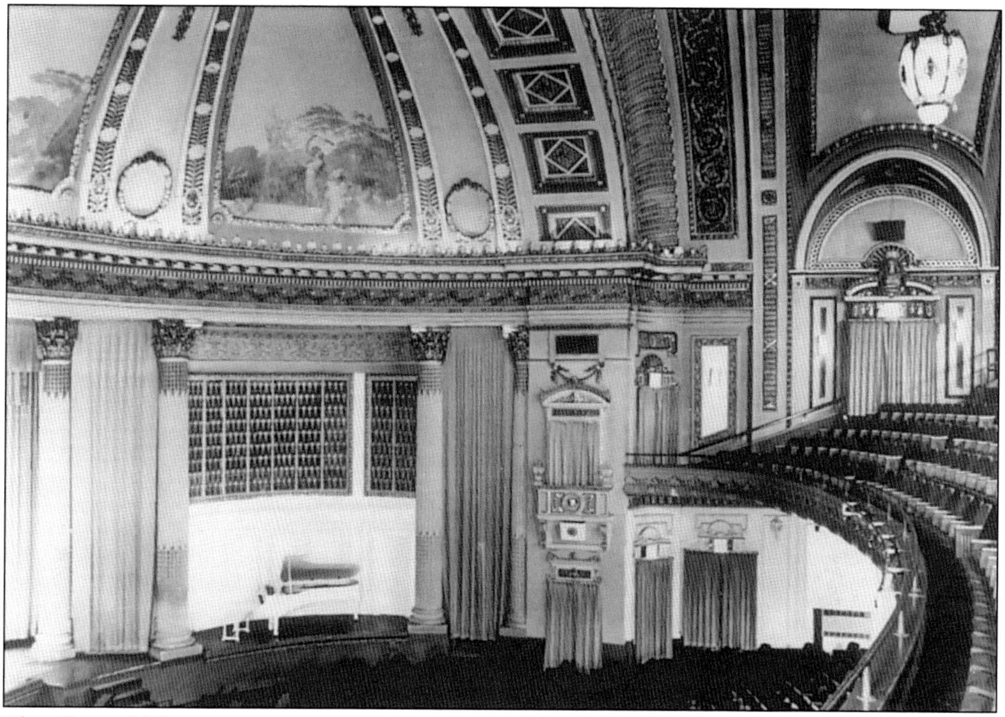

The Capitol Theatre was one of the nation's most elaborate movie palaces when it opened Christmas Day, 1920. The theater continued as a first-run movie house until 1977, when suburban multiplexes forced its closure. Later, it operated as a Spanish-language movie house, and as a country music palace. Its magnificent Wicks organ was recently restored.

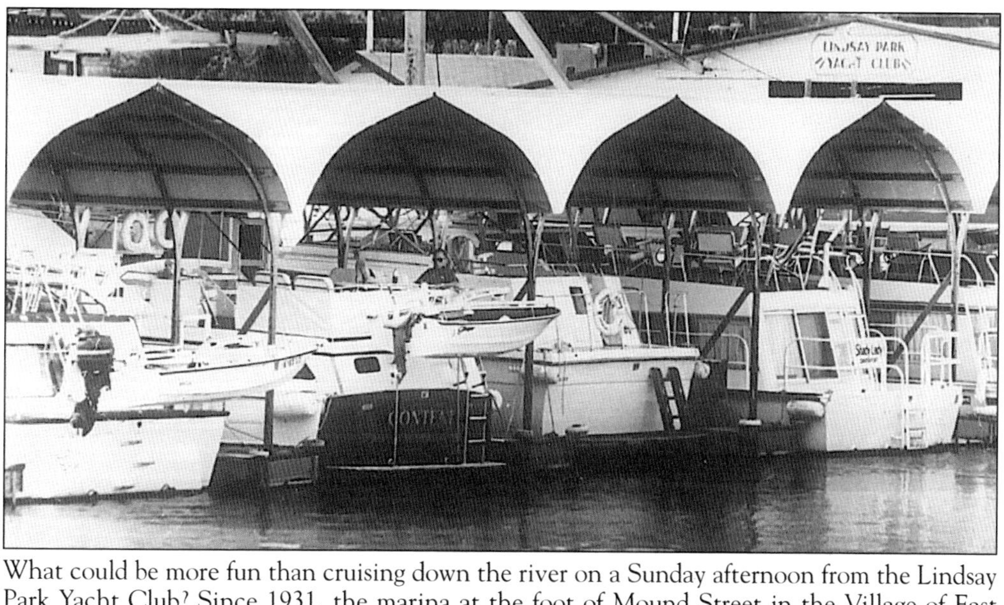

What could be more fun than cruising down the river on a Sunday afternoon from the Lindsay Park Yacht Club? Since 1931, the marina at the foot of Mound Street in the Village of East Davenport has been the center of power boating in Davenport. The marina has 127 slips and a membership of more than two hundred.

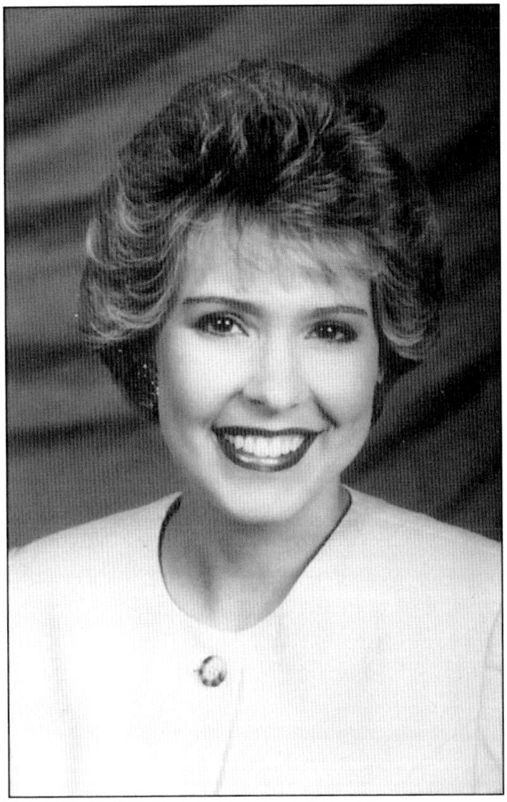

Paula Sands hosts the "Paula Sands Live" show on KWQC-TV, and is also the 6 p.m. news co-anchor. After more than a decade on Quad-City television, she has emerged as one of the community's most popular TV personalities. Her "infotainment" show is a throwback to the golden age of local television, when programs originated live. "I know she could have gone to a bigger job," says Davenporter Angie Peres. "I'm just glad she stayed here."

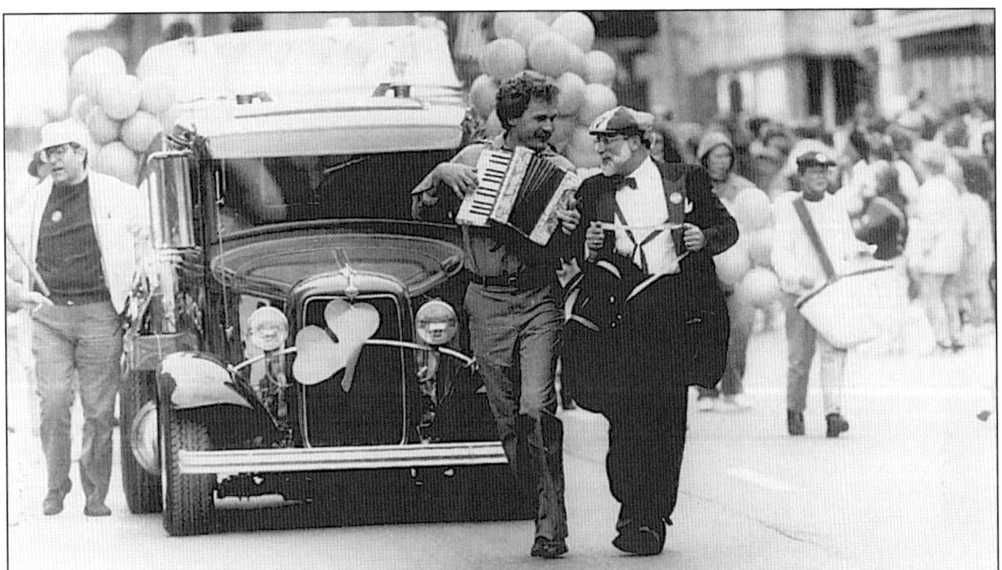

Dr. Joe Seng, a Davenport veterinarian and alderman, and Scott County Attorney Bill Davis display a wee bit o' Irish spirit as they romp in the St. Patrick's Society's annual Grand Parade. The celebration is the nation's only St. Patrick's Day parade that marches through two states. A tradition since 1986, the parade begins in Rock Island and ends in Davenport.

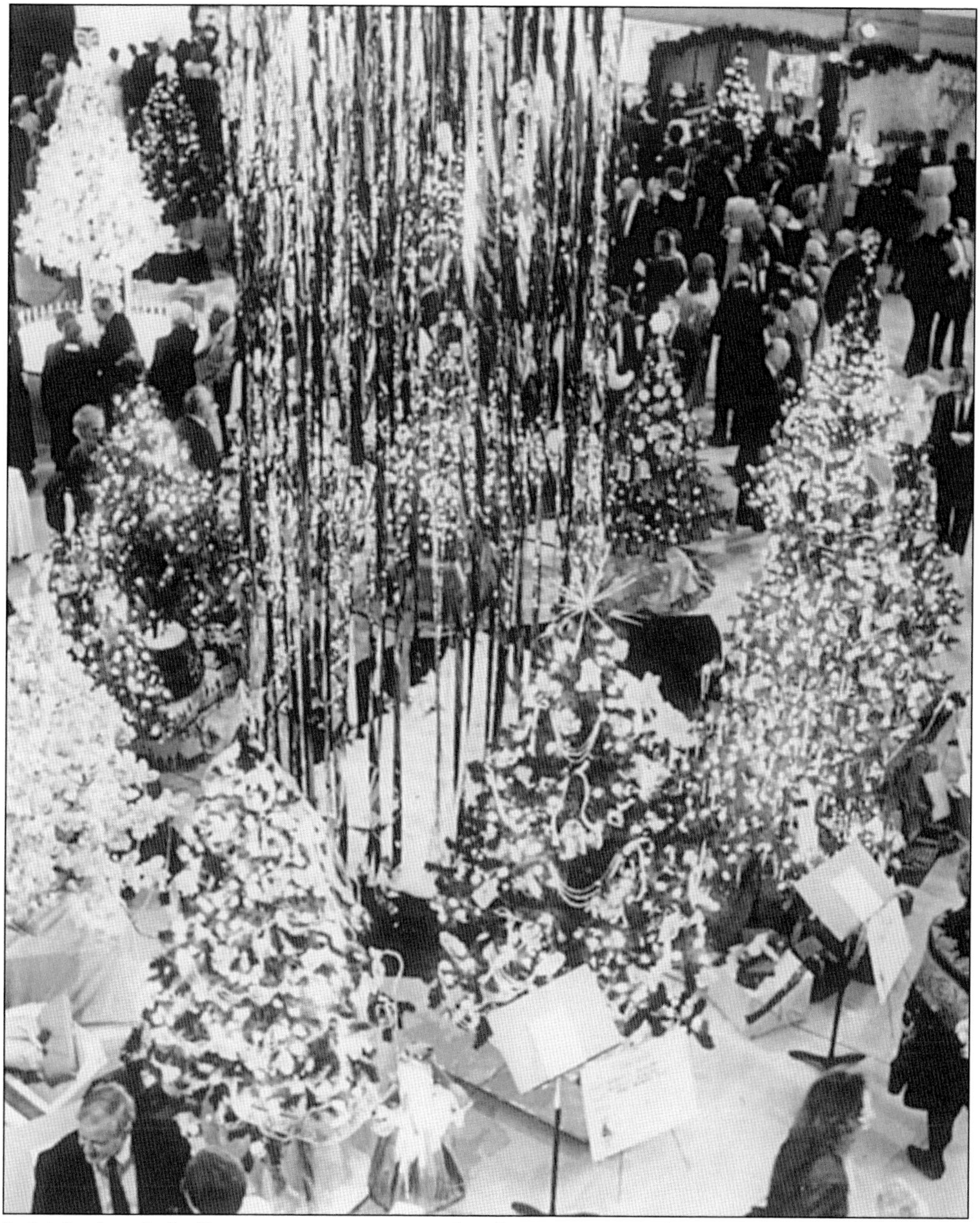

I think that I shall never see a poem as lovely as a tree...Thank you, Joyce Kilmer, and thank you, Festival of Trees volunteers. The Festival of Trees has been a holiday tradition in Davenport since 1986. Thousands of visitors flock to Davenport's River Center to see dozens of decorator trees, hear holiday music, and in general, get in the Christmas spirit. The event, held during Thanksgiving week, also features a popular Holiday Parade with huge helium-filled balloons. "It's just like those parades you see on television," exclaims four-year-old Patrick Johnson. "Except it's right here in Davenport. I like the cartoon characters the best." Six-year-old Amanda Robinson likes the parade "okay," but she loves the beautiful trees. "I never knew a tree could look so beautiful," she says. "My mom gets new ideas every year and tries them out at home." Proceeds from the Festival of Trees help to support arts activities in the area.

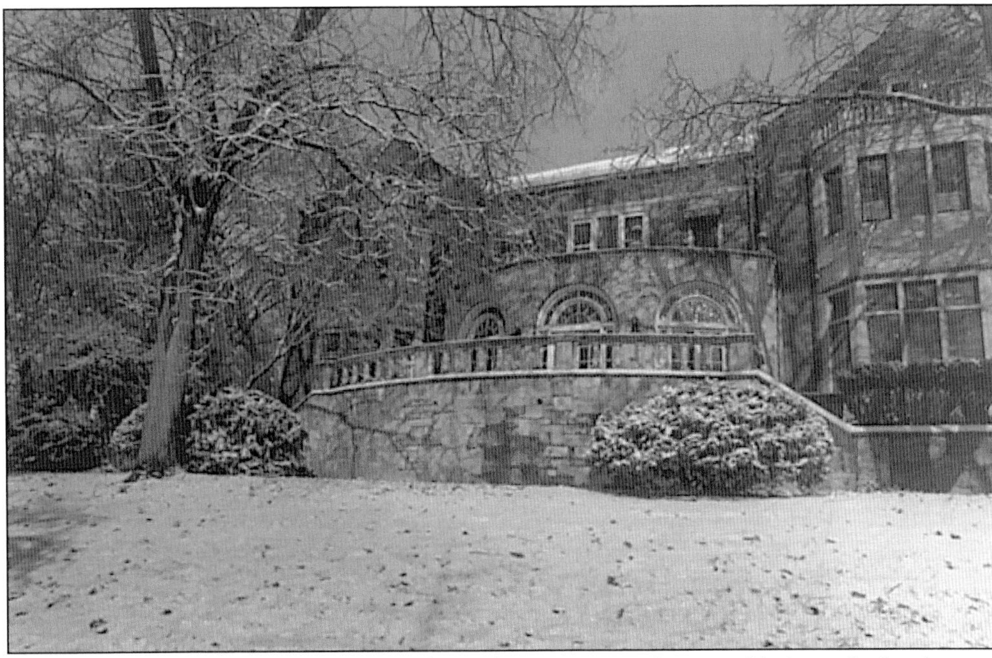

Anyone spending any length of time along the Mississippi River is likely to find a favorite spot, a place where beauty merges with the general atmosphere to form a heaven on earth. In Davenport, it is hard to find a lovelier location than the back patio of the Clifton Manor. From the vantage point there, one can take in the entire sweep of the river as it snakes through the Quad-Cities. Located on the Marycrest grounds, the patio is directly off the grand ballroom. It is a breathtaking view!

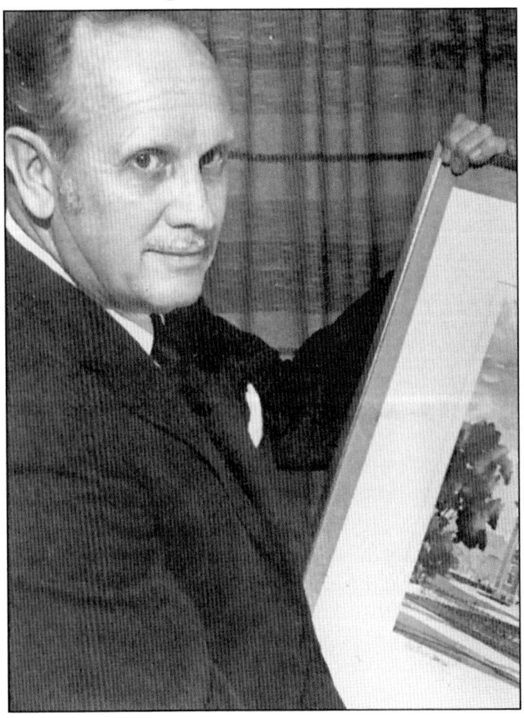

Thanks to this talented man, you can find the Quad-Cities in homes, businesses, and libraries around the world. Paul Norton represented art at its best. He shared his artistic gifts so that although he is gone now, people still admire his work. Norton's fingers could work magic with watercolors, capturing a riverboat, a church, a school, or virtually anything with warmth, sensitivity, and perception. It was not just the way he painted; it was the person he was.

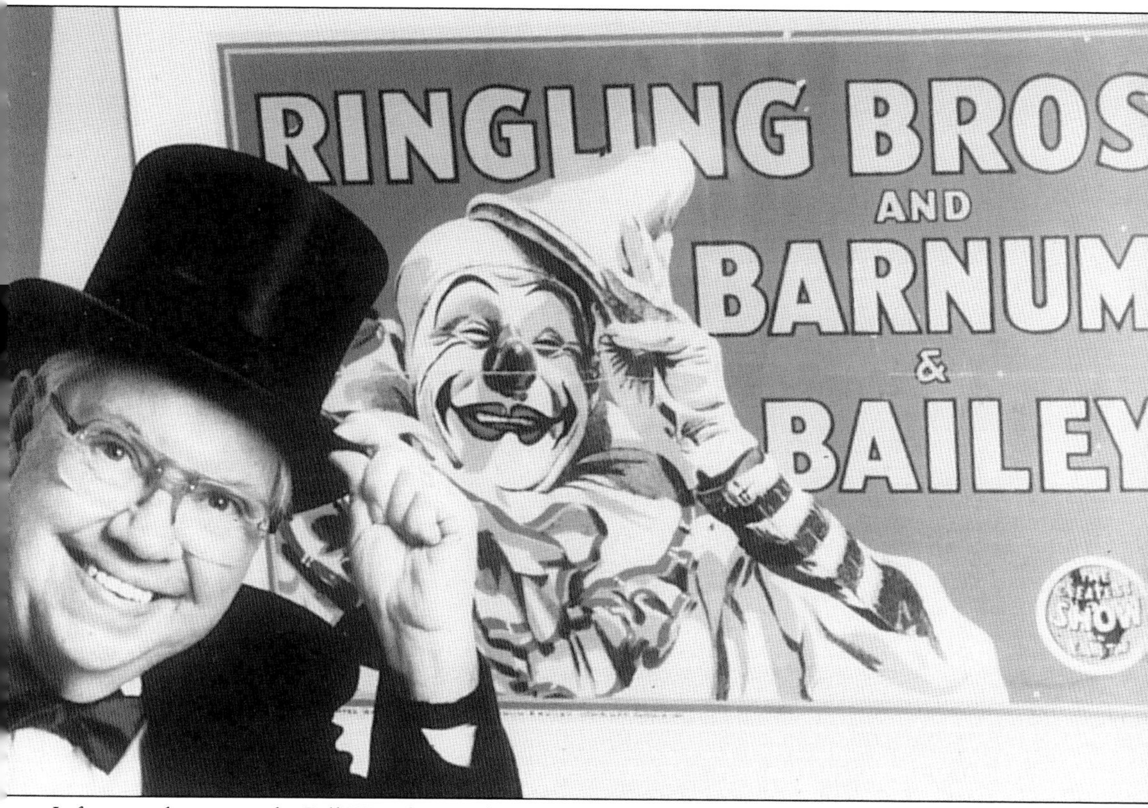

Life is one big circus for Bill Wundram, who writes a daily column for the *Quad-City Times*, and is a 56-year veteran of the *Quad-City Times* newspaper. This past year saw the smiling columnist compiling and writing a giant collection of human interest and historical selections from the past century called *A Time We Remember*. Everywhere he went to autograph books, he was deluged with fans. Nevertheless, he did not complain about getting writer's cramp. Day after day, Bill manages to reach into the mind and heart of the area reader, bringing both laughter and tears. One reader comments that he had never met Bill's late son, Peter, but felt that he knew him well through his father's poignant writing. Yes, Bill, they are listening out there. A circus sign in Wundram's office promises the greatest show on earth. If that is true, then he runs a close second. Perhaps he himself said it best some 30 years ago in a speech to a gathering of high school students. "It's a wonderful life," he told them. "And it never grows dull."

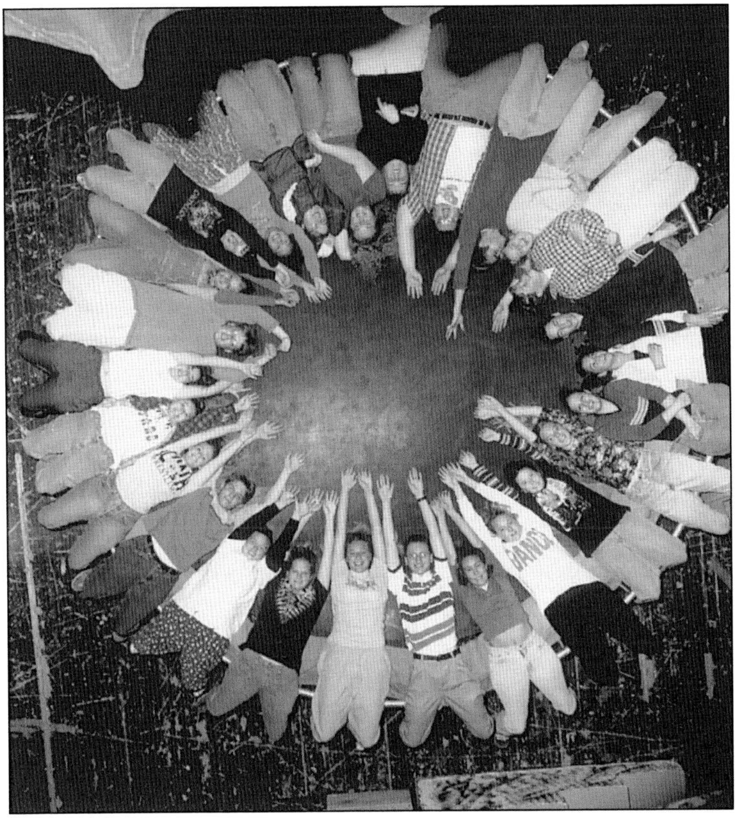

What is this gathering about? Could it be a group of young dynamic Davenporters cheering for their fair city? Maybe it is a new exercise plan, guaranteed to gather body tone. Maybe it's just young people letting off some steam. Actually, this handsome group is the West High Drama Club. Perhaps they are getting ready to try out for a play. If that happens to be the case, break a leg, you hardworking thespians!

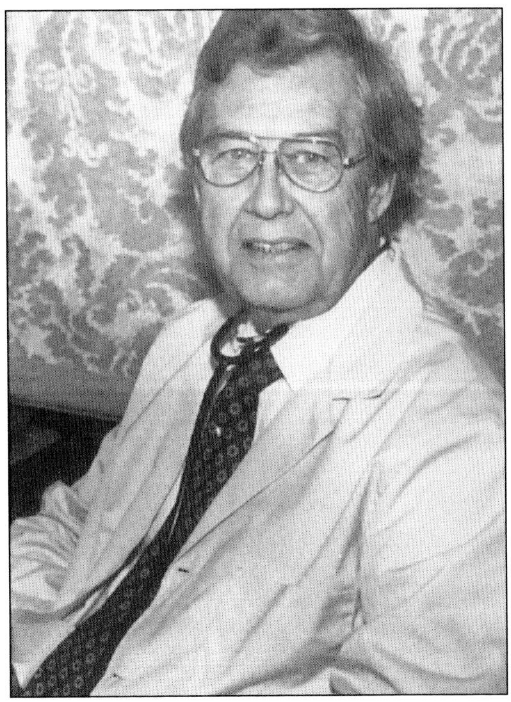

Is there a doctor in the house? Well, if there is, and it happens to be Dr. Jack Sunderbruch, you have the best! Sunderbruch's connections to Davenport go back a long way. The doctor remembers growing up during World War I, when anti-German sentiment dictated the re-naming of all Davenport facilities and streets sporting German monikers. Medically educated at the Universities of Iowa and Michigan, Sunderbruch returned to Davenport where he "doctored" generations of friends and neighbors. He also donated his services to school athletic teams. As special thanks, Assumption High School Auditorium was re-named in his honor.

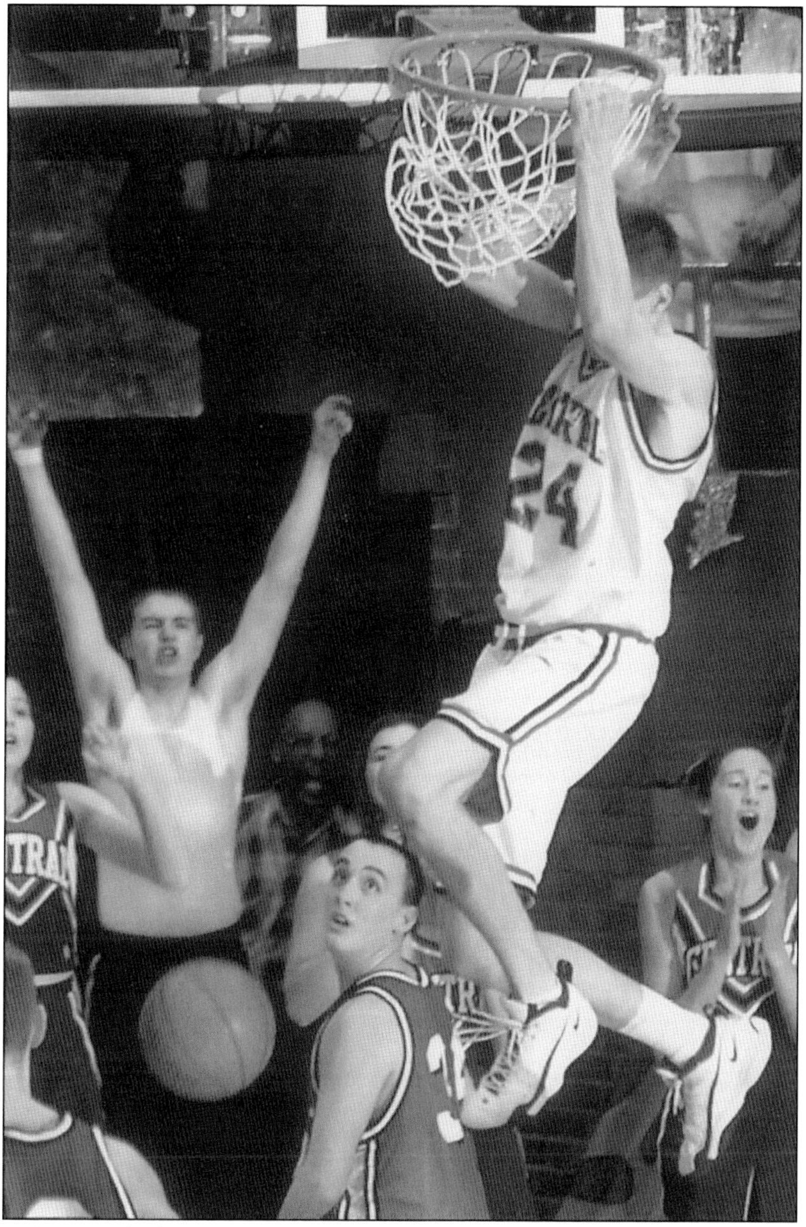

You do not have to look far to find quality sports competitions for girls and boys, men and women, in the Mississippi Valley community. For the huge contingent of dedicated sports fans, there are few better places to look than right in the Quad-Cities. Year after year, quality athletes treat crowds to exciting action, whether it is on the field, on the court, in the pool, or in a variety of other arenas. Davenport maintains a high standard of performance matched by an outstanding level of sportsmanship. The 1999–2000 high school year was no exception. It would be hard to top the February 4th contest between the Central High Blue Devils and the Assumption High Knights. It was one of those games that caused hearts to beat faster on the court and in the stands. Here, Central's Nate Sharp gets an overtime slam to put the Blue Devils into the lead, defeating the Knights 75-72. Nevertheless, people leaving the contest knew they had viewed two winning teams, not just one.

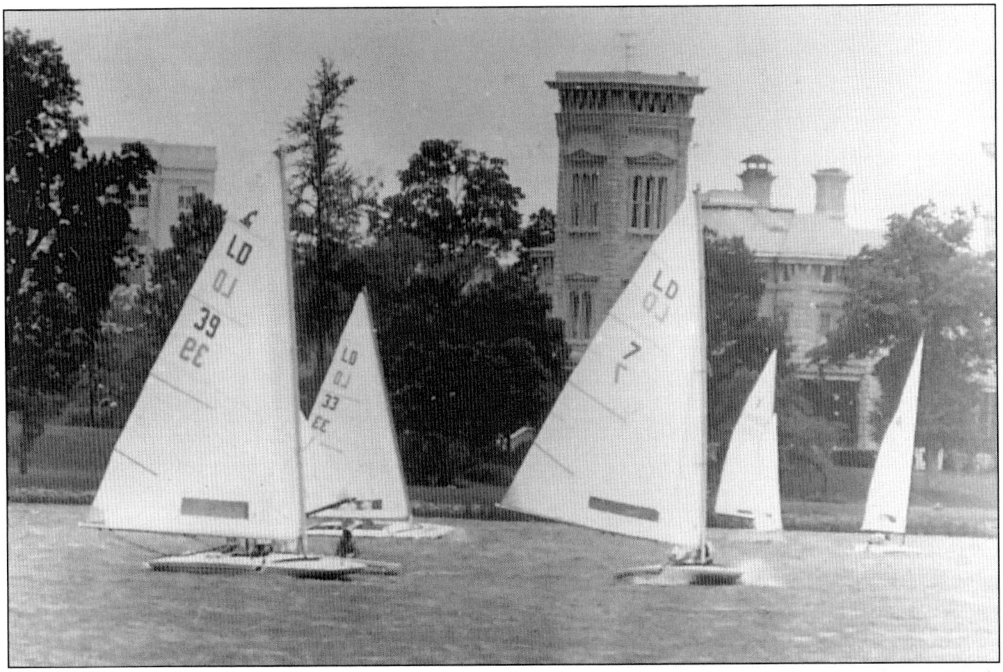

Races by the Lake Davenport Sailing Club add beauty and action to the riverfront. With Quarters One, the commanding general's residence on Rock Island Arsenal as a backdrop, sailboats skim across the river on a Sunday afternoon in May

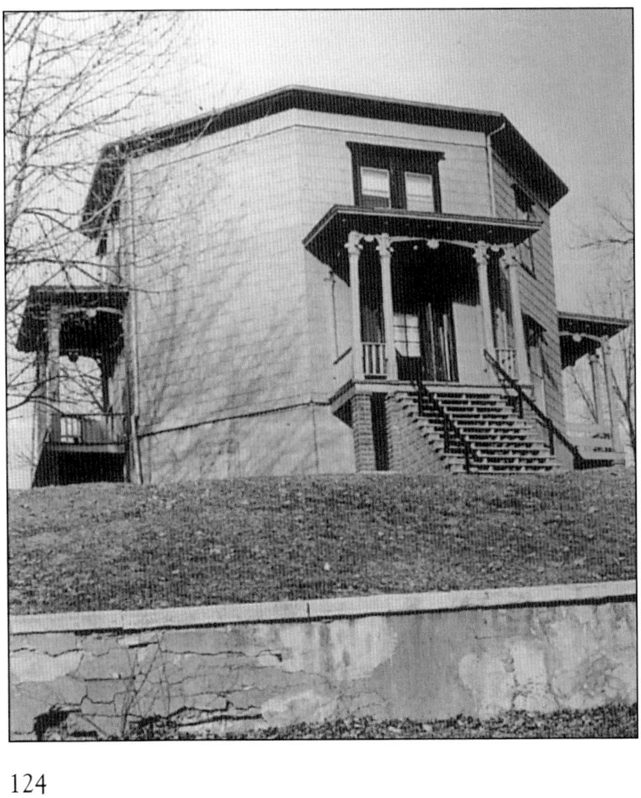

Davenport's architecture reflects a variety of styles. Among the more unusual is this octagonal house located at 512 East Sixth Street, known as the Smith-Murphy House. The architect is believed to have been Willett Carroll, one of the city's first professional architects. The unusual shape was influenced by the phrenologist belief that octagonal shapes were conducive to good health. Today's Davenporters still cherish their Victorian and Edwardian era homes, many of which can be viewed along Davenport's famed Gold Coast and eastern River Drive.

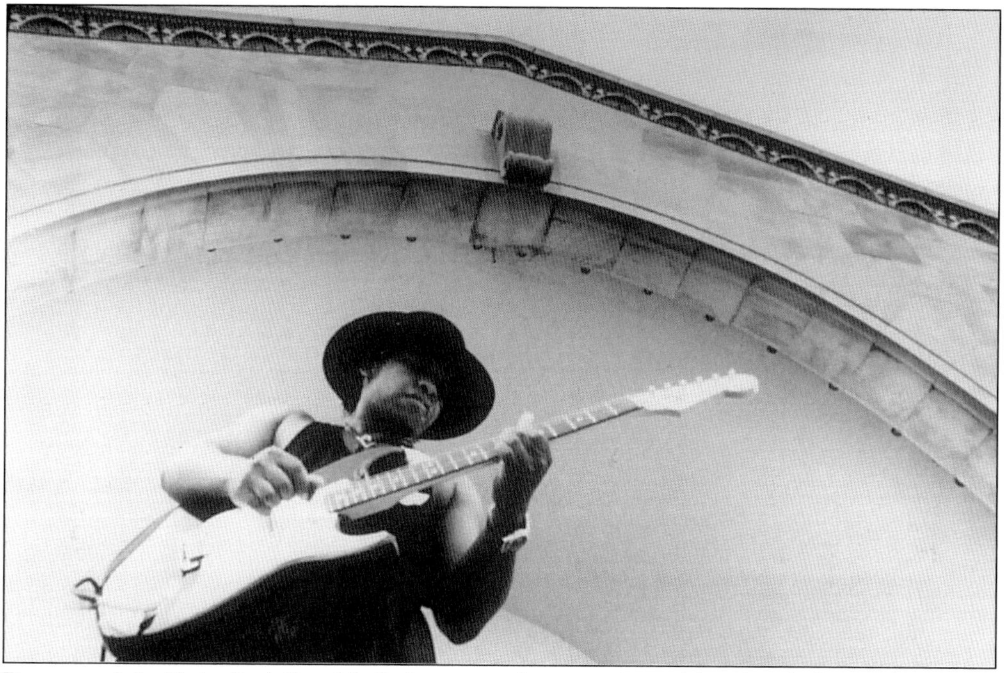

Davenport's LeClaire Park Bandshell showcases the nation's top blues bands during the annual Mississippi Valley Blues Fest. The show's stars have included Baton Rouge blues artist Troy Turner. The Blues Fest is one of several music events that keep people tapping their toes at the historic music pavilion—a fixture on the Davenport riverfront since 1924.

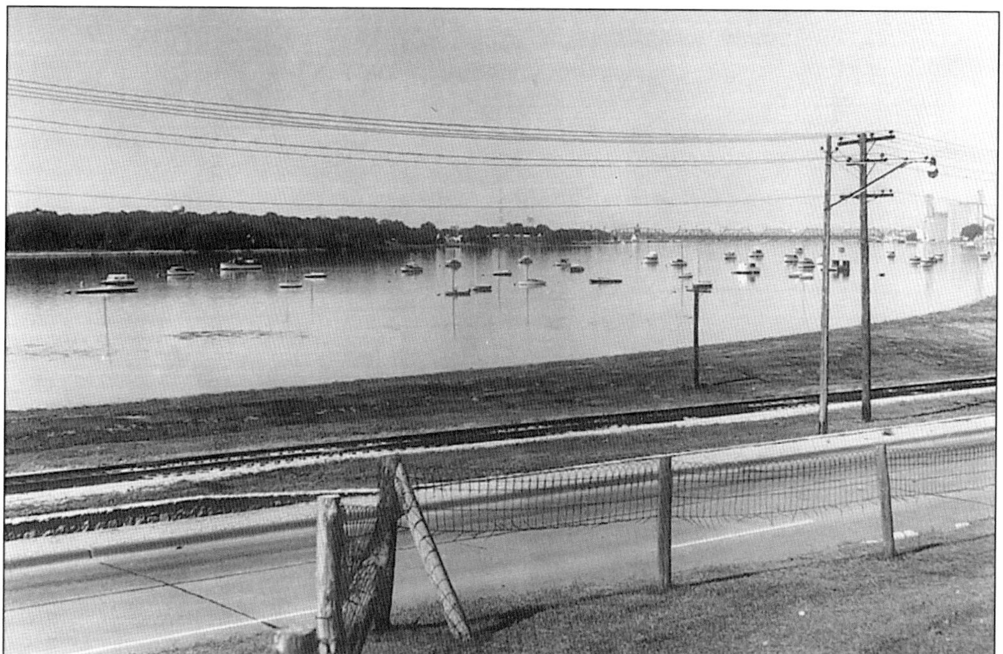

The view of the Mississippi River from River Drive was much different in the 1940s and 1950s, before the Lindsay Park boat harbor was built. Boaters moored their craft on buoys and used dinghies to get back and forth.

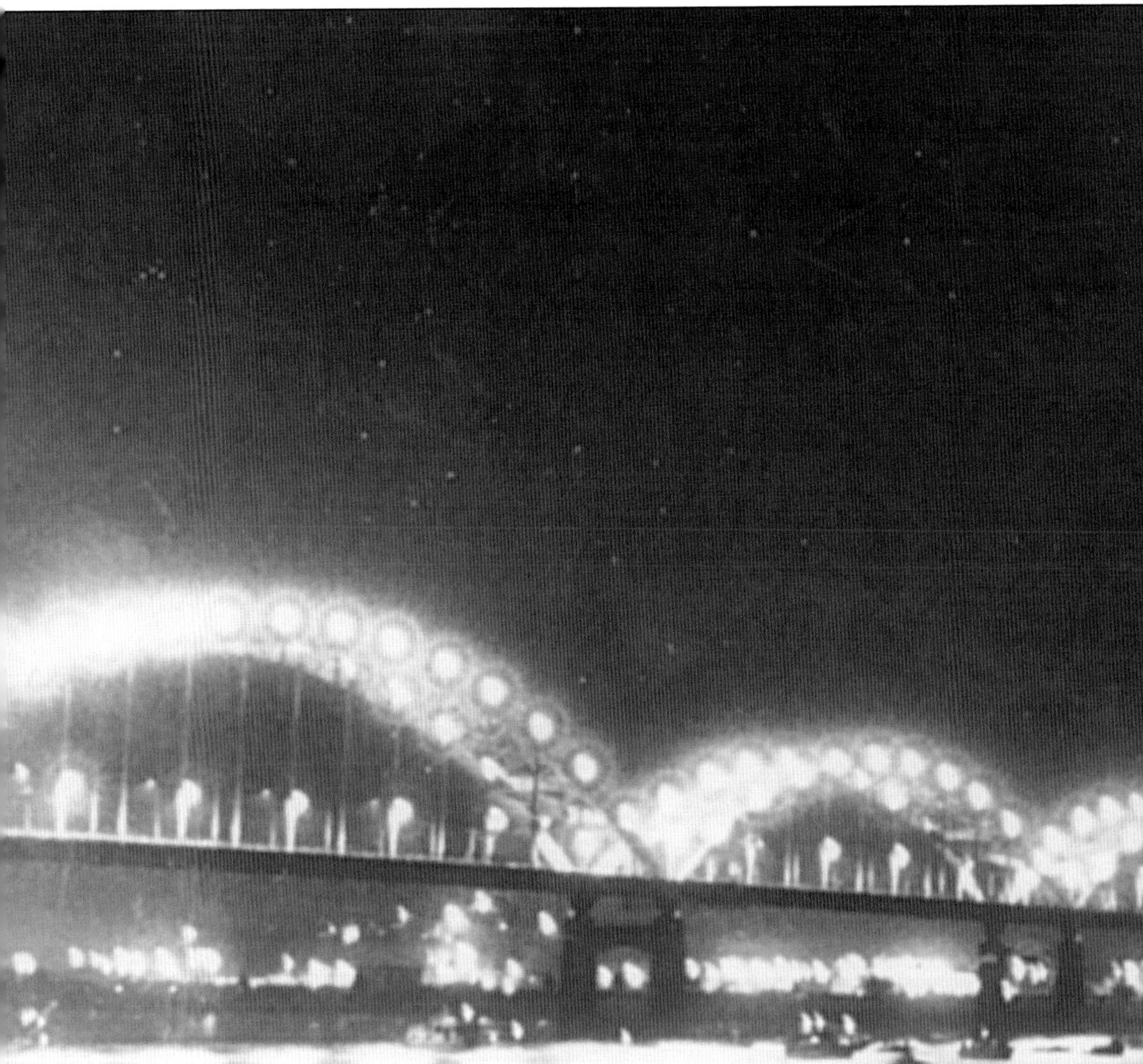

The Centennial Bridge, linking Davenport and Rock Island, sported a dramatic new nighttime look in 1988 when its span was laced with lights. The added illumination and the glow of small boat lights create a dramatic backdrop for riverfront fireworks displays. To the delight of thousands of revelers, the year 2000 was welcomed in with the largest fireworks show ever staged on the riverfront. On that rousing New Year's Eve 1999, aerial bursts were fired from both the Rock Island and Davenport sides of the Mississippi. "I'd never seen anything like it,"

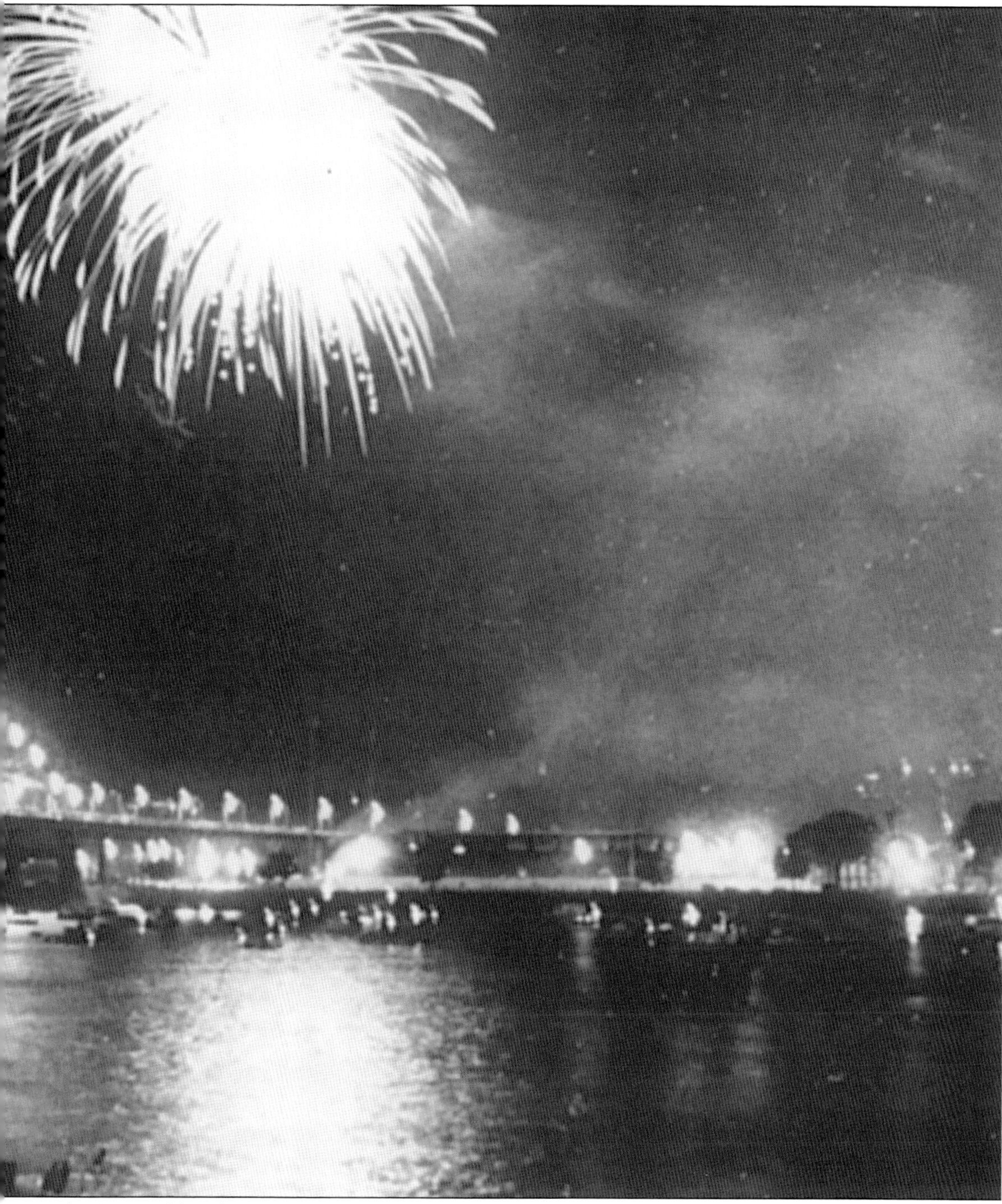

said 85-year-old Esther Salzmann. "I was going to stay home and watch the fireworks from different parts of the world. But I'm so glad I went to see those right here on the Mississippi." Thanks to the bluffs, thousands on the riverfront and the hillsides viewed the display. "I hope we don't have to wait another thousand years to view a display like this one," observed Davenporter Caroline Freeburg.

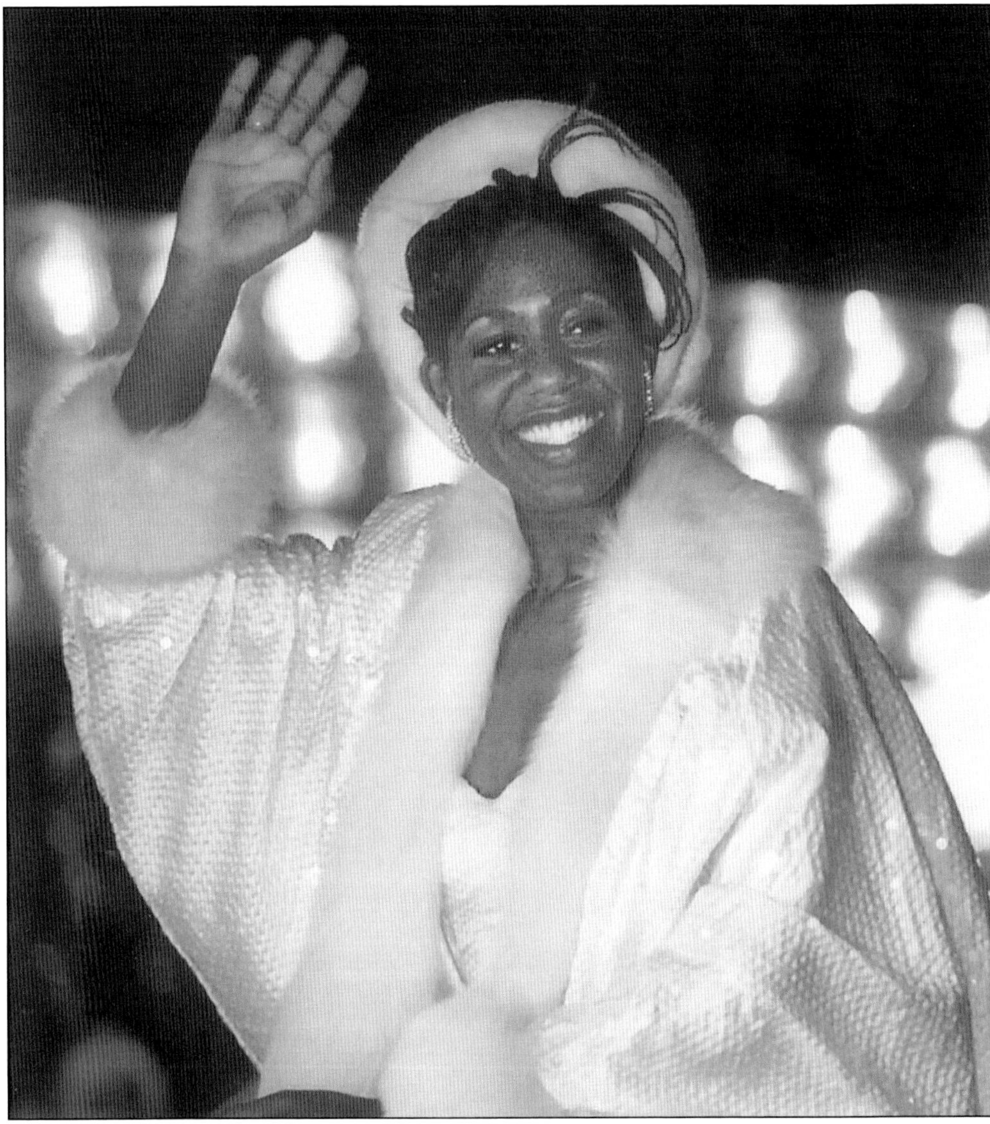

Selecting a photo to conclude a collection of this nature is no easy task. One could choose an image that summarizes, one that sentimentalizes, one that seeks laughter, or one that provides a more solemn reflection. It would be ideal to come upon a photograph of someone waving farewell, now that this breezy look back at Davenport is completed. If only the subject radiated class, warmth, personality, and elegance. That person has to represent the city of Davenport, a sparkling jewel on the Mississippi. Eureka! What better choice than Davenport's own intelligent, gracious, and glamorous Jennifer Caudle, the reigning Miss Iowa! Here she is, flashing a typically royal smile in Atlantic City. Thus completes a visit to a city with a fascinating past, an exciting present, and surely a grand future. Thanks for making the trip!